Takin' Care of Business

Takin' Care of Business

A History of Working People's Rock 'n' Roll

George Case

OXFORD

UNIVERSITY PRESS

OXFORD
UNIVERSITY PRESS

Oxford University Press is a department of the University of Oxford. It furthers
the University's objective of excellence in research, scholarship, and education
by publishing worldwide. Oxford is a registered trade mark of Oxford University
Press in the UK and certain other countries.

Published in the United States of America by Oxford University Press
198 Madison Avenue, New York, NY 10016, United States of America.

Library of Congress Cataloging-in-Publication Data
Names: Case, George, 1967– author.
Title: Takin' care of business : a history of working people's rock 'n' roll /
by George Case.
Description: New York : Oxford University Press, 2021. |
Includes bibliographical references and index.
Identifiers: LCCN 2020032881 (print) | LCCN 2020032882 (ebook) |
ISBN 9780197548813 (hardback) | ISBN 9780197548820 (epub)
Subjects: LCSH: Rock music—Social aspects—History—20th century. |
Working class—Attitudes—History—20th century.
Classification: LCC ML3918.R63 C39 2021 (print) |
LCC ML3918.R63 (ebook) | DDC 781.66086/23—dc23
LC record available at https://lccn.loc.gov/2020032881
LC ebook record available at https://lccn.loc.gov/2020032882

DOI: 10.1093/oso/9780197548813.001.0001

1 3 5 7 9 8 6 4 2

Printed by Sheridan Books, Inc., United States of America

Forget your lust for the rich man's gold.
All that you need is in your soul.

Lynyrd Skynyrd, "Simple Man"

Rich man, poor man, beggar man, thief,
Ain't got a hope in hell—that's my belief.

AC/DC, "Sin City"

Contents

Introduction

Dream On

> Rock, having evolved among the poor, and appealing to the young
> before they learned to cooperate, seemed the music of those who
> could not or would not take part in the orderly business of society. It
> flowed through the air, straight to the nerves, immune to the settling
> influence of any status quo. It appeared to have great liberating po-
> tential: all those people, moving in bliss to the same beat, might ac-
> complish anything.
>
> **Mark Crispin Miller, "Where All the Flowers Went"**

At the 2016 Republican Party Convention in Cleveland, Ohio, the delegates
who ultimately chose Donald Trump as the GOP's presidential candidate
attended a historic political event driven by what critics charged were dangerous currents of xenophobia and demagoguery. Few of the people in the
crowds in the Quicken Loans Arena may have noticed that the official logo
of the proceedings combined the party's traditional symbol of an elephant
with a silhouette of a Fender Stratocaster electric guitar, a reference to the
convention's locale in the so-called birthplace of rock 'n' roll and home of the
Rock and Roll Hall of Fame; the red-white-and-blue design was realized by the
Cleveland firm of Falls Communications. "The elephant marching forward
represents strength with a positive attitude," explained company head Rob
Falls. "The guitar is a proud symbol of the rock and roll history of Cleveland."[1]

The Fender Stratocaster was the instrument favored by celebrated rock
performers including Buddy Holly, Eric Clapton, and the African American
genius Jimi Hendrix. Hendrix, who died in 1970 at age twenty-seven, was the
best-known exponent of the psychedelic sound, a musical style of spacey electronic noises and surrealist lyrics conducive to the hallucinatory perceptions
of listeners experiencing the effects of marijuana and LSD. Hendrix, Clapton,
Holly, and other players of the classic "Strat" were also countercultural heroes,

Takin' Care of Business. George Case, Oxford University Press (2021). © George Case.
DOI: 10.1093/oso/9780197548813.003.0001

whose lives and work had aroused much suspicion among older people for the provocations of their songs and the rebellious implications of their fame. The futuristic cutaways and curves of the Stratocaster, first marketed in 1954, had long been associated with the racial and moral upheavals that had transformed society through the last half of the twentieth century. Yet here was the guitar's outline being employed to advertise the official ascendancy of a man who promised to Make America Great Again—or, to his opponents, threatened to turn back the clock on decades of hard-won social progress.

In the weeks leading up to July's convention, the Trump campaign had also played a number of classic rock tunes at the candidate's increasingly well attended and increasingly controversial rallies. Through representatives, many of the artists issued cease-and-desist notices requesting that their songs not be used at such gatherings. Among the acts whose work had sounded out over venues full of baseball-hatted, media-hating, Hillary Clinton–loathing Trump supporters were Aerosmith ("Dream On"), Queen ("We Are the Champions"), Neil Young ("Rockin' in the Free World"), the Beatles ("Here Comes the Sun"), and the Rolling Stones ("Start Me Up" and "You Can't Always Get What You Want"). That the performers—most of them veterans of drug busts and other debaucheries, and several not even American citizens—would be embarrassed by their appropriation by the Republican upstart was hardly surprising. Less noticed, though, was the remarkable fact that Republicans were celebrating their upstart ascendancy to the accompaniment of classic rock 'n' roll.

What had happened? How had the roiling wave of conservative American populists co-opted the iconography of sex, drugs, and rock music? Or was conservative populism now expressed through electric guitars, and had the co-optation gone the other way?

One possible clue to those puzzles lies in a particular strain of rock 'n' roll itself. With the form now several decades old, spanning several generations of fans and an entire planet of audiences, numerous genre subcategories have emerged: heavy metal, punk, new wave, alternative, folk, and even smaller offshoots within each, like death metal, grindcore, emo, new romantic, power pop, and on and on. Among the most enduring of these tangents is the music that emerged in the late 1960s as a response to the kaleidoscopic indulgences of psychedelia and the acoustic introspections of folk-schooled singer-songwriters. This work maintained the volume and energy of electric rock but coupled it with a down-to-earth fatalism that over the next twenty years and down to our own era has proven enormously appealing to a major segment of the entertainment market—and also, perhaps, to a crucial segment of the electorate in Western nations.

That fragmentation of the listening public, no less than of the artistic choices available to the public itself, might be another explanation of the merging of rock sound and imagery with Republican platforms, as seen in Cleveland in 2016. By the early 1970s, rock 'n' roll had become so popular that scarcely any young person would admit to rejecting the entire medium on general principles; they might eagerly approve of one band but scornfully dismiss another appearing on the same bill. Conversely, the vast baby boom cohort that comprised rock's commercial base was so populous that few in the music industry would present any new act as a one-size-fits-all product. Everyone under a certain age liked rock, but not everyone liked it for the same reasons. Instead, managers, promoters, record company executives, and music writers tried to identify different areas of generational, regional, or cultural preference, just as distinct generations, regions, and subcultures began to understand and articulate what their own preferences were.

The particular preference of a particular audience, it emerged, was for the rock 'n' roll music considered in this book. This ranged from the homespun urgency of Creedence Clearwater Revival to the good-time oafishness of Ted Nugent, Grand Funk Railroad, and Black Oak Arkansas; from the New England snarl of Aerosmith to the heartland grit of Molly Hatchet, Bachman-Turner Overdrive, and the Texas blues of ZZ Top; from the raspy earnestness of Bob Seger and George Thorogood to the more nuanced proletarianism of Bruce Springsteen and John Mellencamp; from the overseas attitude of Bad Company, Nazareth, Thin Lizzy, Foghat, and Motörhead to the twin titans of the denim demographic, Australia's AC/DC and the unrepentant American southerners Lynyrd Skynyrd. All the artists—apolitical but anti-elitist, socially tolerant but sternly ethical, products of both international uprising and local loyalty—provided the anthems of a young working-class contingent that has since grown into a maligned and misunderstood division of postindustrial society.

Those anthems are still revered now, even as their enthusiasts are not. They are songs of allegiance to place: "Sweet Home Alabama," "Mississippi Queen," "Born on the Bayou," "Born in the USA." They are songs of allegiance to no place: "Turn the Page," "Highway to Hell," "Eight Days on the Road," "(We Are) The Road Crew." They are songs of work: "Just Got Paid," "Working Man," "Takin' Care of Business," "Workin' for MCA." They are songs of desperate hope: "Dream On," "Born to Run," "Jailbreak," "Breaking the Law," and songs of bitter resignation: "Lodi," "Against the Wind," "Racing in the Streets," "Rain On the Scarecrow." They are songs of macho bluster: "The Boys Are Back in Town," "We're an American Band," "Run with the Pack," "Bad to the Bone"; songs of puerile lasciviousness: "Go Down," "Wang Dang Sweet Poontang,"

"Pearl Necklace," "Muscle of Love"; songs of grassroots defiance: "Fortunate Son," "Just' Cos You Got the Power," "Stormtroopin'," "Gimme Back My Bullets." Remembered by millions, these tracks comprise the playlist of the forgotten man. Certified classics of long standing, they are the soundtracks of an inchoate insurgency.

Just what that insurgency means, or where it may ultimately lead, is as yet unknowable. More verified today is the long shadow cast by rock 'n' roll over hundreds of millions of citizens around the world—not just over reckless kids but over wage-earning parents and retired elders; not just over student agitators but over registered voters; not just over indignant youth challenging authority but over indignant adults challenging their own definition of it. Not only have the politics of rock drifted surprisingly rightward since 1970, but some rock, at least, has reset the boundaries of left and right themselves. That God, guns, and Old Glory can be paid fitting tribute in a heavy guitar riff delivered by a long-haired reprobate in blue jeans but #Me Too, Occupy Wall Street or Black Lives Matter might not, hints at where those boundaries now lie. The improbability of rock's political realignment across a fifty-year span is matched only by the improbability of the public's.

And though the sound of rock has hailed a lot of good times, some rock, since 1970, has supported its listeners through lengthening stretches of bad ones. Rock 'n' roll was created by the wealthiest populations ever to have lived; it was sustained and elaborated on by populations whose wealth was less secure than they had once thought. This subdivision of the audience evolved into a "base" well before the word was ever applied to poll results, mailing lists, and swing states. They knew what they liked but, equally, what they didn't—and their dislikes included some artists elsewhere critically sacrosanct, and some themes otherwise philosophically inviolable. Seldom recognized for it, their numbers were large enough to sway the operations of the entire music industry, just when many other industries were beginning to falter. And scarcely conceded by music historians, their choices are singular enough to change our reading of the music altogether, just when so much other historic change unfolds. It is these fans, and the objects of their fandom, that *Takin' Care of Business* will consider. To the extent that "working-class populism" describes an authentic political current, it's now beyond a doubt that certain musicians and certain of their songs helped define that current, to both outsiders and to the populists themselves. Assessing the social history of the last few decades, we learn a lot from studying important elections, pivotal legislation, traumatic wars, and transformative new technologies. But we can also learn a lot from picking through a stack of legendary vinyl records.

Yes, this is pretty arbitrary. The same era in pop music covered here, and a lot of the same pop music, could be selectively applied to a completely different analysis. Maybe the spreading attraction of reggae, and the occasional use of South Asian or Near Eastern sonorities in rock songs (e.g., "Norwegian Wood" or Led Zeppelin's "Kashmir"), says something about the rise of multiculturalism; maybe the prominence of female performers like Janis Joplin, Joni Mitchell, Aretha Franklin, and Heart indexes the impact of feminism on Western society; maybe glitter, disco, and Elton John and Freddie Mercury were early pointers toward today's broad acceptance of the LGBTQ community. You can choose a few key names from within any few years of show business history to illustrate just about any wider tide outside it, if you're sure to overlook the contradictions and qualifications that argue the other way.

An overview of rock 'n' roll populism, further, implies an unasked question: whose populism? Is one audience more valid, more *real*, than another? Many of these performers would happily have boasted of playing their music "for the people" (or would happily have press agents and compliant journalists do the boasting for them), but in fact their products were frequently aimed at discrete slices of a much broader clientele. In some cases, artists and audiences were surprised to discover each other and encouraged by the spontaneous community that developed between them. But elsewhere, musicians and fans were artificially brought together by advertising, media opportunism, and self-interest—hype, in other words.

Consider: there has never been a requirement to show a pay stub or a bank statement to get into a Bruce Springsteen concert. Affluent people can like AC/DC too; auto workers can take a shine to Gilbert and Sullivan. Most of the supposedly ordinary-dude musicians described herein are, in fact, rich and famous. The record labels that retailed their output in Middle America, industrial England, and small-town Canada belonged to multinational corporations. There is no section of music stores labeled "Blue-Collar Rock," and music trade publications have never featured special "Working People's Music" rankings. In 1977, for example, Bob Seger's heartland ode "Mainstreet" was on the *Billboard* singles chart a few notches below Marvin Gaye's "Got to Give It Up (Part 1)," Fleetwood Mac's "Dreams," and KC and the Sunshine Band's "I'm Your Boogie Man." It seems unlikely that the same people were buying the Seger record along with those of Marvin Gaye, Fleetwood Mac, or KC and the Sunshine Band, or that the same people were requesting each of those songs to be played on their hometown AM broadcasters—but who really knows? Today such micromarketing certainties are probably possible through online algorithms and web analytics, but forty or fifty years ago the performers, the A&R staff, and the public themselves could only make educated guesses as to whose material meant how much to which people. It's since fallen to music journalists and music historians to sort music into neat (and often false) denominations that conveniently ignore the flukes of timing and taste that produce hit tunes and successful acts. The curatorial selectiveness that isolates "Mainstreet" from "I'm Your Boogie Man," even though both songs were about as popular about the same time, takes some justification and no little amount of personal bias. In that sense, all of this is as much about rock criticism as rock itself.

In some ways, it's not even about rock at all. What makes the music significant is partly the mechanics of the songs and the dynamics of the business, but the changes in the wider society also need to be reckoned with. Some of the reckonings are not pretty: undertones of white racism in an environment where minority rights were advancing, crudely sexist lyrics and stage poses coinciding with feminism's second wave, and an exaggerated masculinity during a time of gay emancipation. In these years, the music industry offered a haphazard, organic preview of the balkanization that cable networks and online news outlets would later promote deliberately and artificially. Rock 'n' roll—and its country cousin—anticipated how every kind of mass entertainment would one day become political, and how politics would one day become a form of mass entertainment.

More broadly, what's considered here is how notions of status and identity were evolving alongside realities of labor, ethnicity, gender politics, and world affairs. Like actors typecast following memorable roles they only played once or twice, the rock 'n' rollers discussed in these pages came to represent outlooks they may never have meant to advocate for. As with movies, television, or novels, it's now possible to pick out trends in the history of the medium to which the artists themselves were oblivious. Eventually, somehow, rock 'n' roll decadence came to be hailed as old-fashioned dignity. Somehow, rock 'n' roll's teenage ardor persisted into its fans' middle age. Somehow, the inherent rebelliousness of rock 'n' roll was adapted to stand for the traditionalist values of a beleaguered economic caste. Somehow, a vital brand of rock 'n' roll was turned into an idealized self-portrait of a vulnerable people beginning a long decline.

Admittedly, few things are as nerdy as a rock critic striving to define what's cool. And nothing says amateur sociology as much as someone sorting his record collection according to ZIP code and income bracket. Devising elaborate taxonomies of pop genres—carefully delineating the subtle differences between glam rock and shock rock, or hotly debating whether to file the MC5 under heavy metal, garage, or proto-punk—is indeed a cliché of rock texts. But not all of those taxonomies have been established retrospectively;

as we'll see, contemporary listeners in 1969, 1974, and 1986 were already classing some soloists and bands by their currency with downmarket white males eager for high-volume, no-bullshit performance. Even back then, the music business had a hand in determining who its wares were sold to: advertising certain acts in certain publications, promoting them in certain venues in certain towns, pushing airplay on certain radio stations, and so on. Sure, there were probably some upwardly mobile MBAs cranking ZZ Top's "Beer Drinkers and Hell Raisers" while they scanned the day's stock reports, just as some factory grunts probably came home and cracked a brew and lit a joint to David Bowie's "Lady Grinning Soul," but some general conclusions about popular music and its diverse consumers remain valid. One is that the diverse consumers of popular music really do favor some kinds of music over others, motivated not by hype or fashion but by genuine conviction. Another is that integrity can't be manufactured, even by a booming, often cutthroat business with millions of customers. And one more is that there really was once such a thing as working folks' rock 'n' roll, just as there really was such a thing, or a lot more of such a thing, as real working folks.

1

Salt of the Earth

> A transitional period, the Sixties witnessed a shift from a society weakly held together by a decaying faith to a rapidly desocializing mass of groups and individuals united by little more than a wish for quick satisfaction; from a sheltered assumption of consensus, hierarchy, and fixed values to an era of multiplying viewpoints and jealously leveled standards; from a naive world of patient deferral and measurable progress to a greedy simultaneity of sound-bite news and thought-bite politics; from an empty and frustrating moral formality to an underachieving sensationalism.
>
> Ian MacDonald, *Revolution in the Head*

Rock 'n' roll had always been the music of poor people. Its antecedents in blues, gospel, and country were songs of Blacks and whites toiling on hardscrabble farms, down dangerous mine shafts, and in hellish industrial mills. They were songs of poverty and humiliation, of release and rejoicing. They were songs of lonesome highways, big steel rails, steady rollin' men, the killing floor, the range, the House of the Rising Sun, and the boss. The folk idioms of labor, struggle, resentment, and resilience were deeply embedded in the words and rhythms of what became the mass-marketed medium of rock.

These roots were not always apparent when the music appeared in the early 1950s. Both teenage acolytes and adult detractors noted only that the new sounds were part of a new affluence, coinciding with the post–World War II economic boom that saw historic levels of material wealth across Western nations. Driven in America by the federal government's New Deal programs designed to alleviate the worst effects of the Great Depression and to prevent future collapses of a similar scale, and by technological innovations in aerospace, electronics, and consumer products, the unprecedented wealth made affordable even such frivolous, faddish trinkets as rock 'n' roll. The commercialized hybrid of rhythm and blues and hillbilly that increasingly seduced the

Takin' Care of Business. George Case, Oxford University Press (2021). © George Case.
DOI: 10.1093/oso/9780197548813.003.0002

ears and minds of young people was merely the most indulgent leisure item yet marketed to the most indulged population of all time.

But underneath the novelty and the outrage surrounding the first era of rock 'n' roll there remained distinct ties to working-class sensibility. In the 1950s almost one in three employed Americans were a member of a labor union, while industrial manufacturing was at the heart of US economic ascendancy. Rock 'n' roll may have been only one ephemeral strand of the entertainment business—in the beginning not even a particularly significant one, in the minds of its corporate sponsors—yet it was nonetheless enabled by the secure jobs and substantial wages that gave parents disposable income enough that their children could spend it on 45 rpm records, jukebox selections, home phonographs, and fan magazines. Whether he knew it or not, the stereotypical suburban 1950s adolescent, cruising his Chevy to the sock hop while AM radio blared Elvis or Chuck Berry or Buddy Holly, enjoyed all the benefits of generous collective bargains, busy assembly lines, and billowing smokestacks. Rock 'n' roll may have been television and tail fins, but it was made possible by foundries and factories. The music was pop culture; its base was proletarian.

Occasionally, that base showed through. Though most of the songs were obviously built around themes of juvenile fun or romance, some material addressed more grown-up responsibilities. Bill Haley's epochal "Rock around the Clock" (1954) applied the language of shift work to its twenty-four-hour party, while Little Richard's "Rip It Up" (1956) started on Saturday night when the singer just got paid; the same year, Fats Domino's "Blue Monday" went through a work week capped by a Friday payday and weekend fun; Chuck Berry's "Too Much Monkey Business" (1956) griped about workin' in both the mill and the fillin' station, and his "Almost Grown" (1959) boasted about that most adult of attainments, a little job; the Silhouettes' "Get a Job" (1957) told an infectious doo-wop story of trying to find one. Clearly, the strains of holding an occupation and the rewards of nights off still resonated with a young audience only beginning to enter the labor market. Rock 'n' roll was not all about living at home on dad's allowance. The artist most identified with this semi-maturity was Eddie Cochran, whose "Summertime Blues" (1957) and "Somethin' Else" (1959) addressed, through Cochran's influential rockabilly guitar style, the basic concerns of earning money, saving it, spending it, not having enough of it, and taking two weeks for a fine vacation.

And it was not only the songs but the singers themselves who gave early rock its blue-collar character. This founding generation of rock 'n' roll stars were all children of the Depression, who had known want and dislocation and who carried at least ancestral memories of economic hardship. Elvis Presley was employed as a delivery driver by the Crown Electric Company in Memphis, Tennessee, when he made his first record; during his childhood his parents, Vernon and Gladys, had occasionally drawn on social assistance and the generosity of neighbors to stay solvent, and father Vernon was regularly in and out of various jobs, at one point losing the family home after an altercation with his boss and landlord. In 1956 he was already amazed at how far he had risen: "My daddy and I were laughing about it the other day," the young Elvis noted. "He looked at me and said, 'What happened, El? The last thing I remember is I was working in a can factory and you were still driving a truck.'"[1] To another reporter he explained his accumulations of cars and clothes: "When you ain't had nothing, like me, you keep count when you get things."[2] Roy Orbison's father worked on Texas oil wells and as an auto mechanic. Carl Perkins was the son of sharecroppers—that is, tenant farmers. Buddy Holly had moved several times while growing up in Lubbock, Texas, in the 1930s, and Jerry Lee Lewis was also a product of a poor rural region of Louisiana.

This working-class aspect of rock 'n' roll was often insinuated its opponents' critiques. Though racial and sexual anxieties were at the forefront of conservative denunciation, there was also the subtler disapproval of personal styles associated with a hitherto compliant menial or agricultural social order. Americans may have preferred to think of themselves as sharing an egalitarian society where origin and accent didn't matter, but their harshest reactions to the new music revealed otherwise. Performers like Elvis were derided as vulgar hillbillies, lowering public taste; they embodied an establishment caricature of the backward, hopelessly tacky southern United States. "Stick to the Heartbreak Hotel, and stay away from the Waldorf,"[3] Milton Berle kidded Presley, none too subtly, when the young singer appeared on the established comedian's television show. Elvis's 1956 detonation, the snare-savage cover of Big Mama Thornton's "Hound Dog," brazenly called out its subject's—by implication, its listener's—spurious claim to be high-class. Sociologists observed that rock 'n' roll appealed to the high school "rough crowd," the teens less academically inclined and more likely to smoke and drink. "Rock and roll is phony and false, and it's sung, written, and played for the most part by cretinous goons," Frank Sinatra infamously complained in 1957. "Rock and roll is the most brutal, ugly, degenerate, vicious form of expression—lewd, sly, in plain fact, dirty—a rancid-smelling aphrodisiac and the martial music of every side-burned delinquent on the face of the earth."[4]

Aside from rock's racy lyrics and broadcast images of white kids cheering flamboyant Black showmen, it was also an affront to bourgeois codes of dress, manner, and language. Its typical listener was portrayed as a "greaser," a drawling garage hand or a seventeen-year-old hoodlum, just as its typical practitioner was an undereducated, garishly dressed guitarist or piano player. The landmark 1955 film *Blackboard Jungle* not only introduced "Rock around the Clock" to a wide viewership but associated the music with inner-city high school thugs. The next year, the trade paper *Variety* added that rock 'n' roll was "suggestive and vulgar, tinged with the kind of animalism that should be confined to dives and bordellos."[5] At a 1956 episode of unrest at a rock 'n' roll show in Saint Paul, Minnesota, it was said that "the general brand of people and type of behavior at the dance were not conducive or beneficial in any respect to the proper environment of juveniles,"[6] and after violence broke out at a 1958 concert in Boston where Jerry Lee Lewis was on the bill, Mayor John Hynes pronounced, "This sort of performance attracts the troublemakers and the irresponsible."[7] Outside a 1950s rock event at a Brooklyn theater, author Jeff Greenfield remembered that his fellow attendees had "the hard faces of the children of the working poor . . . [who] read auto specs at night, not college catalogues."[8]

Into the next decade, rock acquired both a broader audience and a broader authorship. Its class stigma remained, but that reputation was complicated by new names who were neither Black nor indigent white southerners, nor even American. The Beatles and Bob Dylan each released their first records in 1962, at first to divergent markets but, by the middle of the 1960s, together reaching a vast baby boom demographic that became the defining constituency of popular music. Dylan, a middle-class Minnesotan (his father owned an appliance store), was at first tied to the wave of folk music that had become popular with students and progressives; it was also considered "protest music" for its recurring messages against war and racial discrimination. Some heard him as an heir to Woody Guthrie, the great balladeer of marginalized Americana, and the young singer's visit to the hospitalized and terminally ill Guthrie made the comparison inevitable. Though Dylan himself had been a fan of early rock 'n' rollers like Elvis and Little Richard, his initial works bore little relation to what most in his genre felt was an artificial, consumerist product foisted on teenagers, which he mocked in songs like "Talking World War III Blues" and "Bob Dylan's Blues."

Dylan sang of poverty, inequality, and exploitation ("The Ballad of Hollis Brown," "When the Ship Comes In," "North Country Blues"), but few of his followers were poor, unequal, or exploited. He was no fraud, of course—his commitment to civil rights and against militarism was sincere, and to many his most important music, like "Masters of War," "Blowin' in the Wind," and "The Times They Are a-Changin'," came from this period. His strongest support, however, came from the intelligentsia. Folk music itself represented collegians' ideal of the common man, something even those who acknowledged Dylan's originality could see: "More and more [folk singers] are neither rural nor representative of centuries-old family and regional traditions," wrote Nat Hentoff in a 1964 *New Yorker* appreciation. "They are often city-bred converts to the folk style," whose main listeners consisted of "the restless young."[9]

In contrast to the cultish appeal of Dylan, the Beatles' first impact was explosive. Media sensations in Britain and, by early 1964, the US and the rest of the world, they too had been inspired by rock 'n' roll's pioneers but scored most with their own songs, whose music and (especially) lyrics were more inventive than that of their models. At home and abroad, the four were often hailed for a "working-class" irreverence, but their individual origins varied: despite a history of family trauma, John Lennon had grown up in a fairly secure middle-class home, while Paul McCartney (father a cotton salesman), George Harrison (father a city bus driver), and Ringo Starr (mother a barmaid, stepfather a house painter) each represented descending steps on the English socioeconomic ladder. Ringo was the only Beatle who had known the genuine deprivation of Liverpool's slum district, the Dingle. Compared with America, though, all of war-ravaged, empire-divesting Britain was a poorer cousin to the affluent superpower. London's Communist *Daily Worker* newspaper asserted of the Beatles and their hometown peers: "The Mersey sound is the voice of 80,000 crumbling houses and 30,000 people on the dole."[10] "Up the workers, and all that stuff," Paul says to an uptight business traveler in *A Hard Day's Night*. And in a notorious *New Statesman* essay of 1964, conservative writer Paul Johnson lamented that the Beatles' fans were "the least fortunate of their generation, the dull, the idle, the failures: their existence, in such large numbers . . . is a fearful indictment of our education system."[11]

As the rock renaissance flourished through the mid-1960s, though, it was clear that the declassé qualities ascribed to the music ten years before had been obviated. Whatever the reactions to the burgeoning success of the form—which was now dominating the record business and increasingly affecting other entertainments as well—few would have said that rock 'n' roll was merely something by and for small-town yokels, teenage hot rodders, and manual laborers. With the Beatles and Dylan in the lead, pop records were increasingly lauded for their sophistication and their relevance to an educated and prosperous generation adopting new standards of dress and morality. Premarital sex, illegal drugs, antiauthoritarian politics, non-Western spiritualities, long hair and miniskirts—all were encompassed in the revolutionary sweep of rock 'n' roll. Who could resist its momentum?

Certainly not the critics. With the oldest boomers entering postsecondary education, serious writing on rock 'n' roll began to appear in college newspapers and commercial magazines including *Crawdaddy* (founded in 1966) and *Rolling Stone* (1967). Countercultural broadsheets such as the *Village Voice* and the Boston *Phoenix* also set aside ongoing space for coverage of rock releases and events. Until the mid-1960s, few professional music reviewers had much background in youth culture, but as the industry expanded, the opportunities for journalists, scholars, collectors—and advertisers—opened up as well. The first full-time rock writers tended to rate artists and records by aesthetic and sociopolitical standards that seem almost quaint today. They were very earnest, very erudite, and very elevated from the majority of their peers actually buying the discs and attending the concerts. Against a backdrop of the Vietnam War and all manner of social change, they hoped rock would be an instrument of revolution. It was, but not the revolution they were hoping for.

Naturally, the critics tended to focus their analyses on the most "important" acts—Dylan, the Beatles, the Rolling Stones, some of the psychedelic bands emerging from San Francisco, and then phenomena like Jimi Hendrix and the Doors—at the same time as they were complicit in defining for themselves who exactly was important and who wasn't. A few critical ground rules were established: gnomically poetic verses were good; clichéd rhymes were not. Ambitious sonic and musical effects were to be admired, but technique alone was not enough. Expansive albums were increasingly the preferred medium of rock 'n' roll artistry; hit singles were just commercial gimmicks. Authenticity in background or personality was what made performers significant; mere fame was suspect. In the coming years, rock critics like Paul Williams, Paul Nelson, Richard Goldstein, Ellen Willis, Greil Marcus, and Robert Christgau would become gatekeepers of rock 'n' roll respectability.

The irony such figures faced (and at their best acknowledged) in their work was that they were attempting to set the artistic parameters of a field built almost wholly around marketing, promotion, and turnover. They sought the revolutionary potential in capitalist product, and they thought long and hard about works made spontaneously and intuitively. Their publications drew revenue from advertising placements by the record companies whose output was to be judged, and while the problem of payola never surfaced in rock reporting as much as in rock radio, the lures of free tickets and interview access to top personalities could be compromising. Even less than for fiction or film, reviewers of pop music had little real effect on actual public response to available material; as more and more records were retailed and more and more new bands and soloists were put before the audience, critics had to either "interpret" the music (especially the lyrics) with ever-more elaborate explanations or situate the artists within particular sub-categories of style, influences, audience, and so on. They knew they could not effectively recommend buying or not buying a given artist's release, but they could at least offer readers a way to understand what the release meant, and to whom. In the beginning, the tensions between these imperatives—between scholarly appraisal and popular demand, between critical theory and everyday reality, between expert authority and average punter—were easy to ignore.

No doubt, this era of *Aftermath*, *Pet Sounds*, *The Doors*, *Blonde on Blonde*, *Revolver*, *Sgt. Pepper's Lonely Hearts Club Band*, *Disraeli Gears*, and *Are You Experienced?* marked the greatest flourishing of creative achievement and commercial success in the music to date. Indeed, many listeners now called it "rock," implying heavy substance, rather than the old "rock 'n' roll," meaning short-lived good times. Whether for Greil Marcus or Joe Blow, it was a rewarding time to be a fan. Yet in among the pantheon of immortals were many other acts that came and went without leaving much of a legacy. They could boast a suitably psychedelic or acidic identity, but they would never attain the jet-set status of the Beatles or the Rolling Stones; they might score a hit or two, or a much-viewed television spot, but never win the long-term managerial attention and label support that sustained the big stars. Very subtly, a distinction had arisen that separated rock's aristocracy from its serfs. This distinction would later be made explicit in the cataloguing of "garage rock," as in the 1972 compilation record *Nuggets: Original Artyfacts from the First Psychedelic Era, 1965–1968*, featuring gems such as the Count Five's "Psychotic Reaction" and the ersatz Beatles of the Knickerbockers' "Lies." Garage rock, whether termed as such or not, was the music of inexpert young singers and instrumentalists, often recorded in primitive studios and issued to only limited or local exposure. But these were portents of a rift in rock 'n' roll that would widen. While some musicians were courted by the international press (both mainstream and alternative) and widely studied for the lessons they were supposedly imparting to their generation, an underclass of provincials and plebeians was building.

These were the foot soldiers in the swelling ranks of the rock army—the faceless, forgettable players who dutifully stoked public interest in the sound, but from whom no one was expecting the Word. They were the Young Rascals ("Good Lovin'," "Groovin'"), the Box Tops ("The Letter," "Cry Like a Baby"), the Bobby Fuller Four ("I Fought the Law"), the Grass Roots ("Let's Live for Today"), the Standells ("Dirty Water"), and Mitch Ryder and the Detroit Wheels ("Little Latin Lupe Lu," "Devil with a Blue Dress On"). Even a scattering of tracks by earlier performers had somehow become staples of bar bands and teenage wannabes, like the Kingsmen's "Louie Louie" (1963) and the Premiers' "Farmer John" (1964). In a subculture increasingly attending to celebrity, wealth, and newsworthiness, it was these acts' very lack of each that stood out.

By 1968 the fissures in the wider society were penetrating the world of pop music. This was the year of the Tet Offensive in Vietnam in January, which made unmistakable the futility of US military involvement in that country; the assassination of Martin Luther King Jr. in April, triggering a wave of violent Black protest in American cities; the huge student uprisings in Paris in May; the assassination of Robert Kennedy in June; clashes between young demonstrators and police at the Democratic national convention in Chicago in August; and the election to the US presidency of Republican Richard Nixon in November. The polarization between radicals and traditionalists, between the forces of protest and the forces of status quo, between advance and backlash, was no longer just a matter of cultural style but one of political stance. Rock 'n' roll was caught between opposing sides, and the responses to the turmoil were ambivalent.

The Rolling Stones' "Street Fighting Man" implied support for the violence of the antiwar and antigovernment demonstrations, while denying poor rock singers could do much to contribute, and two versions of the Beatles' "Revolution" (45 single and album track from *The Beatles*) carried John Lennon's avowal that he could either be counted in or out of destructive action. Hit songs that year ranged from the reassuring strains of Louis Armstrong's "What a Wonderful World," Dionne Warwick's "Do You Know the Way to San Jose," and Mary Hopkins's "Those Were the Days" to the countercultural kick of the Who's "Magic Bus," Sly and the Family Stone's "Everyday People," and the Doors' "Hello, I Love You." Older people tended to regard all the student generation's music as equally subversive, even as conflicting views on how far subversion should go emerged within the generation itself. But the deeper trend in rock was found less in any lyrical statements as in the overall tonal and visual identity of the artists, both established and new.

In December 1967 Bob Dylan's *John Wesley Harding* album appeared. After an intense period when other acts had repeatedly sought the extreme possibilities of electronic recording tricks and abstract lyrics—*Sgt. Pepper, Magical Mystery Tour*, and the single "Strawberry Fields Forever / Penny Lane," the Stones' *Their Satanic Majesties Request*, Cream's *Disraeli Gears*, the Beach Boys' "Good Vibrations," and numerous other freakouts—the Dylan record was an unexpectedly low-key, acoustic product that harked back to his early folk music. The songs "All Along the Watchtower" and "The Ballad of Frankie Lee and Judas Priest" seemed to reflect a preindustrial, almost atavistic rusticity rather than the hallucinatory fancies of Jimi Hendrix' "Purple Haze," Jefferson Airplane's "White Rabbit," or the Doors' "Light My Fire"; even the cover of *John Wesley Harding* was a sepia-toned outdoor portrait of the artist and some friends, instead of the then-familiar space-age whirl of colors and optical distortion. Given his critical and popular stature as a songwriter and youth guru, the reverberations from Dylan's about-face were considerable.

The Beatles and the Rolling Stones made the clearest comparisons. Both *Beggars Banquet* and the two-record *The Beatles* were issued in the late fall of 1968, each band returning to straightforward, unadorned rock with songs like "Stray Cat Blues," "Factory Girl," "Parachute Woman," "Back in the USSR," and "Birthday." The albums also featured unplugged pastorals such as the Beatles' "Julia," "I Will," and "Mother Nature's Son" and the Stones' blues cover "Prodigal Son," as well as a striking Jagger-Richards original, "Salt of the Earth," which celebrated the hardworking people, uncounted heads, and stay-at-home voters so often ignored in the shifting cultural and political fashions of the day. Psychedelia's moment had passed, at least with the acts that had once personified it more than any others.

Just a few months earlier, the hitherto lysergic Byrds had released *Sweetheart of the Rodeo*, a strongly country-flavored work recorded in the country capital of Nashville and reflecting the input of new recruit Gram Parsons. Parsons was a scholar of folk and bluegrass Americana, whose rural, traditionalist tones, so unhip a year or two before, had now come full circle into antiestablishment coolness: *Sweetheart of the Rodeo's* songs included the traditional "I Am a Pilgrim," Woody Guthrie's Depression ballad "Pretty Boy Floyd," and Parsons' achingly beautiful "Hickory Wind." Acoustic and pedal-steel guitars, honky-tonk piano, and hymnal harmonies were heard throughout. The Byrds' departure was no epic commercial smash (no more than was the Lovin' Spoonful's "Nashville Cats" in 1966), but the potential of their old-new, wooden-electric amalgam was clear. When the group played Nashville's Grand Ole Opry in March 1968, it indicated that a musical style once identified with racists and Republicans had been fully co-opted by drug-taking dropouts. Other LA acts, the Nitty Gritty Dirt Band and former teen idol Rick Nelson's Stone Canyon Band, affected a similar crossbreeding, and San Francisco's Grateful Dead also borrowed hootenanny and jug band devices.

Country rock, so-called, was like most industry developments in being a product of manipulation (who got signed by what label and recorded by which producer) and publicity (how they were described in ads and press writeups) rather than of any conscious ploy by the people actually making it. Perhaps the deeper meaning of *Sweetheart of the Rodeo*, and Gram Parsons' subsequent group the Flying Burrito Brothers, was that young coastal metropolitans were so secure in their place atop the pop mountain that they could do a bit of slumming and sound like hicks. The risks to their popularity with teenagers and college kids were limited—maybe. "Our fans were heartbroken that we'd sold out to the enemy," Byrd Roger McGuinn recalled. "Politically, country music represented the right wing—redneck people who liked guns."[12]

Meanwhile, another trend had arisen in the international pop community: blues rock. The success of conspicuously blues-based acts like the Stones, the Yardbirds, Cream, and Hendrix spurred various new artists who proudly asserted their gutbucket pedigrees: Fleetwood Mac, Free, Chicken Shack, Ten Years After, the Jeff Beck Group, and Savoy Brown from Britain and Electric Flag, Canned Heat, Johnny Winter, and Paul Butterfield in the States. Few scored really big for any great period, at least in their original lineups, but they established a template that would prove highly durable in the coming decade: they updated the licks and riffs of 1950s Chicago and the 1930s Mississippi Delta with distorted electric guitars and powerful rhythm sections; they depicted themselves in the rugged, denim-clad anonymity of truck drivers or ranch hands (albeit with shaggy beards and shoulder-length hair); and they mostly avoided the contemporary politics that preoccupied the rest of their generation. Perhaps most significantly, despite playing songs first developed by Black people, these groups were all comprised of young white men and women. The contrast between the sources of the original material and the audience and performers now embracing its modern editions could be painfully obvious—what did affluent university students and suburban harmonica players really know about the blues?—but the organic appeal of the music was inarguable; even the Beatles' *White Album* song "Yer Blues" commented on it. And there was no doubting the genuine blues feel of guitarists Peter Green in Fleetwood Mac or Mike Bloomfield with Butterfield and his own unit, the Electric Flag. Janis Joplin's wracked vocals on her bitterly comic plea "Mercedes Benz" (from *Pearl*, 1971) were the blues transposed to the tract-home milieu of working hard, nights on the town, and *Dialing for Dollars* on television.

The most popular band to arise out of this trend, Led Zeppelin, soon transcended the purist blues appropriations that marked its competitors (Zeppelin detractors would say they just ran out of blues classics to plagiarize), but leader Jimmy Page summed up the unified message: "I feel that some so-called progressive groups have gone too far with their personalized intellectualism of beat music. Our music is essentially emotional like the old rock stars of the past. . . . We are not going to make any political or moral statements."[13] By not taking an explicit position on day-to-day issues of war and peace, freedom and restraint, youth and age, white and Black, which were stirring the counterculture outside, the blues-rock performers were still taking a stand.

Complicating matters further was the Band. The Canadian-American outfit's debut record, *Music From Big Pink*, came out in July 1968, evoking yet more of the down-home sensibility that marked *John Wesley Harding* and country rock. Critically praised though by no means giant hits, the album and its follow-up the following year, *The Band*, took the rock vocabulary deeper into the Appalachian sounds of fiddles and accordions, as well as guitars, keyboards, and drums, and their song lyrics ("The Weight," "Up on Cripple Creek," "The Night They Drove Old Dixie Down") seemed to have been written sometime around the US Civil War. The Band demonstrated that the old, the rooted, and the timeless had a place in pop music as much as the trippy and the topical. When they won a *Time* magazine cover story in 1969, even chief songwriter Robbie Robertson couldn't quite put his finger on what it was they were doing: "Nobody could figure out what to call our gumbo of sounds. Was it 'roots rock'? 'modern ragtime'? 'Canadian Delta R&B'? 'cinema rock'? 'Americana from Canada'?"[14]

In contrast to the us-against-them, down-with-the-system ideologies that infused a lot of other rock 'n' roll, the Band evinced a maturity, even a world-weariness, unusual in the landscape of youth music. It also mattered that their vocalist on many tracks, including "Up on Cripple Creek" and "The Night They Drove Old Dixie Down," was the group's only American, Arkansas native Levon Helm, who sang with a rich southern accent far truer than the pseudo-blues affectations of other rock front men. "The Night They Drove Old Dixie Down" proudly asserted the singer's lineage as a working man, and *The Band*'s closing track, "King Harvest (Has Surely Come)," went so far as to sing of crop failure and farmers' unions in a scenario straight out of John Steinbeck. "It's just kind of a character study in a time period," Robertson said of "King Harvest." "At the beginning, when the unions came in, they were a saving grace, a way of fighting the big money people, and they affected everybody from the people that worked in the big cities all the way around to the farm people."[15] Having of course previously backed up Bob Dylan and, before him, journeyman barroom attraction Ronnie Hawkins, the members of the group were credentialed hard-partying rock stars in an era crowded with them, but their public personas as woodsy authentics were convincing.

In this heyday of what would later be called classic rock, the size of the market had become bigger than the capacity of any artist, producer, manager, or critic to comprehensively define it. At the same time the Band were releasing their most popular works, newcomer David Bowie issued his folk-futuristic *Space Oddity*, psychedelic stars the Doors put out the jazz-influenced *The Soft Parade*, and the San Franciscan Jefferson Airplane made the insurrectionist *Volunteers*. And those were only rock records; country, soul, and jazz music were also stretching and subdividing in equal measure. It was all mass-produced music, delivered in the strong economies of Western nations and accommodated by a pop culture that was expanding both commercially and artistically. Any single album, movie, novel, play, or television show might have been heralded as part of a portentous social movement. There was no telling which direction the various mediums might turn, or if there was still a single direction for them to go. Many things—anything—seemed possible.

Yet the cultural prospects were countered by a political present in which the upright conservative Ronald Reagan governed the very state where the hippies and the heads most flourished, and the law-and-order Republican Richard Nixon was running for US president. In August 1968 Nixon accepted the Republican Party nomination with a speech praising "the forgotten Americans, the non-shouters, the non-demonstrators. . . . They work in America's factories. . . . They provide most of the soldiers who died to keep us free."[16] The GOP candidate recognized that young Americans, most of them from poorer backgrounds, were still being drafted to fight and die in Vietnam, in place of their wealthier contemporaries on campuses.

At the same time, American cities were still being transformed by "white flight" as residents moved out to the suburbs of Detroit, Boston, Cleveland, Kansas City, Chicago, and elsewhere, leaving Blacks and Hispanics to establish themselves in the inner districts; the nation as a whole was experiencing a shift in population that was broadly migrating from the industrial north and east (Ohio, Pennsylvania, New York, New Jersey) to the south and west (Florida, Texas, Colorado, California). Despite social advances in civil rights for racial minorities and the first stirrings of women's and gay liberation movements, there still remained a sturdy assumption of straight white male superiority— the senior office staff, the astronauts flying to the moon, the faces reading the news on television, the people sitting in legislatures and corporate boards, and the crew of the day shift mostly belonged to the same demographic category.

Rock 'n' roll's most committed partisans extolled its transformative potential, but there remained a lot of transforming to do. Other listeners were less sure of what they wanted to change, and of how they wanted rock 'n' roll to change it. Elvis Presley's top-rated "comeback" NBC television special of December 1968, in which the King reclaimed his throne after a string of cheesy movies and lackluster singles sidelined him in the wake of Dylan and the Beatles, put the greatest of pop culture's southern white boys back in the spotlight shortly after Richard Nixon's election. Elvis performed a medley of early hits such as "Heartbreak Hotel," "Hound Dog," and "All Shook Up," reminding a huge audience of rock 'n' roll's original, undiluted vigor. It was then that the flux of garage rock, blues rock, country rock, the Band, the Byrds, and all the other voices of youth rebellion seemed ready to allow for yet another strain that could somehow reconcile the new instincts with old certainties, the rock spirit without the rock pretense, a strain that might promise a resurrection of the populism implied in older music and that continued to endure in the society at large—might promise, somehow, its revival.

2

Wrote a Song for Everyone

> The American bards shall be marked for generosity and affection and
> for encouraging competitors . . . . They shall be kosmos . . . without
> monopoly or secrecy . . . glad to pass any thing to any one . . . hungry
> for equals night and day. They shall not be careful of riches and priv-
> ilege . . . they shall be riches and privilege . . . they shall perceive who
> the most affluent man is. The most affluent man is he that confronts all
> the shows he sees by equivalents out of the stronger wealth of himself.
>
> **Walt Whitman, preface to** *Leaves of Grass*

Memphis. New Orleans. Virginia. Illinois. Richmond. Porterville. Moline.
Green River. Lodi. The Bayou. The songs of Creedence Clearwater Revival
contain a gazetteer of the American interior, a sometimes celebratory, often
bitter travelogue as documented by the nation's humble and humbled citizens.
CCR established a new archetype of rock stardom and rock music: they had
big commercial hits while retaining an image as industry outsiders, and they
made records that drove the genre forward by looking wistfully back. Back
to a more basic level of artistic craftsmanship, back to a less cynical national
spirit, back to a deeper connection with community and place. They tugged
the student protesters back down toward the earth and made the straights
think back on their fundamental freedoms. An entire shade of the pop and
political spectrum has been colored by Creedence.

The band's official output and working life spanned barely four years.
After a routine apprenticeship of gigging and tentatively recording as the
Blue Velvets and the Golliwogs around their base in the outlying areas of
the San Francisco Bay, the foursome signed a fateful contract with Fantasy
Records and proceeded to hit the US charts with their first single, a cover of
Dale Hawkins's 1957 cut "Suzie Q," in mid-1968, along with a self-titled debut
album and then the major success of their original song "Proud Mary" later
in the year. Into 1969 and 1970 they built a strong case for themselves as one
of the biggest rock groups in the United States and around the world, with the

Takin' Care of Business. George Case, Oxford University Press (2021). © George Case.
DOI: 10.1093/oso/9780197548813.003.0003

albums *Bayou Country*, *Green River*, *Willie and the Poor Boys*, and *Cosmo's Factory* released in the space of twenty-four months, along with constant tours and a performance at the Woodstock festival; the last record with the original quartet, *Pendulum*, came out in December 1970. During this period CCR made a nearly unexampled run of massively popular (and some double-sided) 45s: "Bad Moon Rising," "Lodi," "Up Around the Bend" / "Run through the Jungle," "Travelin' Band" / "Who'll Stop the Rain," "Have You Ever Seen the Rain" / "Hey Tonight," "Fortunate Son" / "Down on the Corner," "Green River"—a formidable greatest hits collection compiled in real time. Creedence Clearwater Revival formally broke up in October 1972, and outside of private functions never played together again.

Critics appreciated CCR as much as the public. Unlike the Band or the countrified Byrds, they did not sell a faintly contrived traditionalism, and unlike the blues rockers, they did not maintain a purist allegiance to format. Their apparent lack of self-consciousness was a refreshing change, not just from the excesses of psychedelia but from the grand ambitions that were now infecting every new rock "statement." A *Rolling Stone* review of 1969's *Green River* acknowledged how songwriter John Fogerty deftly stayed sincere without becoming overserious: "He never makes the mistake of straining to be 'poetic'; he selects ordinary words and images which always manage to be incisive. With a fine sense of economy, he depicts an American landscape that is somehow both older and newer than Chuck Berry's classic rock description of America: older in its nostalgic visions, and newer in its nightmarish perils and traps."[1] The rock aristocracy bestowed their own blessings on Creedence, with Brian Jones repeatedly playing "Proud Mary" at his English home during his doomed last weeks as a Rolling Stone and expressing a foggy wish to start a new group with a similar character, and with John Lennon avowing in his cathartic *Rolling Stone* interview of 1971: "I like Creedence Clearwater. They make beautiful clear water music—they make good rock and roll music."[2]

There were a number of components to Creedence's sound that made them stand out in the collage of late-1960s pop. Though in their day they were often classed as a hard rock act (and were known for their high concert volumes), they did not play distorted single-note riffs or fuzzed-out washes of feedback. Instead they had a trebly, strummy two-guitar signature that more often evoked the rockabilly picking of Scotty Moore or James Burton rather than the overdriven soloing of Jimi Hendrix or Eric Clapton; John Fogerty was a capable lead player, but he rarely took virtuoso spotlights. One of his favored guitars was a Rickenbacker, the same brand associated with the Beatles' jangly early material. Bassist Stu Cook and drummer Doug Clifford were a good but unspectacular rhythm section, and brother Tom Fogerty, who left CCR in 1971, was likewise no more than an adequate complementary guitarist. Creedence Clearwater Revival were seldom funky. The CCR tone was bright enough, and concise enough, to cut through the murk generated by most of their AM and FM radio rivals.

John's avoidance of power chords and wah-wah pedals meant most Creedence songs boasted unusually tight arrangements from beginning to end. In an era marked by instrumental indulgence, here was a band whose work was built around elemental majors and minors, technically simple yet put together with great musical solidity. "When you hear 'Proud Mary' and 'Bad Moon Rising,' it sounds so all-American," Fogerty judged. "People forget that it came out right in the middle of the acid period and the Strawberry Alarm Clock and the Grateful Dead. That's what was all around us, and yet I was preserving my own vision of what I thought rock 'n' roll should be."[3] Creedence's hit singles, and there were a profusion of them, were catchy without being lightweight. They had the intangible quality of sounding like public-domain standards, or at least lost rock 'n' roll gems from 1958, even while they ascended the Top 40 of 1969 and 1970. That ascent was itself a kind of throwback: by then many pop artists were gravitating to the "serious" plat-form of albums rather than 45s, but Creedence issued their most listenable music in the most affordable medium. Even now, millions of people know CCR through constantly rotated three-minute radio cuts, rather than any tracks hidden deep on long-playing vinyl.

The most immediately recognizable aspect of CCR tunes was John Fogerty's voice. Despite his Californian origins, he sang with a twangy drawl that many listeners believed came from Louisiana or Mississippi—his vocal influences included bluesman Howlin' Wolf and Little Richard, the Georgia Peach. It was an affected accent, sure, but a convincing one. Fogerty also had a loud, yelping delivery as a singer that made him effectively the act's acoustic trade-mark (listen to the obvious homage of Allan Clarke in the Hollies' "Long Cool Woman in a Black Dress" from 1972), no matter his slurred and sometimes indecipherable lyrics.

Visually, CCR also stood out. There were no sex symbols in the group. They never relied on the lighting or audio gimmicks that other acts employed at their shows, and it was a point of pride for John Fogerty that Creedence took the stage rehearsed and ready to entertain, unlike their Bay Area peers such as the Grateful Dead, who routinely tuned up and held loose jams in front of their audiences before settling on any particular song. The band's sole recur-ring sartorial effect was John's plaid flannel shirts. There were plenty of com-peting groups also comprised of scruffy longhairs, but CCR was conspicuous by the naturalness with which they wore their scruff and their hair; they didn't affect the shamanic eroticism of a Jim Morrison or a Mick Jagger. Critic Ellen Willis opined that John Fogerty "resembled the solid, sustaining husband who is forever being betrayed for the dashing, undependable lover."[4]

As much as anything, it was the very name "Creedence Clearwater Revival" that established the band's public persona. By the late 1960s the standard article-plural grammar designating rock 'n' roll ensembles had evolved past mere characterizations of the individual members (the Beatles, the Beach Boys, the Four Tops, the Yardbirds) and toward a more abstract syntax that described the players' unity (the Who, Them, the Strawberry Alarm Clock, the Electric Flag), eventually culminating in fully suggestive titles that declared an entire aesthetic mandate of which the music was only one iteration (It's a Beautiful Day, Quicksilver Messenger Service, Blind Faith, Moby Grape, Vanilla Fudge). Tom Fogerty initially floated the word *credence*, after Credence Nuball, a South African apartment custodian known to the brothers, while John briefly toyed with "Whiskey Rebellion" and "Whiskey Revival" until late 1967, when he saw an outdoorsy beer commercial on TV. "It's the water," promised the ad. The final combination of nouns—Creedence, Clearwater, Revival—announced the quartet's identity before a note had been sounded: integrity, clarity, nature, and a commitment to the restoration of older, endangered values.

Once CCR's songs were heard, there was no missing their message. Almost all of them composed and sung by John Fogerty, they sided with their generation's countercultural outlook but out of a sense of heritage, not utopianism; like other songwriters of his cohort, Fogerty often castigated American authorities, only not for being stuck in the nation's past but also for dishonoring it. He named the celebrated (and once blacklisted) antiwar folk artist Pete Seeger as a favorite lyricist, despite dutifully serving a stint in the US Army Reserve himself, after being drafted in 1966. Always suspicious of political leaders, Fogerty obliquely referred to Washington, DC and Richard Nixon in "Who'll Stop the Rain," "Effigy," "Commotion," and "Run through the Jungle" and called out California governor Ronald Reagan as "Ronnie the popular" in "It Came Out of the Sky." In "The Working Man" and "Don't Look Now (It Ain't You or Me)" he also reminded the audience of the ordinary people who weren't included in, or even much considered by, the rock culture. The Fogerty brothers came from a family of five boys whose parents had divorced (father a press operator, mother a nursery school teacher) and had grown up at the low end of the US middle class, which gave John a detached perspective on the idealism around him. "Even though new ideas were being vocalized, and there was all this hopefulness and do-gooderness, and we'd accomplished a lot of philosophical things through demonstrations and protests, my generation wasn't working in the blue-collar mainstream yet, and we weren't doing the kind of stuff that the pioneers who built our country did," he remembered. "So I was saying, 'Don't look now, but it's not you or me. Other people are the ones doing that stuff for us.'"[5] Elsewhere, he made the same point more harshly: "We're all so ethnic now, with our long hair and shit. But when it comes to doing the real crap that civilization needs to keep going, who's going to be the garbage collector? None of *us* will."[6]

CCR songs depicted low-paying menial jobs in other ways, as in the plate cleaning and gas pumping of "Proud Mary" and the bricklaying of "Penthouse Pauper," but the band's bluntest commentary on work, wealth, and social status was "Fortunate Son." Today a virtual anthem of proletarian reproach, the piece was issued on 1969's *Willie and the Poor Boys* album (the title was another acknowledgement of class) and, on the same 45 single as "Down On the Corner," reached no. 3 on the US *Billboard* charts in December that year. It has been featured in numerous films, video games, and even commercials, and in 2014 was added to the US National Recording Registry by the Library of Congress for its historic significance. "Fortunate Son" was Fogerty's attack on privileged politicians who launched wars they and their own children would never have to fight: born with silver spoon in hand, avoiding taxes, and waving the flag, they remain on the safe side of the cannons while the unlucky and the unconnected do the soldiering and the dying. It was a searing testimony released during the bloodiest period of America's involvement in Vietnam, even though no actual war or elected officials were mentioned specifically. "You'd hear about the son of this senator or that congressman who was given a deferment from the military or a choice position *in* the military," Fogerty explained. Since he had already done his required hitch (as had drummer Clifford) and had no VIP relatives to lean on, he shared his audience's resentment toward a patrician elite whose sons were made exempt from national service. "Usually I strive to make my songs more general, but that was one case where, when I said 'It ain't me,' I literally meant me."[7]

And "Fortunate Son" was all the more effective because it was presented as uptempo rock 'n' roll, by a group that just as often played straightforward party music like "It Came out of the Sky," "Hey Tonight," or, indeed, the tune's flip side, "Down on the Corner." Coming across as a fed-up burst of anger from people who would rather be having fun, its righteousness was believable in a manner that more preachy takes on similar themes (say, John Lennon's "Give Peace a Chance," or Buffy Sainte-Marie's "Universal Soldier") sometimes weren't. "Fortunate Son" was not a sermon but a model for future hymns to common-man frustration: the blistering denunciation of social injustice by musicians usually content to play on and resign themselves to it.

Its composer's achievement was in blending the inarticulate and immediate iconoclasm of rock's originators with the urgent, adult causes of the 1960s. "I'm a guy who admires 'Wooly Bully' as much as 'The Times They Are a-Changin','"[8] Fogerty declared.

Sadly, the dissent that was manifest in CCR songs was also a factor in the band's professional trajectory. As singer, songwriter, lead guitarist, and producer, John Fogerty was one man doing the work that most other groups of their stature shared among at least two or three, which birthed bad feeling on the part of his brother Tom, as well as the backup of Cook and Clifford. The Creedence ethos espoused grassroots democracy, but they didn't function as one. On top of the personal dynamics between the players, they were also locked into an egregiously inequitable contract with the small Fantasy label, which went on to mismanage or misallocate their substantial grosses and John's legal rights to the catalog of classic songs he had authored. A similar fate befell a lot of other young and innocent rock 'n' roll stars, but it destroyed the relationships within CCR. John Fogerty spent decades trying to recover his copyright and battled with the remaining Creedence members (Tom died in 1990) over earnings and licensing. The act that had enfranchised rock's regular guy got screwed over by the lawyers and the money men. It was an ironic finish to their short active life, even as "Proud Mary," "Bad Moon Rising," "Fortunate Son," and all the others enjoyed posthumous immortality.

Creedence Clearwater Revival's status as purveyors of hit singles and authentic Americana pointed to the ongoing transformation of rock from show business to cultural signifier. As the new decade opened, artists were becoming known less for their songs or their concerts than for what they seemed to mean to their core audience—or, taking another step back, for who their core audience was perceived to be. Once a distinct sideline of the entertainment market, rock had become as pluralistic as the society it entertained. Merely to put out a record or have a song played on the radio or appear on television was not what defined an act for potential consumers. The artist had to have a broader symbolic meaning for that artist to matter, critically and socially. The orthodoxy of this veered toward the perverse, insofar as artists who by any measure had never been heard by many people were elevated into cult heroes, while at the same time you could sell a million records and still be put down as "irrelevant." In his 1997 book *Mansion On the Hill*, music journalist Fred Goodman recalled the epoch's increasingly diverse community of connoisseurs: "There was something conveyed by the attitude of the bands and their records that stood apart from the music, and the way you spoke that language told people how you felt about the world. . . . For instance, a passion for a perfectly acceptable but lightweight group like Steppenwolf showed a certain genial rebelliousness but suggested a lack of depth; a girl who listened to a lot of Joni Mitchell could probably be talked into bed but you might regret it later; a single-minded focus on the Grateful Dead and the New Riders of the Purple Sage was a sure sign of a heavy dope smoker."[9]

Steppenwolf, as Goodman put it, was an act that drew just the sort of non-committal freaks and dropouts amassing around the edges of the hardcore antiwar marchers, militants, and sitters-in. Los Angeles-based but with roots in Canada, they might have remained only one among dozens of competent but unexceptional blues-rock groups plying their trade in clubs, studios, and campus bars around North America, except for an original song crafted by Steppenwolf guitarist Dennis McCrohan, aka Dennis Edmonton, aka, naturally, Mars Bonfire. The song was "Born to Be Wild." Released as a single from Steppenwolf's eponymous first album in mid-1968, it rose to no. 2 in the *Billboard* singles ranks by August and then received a further enormous push with its appearance on the soundtrack of the milestone "antiestablishment" movie *Easy Rider* the following year. A second Steppenwolf cut, "The Pusher," was actually the first song heard in the film, over shots of drug money being stashed in the gas tank of a Harley-Davidson, before "Born to Be Wild" accompanied the title sequence of Peter Fonda and Dennis Hopper taking to the open road on their choppers. "*Easy Rider* is the only film I know that not only uses rock well—though that is rare enough—but also does justice to its spirit,"[10] wrote Robert Christgau in the *Village Voice*. The back-to-back inclusion in a cinematic milestone was perhaps the peak of Steppenwolf's career, as they fragmented and reformed numerous times over the next years, continuing largely on the strength of their fistful of late-1960s successes, which also included the hits "Magic Carpet Ride," "Sookie Sookie," and "Hey Lawdy Mama."

But "Born to Be Wild" was more than a lucky break. "Certainly [the song] had a drive, an urgency with solid drumming and great guitar riffing," vocalist and leader John Kay would recollect. "Another key factor was timing. It was summer time, kids were out of school and wanted to hear more exciting, get it on, high-energy music. . . . The song's lyrics and message spoke to a generation which craved some excitement and some escape from the downer that America had become that year."[11] With its *Easy Rider* association, the number was soon identified with leather-jacketed desperado motorcyclists and for its pioneering use of the term "heavy metal" in its lyrics, which became the standard description of any fast and heavy guitar-based music. Now rock had isolated a demographic that was seen to be just as rebellious as the tie-dyed peaceniks of Woodstock or the VW van riders of San Francisco—as well as more dangerous, and probably more criminal—despite their expressing no obvious opposition to Vietnam, or pollution, or capitalism. Although Steppenwolf did in fact carry more pointed messages on their album cuts, such as "Draft Resister" and "America," and though they also did softer acoustic songs like "Spiritual Fantasy," both "Born to Be Wild" and "The Pusher" were important for how their rejection of mainstream values and lifestyles, and even those of their young contemporaries, was more implied by their overall sound than literally stated in their verses. Kay's guttural inflections took the language of rock 'n' roll outlawry to a new level. Steppenwolf didn't have to spell out their badassery; as far as average fans could tell, they were already living it. "No matter where—Canada, Scandinavia, Australia or at home—bikers have always supported the Wolf,"[12] Kay said. It was ironic that the singer himself, compromised by long-term visual impairment, had never driven anything more dangerous than a bicycle.

The biker contingent cast as Steppenwolf loyalists comprised a disconcerting sliver of the youth movement. They liked rock 'n' roll but had little interest in folk or soul; they liked sex and drugs but weren't so keen on peace and love; they had long hair, but they also had tattoos; they didn't want to overthrow the government, only to get it out of their business. They were not college kids clashing with their parents but working men letting off steam and living in a paramilitary spirit of camaraderie that inevitably drifted into organized crime: drug dealing, prostitution, and violent hits on rivals or renegades. The bikers were almost wholly white. *Easy Rider* confirmed their place in mass consciousness, as had more exploitative motorcycle pictures like *The Wild Angels*, *The Glory Stompers*, and *Hells Angels on Wheels*; gonzo journalist Hunter S. Thompson's landmark nonfiction book of 1966, *Hell's Angels: The Strange and Terrible Saga of the Outlaw Motorcycle Gangs*, further added to their cachet. In a 1968 think piece for the *Saturday Evening Post*, "I'm Going to Be a Movie Star," essayist Joan Didion noted the bikers' rise: "Bike movies are made for all these children of vague 'hill' stock who grow up absurd in the West and Southwest, children whose whole lives are an obscure grudge against a world they think they never made. These children are, increasingly, everywhere, and their style is that of an entire generation."[13] A few members of the Straight Satans gang were hanging around the Charles Manson Family's Los Angeles compound when the savage murders of August 1969 were committed (a couple of Straight Satans eventually gave evidence against Manson and his people), and a San Franciscan Hells Angels chapter wreaked havoc and homicide at the Rolling Stones' disastrous Altamont concert in December. At Altamont, Marty Balin of the Jefferson Airplane had been punched in the face by an Angel when he tried to stop an Angel assault in front of the stage where he was singing. "I ain't no peace creep, man,"[14] Sonny Barger of the San

Francisco Hells Angels later said. The bikers were a fringe of a fringe, a grittier, older, less placid element of the rock culture, whose presence in the coming years would become more noticeable.

Across the Atlantic, a parallel splintering in pop music was underway. The Beatles were descending into a litigious breakup, while the Rolling Stones were eyeing a tax exile away from their British base. The Kinks, prevented from touring the United States by a union dispute, were crafting a suite of songs celebrating common Britons and their place in a slowly ebbing imperial order. "He's just like so many guys who are pushed through life within the confines of the establishment,"[15] songwriter Ray Davies said of his title character in 1969's *Arthur (Or the Decline and Fall of the British Empire)*. Davies had already displayed a knack for portraying the lives of ordinary people, as in "Autumn Almanac" and the gorgeous "Waterloo Sunset" (both 1967), even though, as his co-Kink guitarist brother Dave put it, "It was all the rage to discard everything old: old ways, old styles, old people, too! But we weren't like that."[16] In fact popular songs in the United Kingdom of the time included such retro, old-time bashes as Dave Edmunds's "I Hear You Knocking," Norman Greenbaum's "Spirit in the Sky," and Free's "All Right Now"—simple, blues- and gospel-derived melodies by non-superstar, non-revolutionary performers who only wanted to give the public a good time. Here too the market had been stretched and balkanized out of whatever unity it had once enjoyed. No longer could one or two (or three or five) acts set the pace for all hip young listeners to follow, as disillusion and disintegration looked to be the singular trends of the new decade. Even if characterizations of cultural mood into ten-year divisions were arbitrary journalistic tropes, the months straddling 1969 and 1970 really did feel to have marked the end of the sixties.

Perhaps no single musical performance of that time encapsulated the instability of politics and pop culture more than Jimi Hendrix's rendition of "The Star-Spangled Banner" on a Fender Stratocaster at the Woodstock festival on the morning of August 18, 1969. Released in edited form on film and album the following year, the fuzz-, feedback-, and vibrato-laced solo take on the US national anthem is one of the rare moments of the rock era to deserve every application of the overused adjective "iconic." Hendrix's Woodstock set was the last of the entire event (in a somehow meaningful juxtaposition, he was preceded by the 1950s retro act Sha Na Na) and included several of his well-known pieces, like "Foxy Lady" and "Voodoo Chile (Slight Return)"; at Woodstock the Francis Scott Key song segued into the guitarist's own anthem, "Purple Haze." Hendrix had played similar versions of "The Star-Spangled Banner" prior to this date, but it was this one that became the most celebrated, and the most reviled. For all subsequent listeners, it turned into a sort of political Rorschach test: Was it a screeching anti-American insult or young America's articulation of patriotism? Was it a critique of Vietnam, assassinations, and ghettos or a dream of transcending them? Was it meant to offend or uplift? "I am no great admirer of our national anthem for either its artistic or patriotic merits," wrote the conservative *National Review*'s film critic John Simon of the 1970 *Woodstock* documentary, "but to hear and watch what Jimi Hendrix does to it—something ineffably ugly, inhuman, and hate-riddled—almost had me running for shelter to the nearest American Legion post."[17] Hendrix, who had briefly served in the US Army and who supported the American soldiers' Vietnamese commitment, never explicitly stated his intentions. Responding to press conference questions three weeks after Woodstock, he only offered, "We're all Americans. . . . It was like, 'Go America!' . . . We play it the way the air is in America today. The air is slightly static, see."[18]

Around the Western world, forces of change and convention circled in a complicated dance. For every outrageous gesture from this or that mod celebrity—every literary or cinematic or musical taboo broken, every traditional showbiz custom flouted, every sensational drug bust, nude scene, or contrived controversy—there was a retaliatory reaction from a suit-and-tie politician, clergyman, or academic. In Britain in April 1968, Conservative Member of Parliament Enoch Powell had spoken of potential "rivers of blood" in the wake of increased Asian immigration to the island kingdom (a Beatles tryout of "Get Back" in early 1969 had Paul McCartney joking about Pakistanis taking jobs away). In October 1970, Canadian prime minister Pierre Trudeau invoked the War Measures Act, suspending civil rights in the province of Quebec following a kidnapping and murder by Quebecois separatists.

The most ominous of these reactions was US president Richard Nixon's broadcast speech from the Oval Office on November 3, 1969, when he called on "the great, silent majority" of American citizens to back him in his continued prosecution of the Vietnam War. "I know it may not be fashionable to speak of patriotism or national destiny these days," Nixon intoned, "but I feel it is appropriate to do so on this occasion."[19] Nixon's oratory has been interpreted in some quarters as a coded appeal to white racism or a veiled threat by the many against the few, but the deeper consequence may have lain with his modifier *silent* rather than his noun *majority*. As he had in his 1968 acceptance of his party's nomination, the president was singling out the Americans who were largely inaudible to the news media and to Hollywood, and certainly to the airwaves of Top 40 AM and underground FM radio. You aren't getting much attention, Nixon implied, but I know you are there. The long-term strategy gradually taking shape in his administration was to win the workers' support away from the Democratic party—usually backed by organized labor—on the basis of cultural rather than economic appeal. With the right message, hard hats would vote their personal morality rather than their pocketbooks.

In a sense, though, Nixon had misread his own constituency. If most Americans were not marching against the Vietnam War, and if most had more circumspect views on civil rights and women's liberation than the activists and demonstrators on the TV news, that didn't mean they didn't want to make some noise themselves. Nixon had assumed the longhairs and dope smokers were all on the other side of the political divide; he didn't see that some of them still held on to the unfashionable ideals of patriotism and national destiny he invoked in November 1969. Older supporters of the president made no distinction between the rock generation and the protest generation, when in fact rock was inspiring many more young people beyond the shouters and the demonstrators. Put another way, antipathy to rock 'n' roll would turn out to be more about age than attitude. The phrase "silent majority" had actually been kicking around for a while in American public discourse. Oddly, it had appeared just the day before the presidential address, in a popular rock 'n' roll foursome's slow, sad song that was newly released, in which the singer cautioned bleakly that the silent majority wasn't keeping quiet anymore. The song was "Effigy," from the record *Willie and the Poor Boys*, by Creedence Clearwater Revival.

3
Free for All

When I hear a college kid say, "I'm oppressed," I don't believe him. You know what I'd like to do for one year? Live like a college kid. Just for one year. I'd love to. . . . Wow! Sports car! Marijuana! . . . Somebody has to do this work. If my kid ever goes to college, I just want him to have a little respect, to realize that his dad is one of those somebodies.

Mike Lefevre, quoted in Studs Terkel, *Working*

In 1969 the city of Detroit was already beginning its painful passage from America's industrial powerhouse to hollowed-out Rust Belt wasteland. Its chief business of auto manufacturing was increasingly affected by automation, decentralization of facilities, and competition from foreign builders such as Volkswagen and Toyota. Detroit's fabled manufacturing productivity, which had rolled out thousands of bombers and tanks during World War II, had fallen behind the output of its wartime enemies: the city's plants built ten vehicles per worker annually, but in Japan, Toyota's built fifty. Adding insult to injury, the "Big Three" employers of Ford, General Motors, and Chrysler each faced challenges from consumer advocates like Ralph Nader, as well as the general public, for making inefficient, unsafe, and environmentally destructive cars. Meanwhile, despite federal efforts to desegregate, the metropolitan region became more and more divided into all-white and all-Black neighborhoods. Two years before, a major race riot had claimed the lives of forty-three citizens and had necessitated the intervention of the state National Guard. The July 1967 violence in Detroit's urban core accelerated the ongoing exodus of white residents to the suburbs of Sterling Heights, St. Clair Shores, Livonia, and elsewhere, shrinking the local tax base and thereby reducing city services, thus spurring further depopulation, in an ongoing cycle. It was only as recently as May 1964, in nearby Ann Arbor, Michigan, that President Lyndon Johnson had announced a national goal of building "the Great Society." Nothing so promising could be anticipated from the social and economic situation of Detroit as the decade turned.

Takin' Care of Business. George Case, Oxford University Press (2021). © George Case.
DOI: 10.1093/oso/9780197548813.003.0004

Except, perhaps, in its music. The Motor City was still home to Berry Gordy's Motown Records, the label of the Supremes, the Miracles, Stevie Wonder, the Four Tops, Marvin Gaye, and a roster of other stars whose up-beat soul had become a fixture of international pop. Motown wasn't just the name of one studio or distributor; it was an entire genre. Such was Motown's success that Gordy had begun to sign white acts alongside his traditionally African American lineup of performers, including Rare Earth, who eventually had hits covering the Temptations' "Get Ready" and "(I Know) I'm Losing You." Detroit was also home to white artists emerging outside of the Motown brand, such as Mitch Ryder and the Detroit Wheels, Frijid Pink, the Amboy Dukes, and the politically radical Motor City Five (MC5), whose onstage order was "Kick out the jams, motherfuckers" and whose private imperative was "rock and roll, dope, and fucking in the streets." Their 1969 live album *Kick Out the Jams* featured the slow blues rebellion of "Motor City Is Burning." A second gang of Michigan provocateurs was the Stooges, who like the MC5 also premiered in 1969 on the Elektra label, with their own variation of lo-fi, DIY garage rock in "No Fun" and "I Wanna Be Your Dog."

But despite the approval of the rock press (*Rolling Stone* ran a profile, "Toking Down with the MC5" in January 1969) and future rock historians, neither the Stooges nor the MC5 were anywhere near the most popular white rock act out of the Detroit area. That distinction went to Grand Funk Railroad. Grand Funk was formed in the satellite auto manufacturing center of Flint, a short drive northwest of the Motor City. In contrast to Ann Arbor, where the MC5 and the Stooges were based, Flint was not a college town: its main employer was General Motors rather than the University of Michigan. That's not to say that the Grand Funk members were real working men while the other groups were student poseurs, but it's as handy a stereotype as any. "It's kind of like . . . they were rock snobs," was how Grand Funk's Don Brewer made the distinction between the two cities. " 'Oh, they're just that band from Flint.' We were being written off."[1] GFR's Mark Farner was to recall of his high school years in Flint, "As things went in that school we had the uppity people with their noses up in the air and then there were the rich kids. . . . Then there was us—all the middle class and lower class kids who fell into the same category."[2] Their trio configuration of Farner (guitar and vocals), Brewer (drums and vocals), and Mel Schacher (bass) was designed in emulation of the influential British threesome Cream, although GFR didn't, or couldn't, try to match Cream's prowess at dazzling instrumental workouts.

The most important factor in Grand Funk Railroad's rise, in fact, was less the abilities of its musicians than the strategy of its manager, fellow Flintian Terry Knight. "He had the gift of gab and could really hype something,"[3] Farner acknowledged, and Brewer agreed: "Terry really knew how to stretch the truth and make everything bigger and louder than real."[4] Knight was himself a young singer and DJ who had kicked around the rock scene for a while but drew Farner and Brewer out of his own group, Terry Knight and the Pack, and pulled Schacher from a later edition of the novelty act ? and the Mysterians. GFR made a well-received national debut at the Atlanta Pop Festival in July 1969 and a month later at the Texas International Pop Festival, each time playing in front of over a hundred thousand receptive youths gathered to see a slate of better-known artists. Other big festival gigs followed. Knight channeled these fortuitous exposures into promoting the Grand Funk albums *On Time* (1969), *Grand Funk*, aka "The Red Album" (1969), *Closer to Home* (1970), *Survival* (1971), and *E Pluribus Funk* (1971). He also made much of the band's connection with its audience, over its usually negative reviews from the mainstream and youth press. What fans got from a typically loud and boisterous Grand Funk show, he stated, was that "It allows them to forget for ninety minutes that their brothers are being killed in Vietnam. . . . GFR's message to all people is 'Look at me—I'm free!' "[5] The inner sleeve of the 1972 compilation record *Mark, Don and Mel* featured a collage of scathing press clips from those who couldn't dig it.

During these short few years, Grand Funk Railroad was probably the biggest-grossing rock 'n' roll band in America, in both record and ticket sales. They played a packed Shea Stadium in 1971, selling the venue out faster than their Capitol labelmates the Beatles had six years prior. But the critical assault continued: "Grand Funk has continued to be such an unprecedented musical phenomenon despite the utter worthlessness of its music," ran one writeup, while another slagged them as "almost certainly the vilest phenomenon in rock's recent history. . . . Exploiting the distressing fact that the teenage audience it gears itself toward is incapable of distinguishing either hideous noise from music or perverse exhibitionism from real emotion, Grand Funk deals with the former in both regards."[6] For "serious" rock journalists and listeners—most of them more educated and certainly older than the album buyers or concert attendees whose tastes they disparaged—GFR were indisputably an indication of the music's decline. "You don't think something that's as obviously bad as Grand Funk Railroad has an effect on the overall quality of the music?" ex-Beatle John Lennon was queried about the state of rock in 1971. Lennon didn't take the bait. "I don't think it does," he replied. "More people can assimilate more shit, but the shit is relatively the same as it ever was."[7] Grand Funk's archenemy *Rolling Stone* was unusually generous in saying, "They are to real rock and roll what a PTA versifier is to poetry, but there is no more reason to decry their ascension than to moan about hula hoops or beach blanket movies or any of a hundred other fads which have captured huge audiences in the past."[8]

Contrary to reputation, however, at least a few contemporary writers were willing to express a tentative sympathy toward Grand Funk's obvious public appeal versus their artistic failings. After all, wasn't rock 'n' roll *supposed* to be populist entertainment that outraged stuffy outsiders? Weren't the earlier generations of rock performers, including those now revered as innovators and geniuses, once dismissed by adults too? If millions of ordinary kids were into it, how could they be wrong? Robert Christgau in the *Village Voice* admitted of *Closer to Home*, "Maybe I'm beginning to appreciate—I said appreciate—their straight-ahead celebration of beat, amplification, and youthful camaraderie,"[9] while in the same publication, Ellen Willis granted of Grand Funk, "I'm glad they're around as an antidote to James Taylor and the other upper-class brats; their adrenaline is bound to do us all good in one way or another. . . . Mark Farner's political clichés are fallout from counterculture fantasies that were exciting because taboo and later embarrassing because naive."[10] The assessments were a musical version of the what's-the-matter-with-Kansas political conundrums that would stump American progressives in the coming years: Of course we stand with the noble common folk, but why can't the bumpkins realize what's good for them?

Perhaps the biggest indictment of Grand Funk was that their huge success derived from a sound, visual style, and lyrical attitude that would have been shockingly confrontational just a few years before but that now was blithely accepted by a broad cohort of adolescents. To detractors, they and Terry Knight were mere yahoos taking oblivious advantage of cultural changes that earlier waves of rock ensembles had fought hard to bring about. "Grand Funk took our spot," said Dennis Thompson of the Motor City Five. "Had the MC5 not made some of the tactical mistakes we had made in the business community and in philosophy, we would have been bigger than Grand Funk."[11] (One big mistake was when members of the MC5 developed heroin habits.) "We were the people's band,"[12] Mark Farner claimed, echoing Knight's ad copy and liner notes—except the GFR people were teenagers in 1971, not 1965 or 1959, which made all the difference. Grand Funk was not really in the same musical league as fellow hard rockers Led Zeppelin, whose breakthrough first records and tours were competing with theirs (the two bands shared a bill at Detroit's Olympia Stadium in 1970), but at the time each group faced a comparable ageist snobbery. As Zeppelin biographer Stephen Davis recognized, "Already Led Zeppelin was in trouble because it was the younger kids, the little brothers and sisters of the great sixties generation, who loved Zeppelin the most. . . . Its popularity wasn't just confined to the world of rock, but to a despised segment of the rock audience—young, mostly male, mostly working-class cannon-fodder youth."[13] Grand Funk capitalized on a similar reception by the identical market. Numerous later acts would come in for parallel complaints, uttered without irony from paying consumers of mass-merchandised pop music: "Those guys suck—too *commercial*."

GFR were never completely apolitical—*E Pluribus Funk* had songs called "People, Let's Stop the War" and "Save the Land"—but they more often delivered a kind of innocuous electric stomp, at once blustering and bland, that made little pretense to social commitment or blues authenticity. Their most enduring singles came after they split with Knight over a management dispute in 1972: covers of R & B gems "Some Kind of Wonderful" (1974) and the Gerry Goffin–Carole King–penned "Loco-Motion" (a Number One the same year), and the Don Brewer original from 1973, "We're an American Band," which summed up them and their community. Notwithstanding its title, the song wasn't about national pride, but instead about the routine adventures of a group admitting to be basically little different from any other touring rock 'n' roll act: *a* band, not *the* band, or the *Band*, or any other special people. "We're an American Band," a classic rock radio staple to this day, offers its own landscape of the US heartland—Omaha and Little Rock—and references their opening act the great African American blues guitarist Freddie King, as well as the infamous Arkansas groupie Connie Hamzy. "That's really what we were doing," Brewer remembered. "We were coming into town and we *were* the party. . . . It wasn't to wave the flag or anything, it was just simply what we were."[14]

Aside from Grand Funk Railroad, the biggest influence on rock to spring from the industrial sector of southern Michigan was not a band but a magazine. During this period a small library of youth, music, and countercultural periodicals crowded the shelves of record stores and college reading rooms everywhere—many came and went after a few issues; some were renamed or remade over their run; some never broke out of regional markets, while a handful were distributed across North America. *Rolling Stone* was the most visible, but *Crawdaddy, Hit Parader, National Lampoon, Stereo Review, High Times, Circus,* and numerous others catered to the same young baby boomer clientele with time and discretionary income on their hands. In March 1969 the first edition of *Creem* was published and retailed out of a Detroit head shop.

Over the next few years, *Creem*'s format grew slicker as its success attracted a masthead of talented contributors and a following around the United States. *Creem* staked out a singular identity within the field of rock journalism and vied with the established *Rolling Stone* as the preeminent music magazine for young people. The two journals were not polar opposites: to a large extent they shared readerships, advertisers, and, at different times, staff. Writers whose work ran in both magazines included Cameron Crowe, Dave Marsh, Greil Marcus, Robert Christgau, and Lester Bangs, who served as *Creem*'s editor during its glory years from 1971 to 1975. *Creem* did not automatically endorse what *Rolling Stone* disliked, or vice versa. But the Detroit publication was all over noisy upstarts like the MC5 and the Stooges and didn't genuflect before the introspective *Rolling Stone* darlings of Bob Dylan, James Taylor, and Joni Mitchell. "It was about hard-core rock and roll rather than what was going down in California," said Robin Sommers, a friend of *Creem* founder Barry Kramer. "It was the real deal about the music—that's what got Lester Bangs and these guys. It was no bullshit."[15]

Whereas *Rolling Stone* commissioned lengthy forays into political and social reportage (for example, regular contributions from the notorious Hunter S. Thompson), *Creem* was all about rock. Whereas *Rolling Stone* expended much of its column space on substantive articles and reviews, *Creem* featured more glossy photos, punchy captions, and contest and award pages. Whereas *Rolling Stone* gradually expanded its coverage to include film and television celebrities, *Creem* stayed rigorously attentive to musicians, even musicians far down from any showbiz A-list. Most importantly, whereas *Rolling Stone* cast itself as the responsible record of countercultural news and ideas, *Creem* took an irreverent, at times almost satirical view of rock 'n' roll, along with its followers, its scribes, and its stars. "We do not think of ourselves as professional journalists and we do not want to adopt that distant, oracular stance of professional journalists," ran a 1970 *Creem* editorial cowritten in part by Barry Kramer and Dave Marsh. "We do not want to be another Rolling Stone."[16] Given its headquarters in Detroit, the magazine was not so much blue-collar as midwestern in its outlook, seeing performers and their concerts as an average fan from Ohio or Nebraska might see them, rather than as a media vulture from New York or Los Angeles. *Creem* approached its subjects for what they usually were—itinerant entertainers trying to drum up business as they slogged across the country—instead of the Next Big Things their publicists on the coasts touted them to be. *Creem* was rarely as dazzled by big-name glamour as *Rolling Stone*.

By the early 1970s there were many such rock bands drumming up business as they slogged across the country. With the largest population in America consisting of adolescents and young adults, the sheer size of the market turned rock 'n' roll into a considerable industry, to the eternal regret of the diehards who cherished visions of a post-capitalist utopia serenaded gratis by the Grateful Dead and the Rolling Stones. Record companies, recording studios, record shops, FM radio stations, stereo and instrument manufacturers, and print commentaries like *Rolling Stone* and *Creem* all spun off from the vast cultural and commercial force that rock had become. But no aspect of the boom was as loud or amplified its impact as literally as the concert business. With so many prospective ticket buyers wanting to see so many acts competing for their attention, it was inevitable that the great infrastructure of the touring rock enterprise took shape. Broadcasting, films, and magazines could spread the news about rock 'n' rollers, too, but the most effective promotion was still the live performance. Even with the growing reach of corporate media, there remained parts of North America where no rock documentary or *Rolling Stone* cover could win converts as persuasively as in-person appearances. For that, bands had to travel, and to travel, bands had to have places to play.

Up until this time rock 'n' roll tours were haphazard, ad hoc arrangements between artists' managements and a varied gaggle of local promoters. Acts often had to scramble for individual gigs one at a time in unpredictable and often geographically illogical sequences. Payment, accommodation, and the logistics of transport were just as erratic. Gradually, however, sharp-eyed businessmen saw the prospective revenue from organized itineraries preplanned from a central location. The key figure here was Frank Barsalona of New York's Premier Talent, the first American booking agent to specialize in rock. "When I first started to become an agent, contemporary music was the armpit of the business," Barsalona recalled. "You used a hit record as, at most, a first stepping stone to television or motion pictures. . . . A hit record was useful only to get you bookings on *The Ed Sullivan Show*, at the Copa or in casinos."[17]

Barsalona's innovation was to link up the trail of regional players into viable networks of venues that could then be negotiated at rates that made road work worthwhile for acts who weren't otherwise getting much press. Indeed, he believed that mass media coverage by itself could prove harmful in the long run, and he recommended his clients limit their appearances to live concerts at select times and places: the trick was to maintain unfulfilled demand as long as possible, rather than oversell through TV. His efforts on behalf of British groups like the Who and Herman's Hermits in the mid-1960s had established his name, and he went on to book tours for many hungry new bands willing to put in the hours and mileage required to build an audience—everyone from Mitch Ryder to Led Zeppelin. "Frank pretty much dictated who would be successful and who wouldn't,"[18] said Chip Rachlin, another agent who had been employed by concert impresario Bill Graham. Barsalona was also among those who detected, and capitalized on, the generational divide that had opened up between the strident class of '67 and the less revolution-minded youngsters growing up in their shadow. "In the States I think this is one of the reasons for the popularity of a Grand Funk Railroad," he said in a *Billboard* interview of 1970. "They have been put down repeatedly by the underground press but the younger kids are not letting the press tell them what to like."[19]

Because a schedule of concerts could now be coordinated with at least a semblance of predictability from city to city—guaranteed fees or percentages of the gate, prearranged airline flights or van rentals, a reserved floor at the local Holiday Inn for the players and the crew—the road became a kind of job. Doing gigs was of course more fun and, measured by money made per hour of paid labor, more lucrative, yet regular touring made for a kind of identification between players and spectators. The musicians felt the nightly strains, drudging down times, and physical exhaustion of their routine, even as the punters could see that, like the Grand Funk Railroad of "We're an American Band," the most durable groups were providing solid value for entertainment dollar. Few of the kids going to the shows were really expecting (or, for the most part, really seeking) a message of insurrection from whatever trio or quartet or quintet was in the spotlights—they just wanted an assurance that the bands plied their trade onstage as diligently as they or their parents did at the factory.

Touring, then, didn't just pay off for the artists and the promoters. Professionalized circuits of gigs meant rock 'n' roll shows could be viable in locations far from the coastal scenes with their psychedelic ballrooms or hip nightclubs. The revelation of the road was that the rock culture had taken hold far beyond Swinging London, the Sunset Strip, or Haight-Ashbury. A hard-working group might find itself pulling crowds in plain old Indianapolis or Pittsburgh, not just the big college town of Boston; you could profitably blow through Des Moines or Denver on your way to the Fillmore in San Francisco. The fans in those places appreciated the access to live music and, vicariously, to a way of life they might never have encountered firsthand. It didn't matter if the performers weren't international sensations. It didn't matter if they didn't have a familiar catalog of hit records. It didn't matter if they hadn't appeared on TV. It was enough that they were coming to town, offering a good time and a taste of big-city decadence on a Saturday night.

Again, with the size of the audience swelling with the teen years of the baby boom, the capacity of the buildings where acts were booked grew accordingly. A local theater or hall, purposely designed for musical performances, could not accommodate everyone wanting to see an up-and-coming artist, but only the biggest names (e.g., the Rolling Stones) or all-star festivals were filling outdoor stadiums. Indoor ice arenas struck the preferred balance between the two. So a successful set of American dates for a rising rock 'n' roll band in 1974 might include appearances at the Baltimore Civic Center; the Cumberland

County Civic Center in Portland, Maine; the State Farm Show Arena in Harrisburg, Pennsylvania; the Veterans Memorial Auditorium in Providence, Rhode Island; Cobo Arena in Detroit; the Cincinnati Gardens; the Winterland Arena in San Francisco; the San Diego Sports Arena; and the Greensboro Coliseum in Greensboro, North Carolina. A real sign of making it would be a night at Madison Square Garden in New York City. Venturing north of the border, the band could play Maple Leaf Gardens in Toronto, the Forum in Montreal, and out to the PNE Agrodome in Vancouver. All such sites could seat anywhere from a couple of thousand to twenty thousand people, paying anywhere between five and ten bucks to get in. Once the roadies packed up and the tour moved on, a hockey or basketball game, or a trade convention or a dog show, might be the next day's event in the same facility.

Touring arenas affected not only artists' careers but also their sound. These were not intimate performances. Amplification and public address systems of the era could not do justice to the tonal subtleties of acoustic guitars or close harmonies; the reverberations and aural temperament of the buildings themselves meant that overly complex or subtle playing—if not executed with care—would degenerate into a booming murk of echo or feedback, or simply go unheard. Acts who became familiar with the sonic properties of arenas learned to highlight music that carried from the stage over the hubbub of the audience and to the furthest bleachers without undue signal loss. This required a significant backline of equipment carried by the band themselves, which would then be situated right with them on the boards and which was incorporated into an essential part of their visual presentation: a Marshall stack or a Fender Twin Reverb was no longer a backup accessory nobody needed to see but an integral element of the spectacle. The songs too were increasingly built on bass-heavy guitar riffs and backbeats, and the long projection of quasi-operatic vocal effects. "Arena rock" was not just anything played in arenas but a particular subcategory crafted to work best specifically within the buildings' audio parameters.

A quick rundown of the traveling rock 'n' roll lineups shaking the rafters of North America in the first half of the 1970s lists a who's who of living or eventual legends, along with a "Where are they now?" file of also-rans. Argent; Hot Tuna; Wishbone Ash; Cactus; Sir Lord Baltimore; Dust; Poco; they were crisscrossing the continent at the same time as the Who, Bob Dylan, the Band, the Grateful Dead, Johnny Winter, the James Gang, Traffic, Santana, Steve Miller, Fleetwood Mac, and Grand Funk Railroad. Within that firmament of star power, bright futures, and fading glows, fans could still distinguish between the social or even economic identities of rival acts. The Beatles had broken up and rarely came down from their separate summits (Paul

McCartney and Wings made a much-publicized return to the United States in 1976), while the Stones made huge US tours in 1972 and 1975. Led Zeppelin played the States annually until 1973, after which they only performed only in 1975 and 1977. No matter what the musicians got up to during those intervals—recording an album, forming a vanity record label, ending a marriage, deepening a drug dependency—such gaps represented a long time in the life of a typical eighteen-year-old suburbanite in Illinois or Florida. It was then that the newer, keener bands made their name.

Years later, critic Ann Powers sketched a composite of these concertgoers: "The prevailing stereotype of the arena rocker depicted a party animal, occupying the lowest rung on the ladder of American pop culture. Even other rock fans saw them as pot-smoking dropouts who had betrayed rock's countercultural potential. . . . Arena rockers gave their male working-class fans a way to believe in themselves when others degraded them."[20] Without especially rejecting the more famous artists, audiences of American high schoolers found they wanted a Rolling Stones without the celebrity glamour, or a Zeppelin, Jethro Tull, and Deep Purple with the mysticism turned down, or a Pink Floyd and Yes without the progressive pretensions. It's conceivable, too, that this mostly white cohort wanted the guitar showmanship of Jimi Hendrix without having to cheer a Black man at center stage. Maybe the fans just wanted cheaper tickets, or to see a show in their home town rather than in the big city a day's drive away. Whatever they weren't getting from the rock royalty, there were plenty of commoners willing to provide it in their stead.

Humble Pie was just such a band. A reliable draw in America during the first half of the 1970s, they had come from Britain under the aegis of A&M Records and Frank Barsalona's Premier Talent and were drilled in the expectations of the road by manager Dee Anthony, formerly of the Bronx. Humble Pie's drummer Jerry Shirley recalled the orders given the group by Barsalona and Anthony: "Okay, guys. We're gonna go ta woik. We're gonna woik and woik and woik. And when we're done woikin', we're gonna woik some more."[21] They never topped the charts, starred in a movie, or made the cover of *Rolling Stone*, but no one minded. The Humble Pie sound was quintessential skinny English kid blues, typified by their irresistible "Thirty Days in the Hole" and covers of R&B gems like Ike and Tina Turner's "Black Coffee," Muddy Waters' "I'm Ready," and Ray Charles's "I Don't Need No Doctor." Material like this, delivered in places that had been used as skating rinks and business conventions a few hours before, were what got attendees out of their seats in 1972: high-energy electric boogie unburdened by deep messages or political meaning, beyond getting it together and feeling all right.

Humble Pie won a choice spot opening for Grand Funk Railroad at the GFR Shea Stadium show in 1971, but their most valuable asset was singer-guitarist Steve Marriott's voice. Marriott had an exhortatory zeal that emerged both during songs and between them, urging on his audiences with an evangelical fervor that was almost a parody of the Black gospel tradition: *Are you ready? I said are you ready? Even you people at the back of the hall? Whoa-yeah!* It was a style that became de rigueur for every hard rock act since—the exuberant frontman imploring the crowd to put their hands together and have a good time, even as he had urged the exact same directive to another crowd in another city the previous night and wasn't quite sure how he'd gotten from one point to the other (particularly for the hard-partying Marriott). From the bleachers and the floor, Marriott's preaching won a lot of converts, at least for the time he was onstage. Where they had once been cathartic ceremonies of adolescent female desire, then reverent gatherings of the stoned and the tripping, concerts were now becoming secular festivals of sheer celebratory release, driven by the high-decibel sensory impact put out by the likes of Humble Pie.

Canada produced its own contribution to arena rock. Bachman-Turner Overdrive was a splinter of the previously successful Guess Who, singer-guitarist Randy Bachman forming his own quartet after breaking with the Guess Who's vocalist, Burton Cummings. With Randy in the spotlight and his brothers Tim and Robbie to the side along with Fred Turner, this early lineup was called Brave Belt but adopted the BTO tag once signed to the Mercury label and after the players had spotted the word "overdrive" on a trucking magazine in the Canadian auto city of Windsor, Ontario, across the border from Detroit. "The universal appeal of their music was that it was understandable rock 'n' roll," said Charlie Fach of Mercury. "It was workingman's rock 'n' roll."[22] "BTO was a blue-collar band, that was its base of appeal," agreed Randy Bachman. "Our songs were about average guys. . . . During the time of glam rock and platform boots we weren't wimps or pretty boys."[23]

The Bachmans came from the prairie capital of Winnipeg, Manitoba, and over the next few years of constant touring, BTO built a solid core of support across the grasslands and river valleys of North America. They had a string of crunching rock hits, whose titles alone declared a loyalty to the loading dock and the punch card: "Let It Ride," "Takin' Care of Business," "Not Fragile," "Blue Collar," "You Ain't Seen Nothing Yet," and the inevitable road anthem, "Roll On Down the Highway." Their band logo was a rotary gear. Though the saying wasn't Bachman's invention, the popularity of the three-chord nine-to-five rocker "Takin' Care of Business" made it a national catchphrase for anyone completing any kind of job. In its review of 1974's *Not Fragile* album, *Rolling*

Stone called the group "a lowest-common-denominator rock band. . . . It's a very simplistic operation, but what BTO lack in imagination, subtlety, technique, structural dynamics, flash et al, they more than compensate for with lots of volume."[24]

Randy Bachman, in fact, was a talented guitarist whose influences included the brilliant Winnipeg jazz player Lenny Breau, and as a practicing Mormon he was an almost superhumanly self-denying participant in the rock business of the 1970s (his less devout brother Tim was in time sacked and replaced by Blair Thornton). Having seen the Guess Who disintegrate under a variety of business and personal pressures, he took pride in his straight-arrow lunch-bucket career ethos. "I'm a conservative guy," he told *Rolling Stone* correspondent Cameron Crowe in a skeptical 1975 interview. "I don't do anything wild or freaky. I like solid, dependable people. I like a solid, dependable way of living. I like to play solid, dependable guitar. I'm Mister Middle-of-the-road."[25] If this attitude did little to endear him to the arbiters of rock 'n' roll cool, it did create an affinity between BTO and their audiences in Fargo, North Dakota, or Sioux City, Iowa, where the abstemiousness of Bachman and his bandmates meant they could lucratively play markets that didn't pay enough to cover the cocaine expenses of more libertine acts. "In the early months we would play anywhere," Bachman remembered. "We would do drive-in theatres with a stage in front of the screen on a Saturday afternoon. People would sit out on their car hoods like it was a picnic."[26] Bachman could not compete with other performers for drugged-out depravity, but he and BTO could deliver a sanitized, truck-stop variation of it that was as much as could be handled in small towns around the Great Plains or the Great Lakes.

For true drugged-out depravity, you'd want early Aerosmith. During the 1970s, Aerosmith too was another band steadily riding the long highways and hitting the rec centers and municipal gardens of the flyover states—only they weren't Mormons. They'd started gigging around their home turf of New England, but after signing with Columbia Records and putting out a debut album in early 1973, they were quickly dispatched working the entire country. For five young men in their early twenties, ambition and adrenaline were enough to keep them going at a grueling pace, although other stimulants were added to help out.

At first the strongest pull of Aerosmith was just that they were *there*. By the mid-1970s their clear models of the Rolling Stones and Led Zeppelin were unimaginably distant figures whose US appearances came only every couple of years and whose concerts were guaranteed sellouts of huge outdoor spaces. The 'smiths were a slouchy and conspicuously stoned quintet (like the Stones) who played groove-laden hard rock (like Zeppelin), already on their way to

FM radio immortality with "Dream On": they had fairly approximated the visual and musical elements of the two big British bands, but unlike the Stones and Zeppelin they were actually performing an almost continuous regular engagement of the continent. "The touring never stopped," guitarist Joe Perry recounted. "We never stopped playing Detroit. We never stopped playing Columbus, Fort Wayne, Cincinnati, Cleveland. We felt like if we could win the heart of America, the rest of the country would follow."[27] In those days, with hardly any rock-oriented television showcases and before MTV, touring was how records were marketed. The shows themselves, however enjoyable for the fans and inspiring to the players, might barely earn enough to cover the costs of travel and stage sets. But they made word-of-mouth reputations that got kids flipping through the record racks at Walgreens or K-Mart. They were occasions for local autograph sessions or radio interviews that sold 8-track cartridges in the downtown music store. They turned idly curious people who'd spent five dollars for a ticket into true believers who'd drop another five for the album. The touring never stopped.

Just like Humble Pie, Bachman-Turner Overdrive, and any number of other artists they shared booking agents and (indirectly) venereal diseases with, Aerosmith was inventing arena rock by trial and error, helping to codify the medium in which they worked. The walls of Marshall, Fender, Hiwatt, Ampeg, Laney, or Orange amplifiers; the racks of backup Strats, Les Pauls, SGs, and Flying Vs; the impregnable Ludwig or Premier drum kits; the volcanic opening numbers (say, "Toys in the Attic" for the 'smiths) and the celebratory encores (maybe "Mama Kin"); the stand-alone guitar and drum solos; the vocalist and lead guitarist leaning together at a single mic and harmonizing on the choruses; the big showstopping hits; the singer's leering stage patter referencing the hometown crowd; the flicked lighters; the cloud of pot smoke wafting up to the ceiling—they all became indispensable elements of the experience. And groups like Aerosmith discovered that what was effective in a studio didn't always translate well to live recital in a large space; conversely, an ex tempore jam that closed a set could turn out to be absolutely devastating when later committed to tape with lyrics added. Perry said he was given valuable lessons in orchestration by Led Zeppelin, who'd been playing the same mid-sized, middle American barns just a few years before him: "We learned a lot in terms of playing big places with the echo. . . . Rock 'n' roll, a lot of it, is all about sex and the tribal rhythms, and there are certain tempos that work better in a big, echoey hall. It may sound great and exciting when you listen to it on record in your living room, but live in a great big arena it doesn't sound the same. . . . And they knew how that kind of music, if you played it a certain way with certain rhythms, was going to work better."[28]

Aerosmith was also smack in the middle of an America roiling under the combined effects of Watergate, inflation, and gas shortages (eventually Aerosmith would only be in the middle of smack). By then the mines, steel mills, and manufacturing plants of Ohio, Michigan, Indiana, New York, Massachusetts, and Pennsylvania were either drastically laying off or embroiled in bitter worker-management battles during the twilight of American organized labor's collective influence. The rock 'n' roll audience in the industrial Northeast, even if they weren't yet wage earners themselves, were living in an inexorable economic decline for which the classic run of whiplash funk rock by the original Aerosmith—"Sweet Emotion," "Walk This Way," "Train Kept a-Rollin'," "Same Old Song and Dance," "Round and Round," "Nobody's Fault," and all the rest—became an unintended accompaniment. The band's young demographic teetered uneasily between the crumbling unionized job security of their fathers and the complacent consumerism of their suburban shopping plazas. Coming through town every few months, the band sensed as much. "For the most part, our fans were college kids or working guys who liked to party to hard rock and roll," Joe Perry acknowledged. "We wrote, recorded, and played to please that audience."[29] And singer Steve Tyler likewise understood where his base was coming from: "Aerosmith had been big in Detroit from the beginning. We had a loud, flashy, gritty, metallic vibe. *Rolling Stone* called us greasers, 'Wrench Rock.' . . . But they did love us in the rust belt towns: Toledo, Cincinnati, Cleveland, Detroit. . . . We were the voice of the mills and the malls. And those working-class towns were the places that embraced us early on."[30] Plotting his 1972 reelection campaign, Richard Nixon had told his aides, "We should set out to capture the vote of the forty-seven-year-old Dayton housewife,"[31] not considering that the housewife's kids would soon be turning up the volume on *Get Your Wings* and *Toys in the Attic*.

Certainly there was as yet little to associate Aerosmith with the prevailing image of Republican hard hats. Even atavistic groups like the Band or Creedence Clearwater Revival would have been heard as "acid rock" by citizens who'd lived through the Great Depression or World War II; if the Band's "Shape I'm In" and the middle section of CCR's "Suzie Q" were still pretty trippy for their time, then the proto–sex raps of Aerosmith's "Walk This Way" or "Lord of the Thighs" were no more reassuring. For most Americans, rock 'n' roll audiences were irresponsible kids who wore beards, sandals, and no bras, while crew-cut, beer-gutted steelworkers and VFW members were personified in the title character of the 1970 film *Joe*, about an angry blue-collar conservative (Peter Boyle), or in Archie Bunker, the antihero of the hit sitcom *All in the Family*, which aired from 1971 to 1979. Archie (Carroll O'Connor) was a middle-aged shlub from Queens who weekly waxed nostalgic for the way Glenn Miller played in the show's theme song. He was also a reactionary bigot viewers either laughed at or with, depending on their own leanings. That a rock musician might come from and play for the same kinds of people portrayed in *Joe* or *All in the Family* would have seemed self-evidently absurd in 1975. What could Archie Bunker possibly have in common with Aerosmith? More than you'd think, it turned out. Within another ten years or so, generational divides would be obviated by class cohesion.

The music business responded to the sort of regional and socioeconomic appreciation awarded to Aerosmith in various ways. On the one hand, agents, managers, and record company A&R staff were recognizing that Milwaukee, Pittsburgh, and St. Louis could be just as decisive to their clients' fortunes as New York, Los Angeles, and San Francisco. They diligently courted radio DJs and concert promoters no matter where they lived—a buck was a buck, whether earned through a laudatory review in the *New York Times* or from tearing down the Roberts Municipal Stadium in Evansville, Indiana. In a 1970 *Billboard* article, Chicago-based Mercury Records' president Irwin Steinberg had plugged, "In Chicago, you are within 700 miles of reaching 75 percent of the record buying public,"[32] while just a few years later, the same publication heard from Warner-Elektra-Atlantic (WEA) promoter Doug Lee, who assured the trade paper's readership, "There is vitality in the secondary, or median markets of the Midwest."[33] Critics, however, could be unimpressed with the preferences those markets revealed. In a *Rolling Stone* essay on what was then broadly classed as heavy metal, Lester Bangs sneered that "[American] metal merchants have, for the most part, remained solidly Industrial Working Class. . . . The Boogie Bands . . . are almost defiantly apolitical (not to mention atonal). Their raison d'être seems to be the reiteration of the simplest riffs, for the sake of 'partying.' "[34]

Aerosmith in those days was only one of many metal merchants and boogie bands doing their thing through the corn belt and the Rust Belt of the recessional United States. Most people over the age of twenty-one had probably never heard of them, couldn't name one of their songs, and couldn't have picked Steve Tyler or Joe Perry out of a lineup, never mind their accomplices Brad Whitford, Tom Hamilton, and Joey Kramer. Same with BTO, Humble Pie, and even Grand Funk. But during this era one new rock 'n' roll group actually did become a household name with moms and dads as well as their sons and daughters in junior high; there was one American rock act that inflamed the middle of the country just as much as it caught the attention of the coasts. It turned out that the old showbiz adage applied to electric guitars as much as to vaudeville comedy and B-movies. For a few short years, there really was no such thing as bad publicity for Alice Cooper.

The Alice Cooper band—and originally it was a band, not a person—had formed in Phoenix, Arizona, from a gang of middle-class high school buddies who'd been doing their own not particularly inspired covers of British Invasion blues. They could have been Creedence Clearwater Revival or Steppenwolf, or a thousand garage and bar ensembles sprouting up in cities around the Western world. But when they moved to Los Angeles and met up with Frank Zappa, then got Shep Gordon as their manager, and finally got Bob Ezrin to produce their third album, the morbid theatricality of their stage act was more and more complemented by the sleazy innuendo of their music. The members of Alice Cooper were hardly the best instrumentalists around, just as front man Vince Furnier's voice was no great shakes, but Gordon and Ezrin had distilled the Dadaist surrealism Zappa first noted into a calculated offensiveness that was soon dubbed as its own subcategory: shock rock.

By 1973 Alice Cooper was launching a massive tour of the United States, after already scandalizing the country the previous year and even causing a stir in Britain. The reasons for the notoriety were obvious: the players wore extremely long hair and posed in makeup and women's clothes, while the singer carried a boa constrictor onstage and, through old-fashioned stage trickery, was nightly executed by his mates in climactic rituals of hanging or decapitation. Baby dolls were crushed in performance. The songs, as well, were patently reaching for maximum juvenile crudity, with an extra touch of feigned sexual deviance thrown in for good measure: "School's Out," "I'm Eighteen," "Is It My Body," "No More Mr. Nice Guy," "Under My Wheels," and "I Love the Dead." "Dumb it down," Bob Ezrin had told them while they woodshedded in their second home of Detroit. "Hit them on a basic level."[35] Furnier's raspy vocal timbre made every lyric sound like a lewd suggestion, while the chord progressions, mostly by guitarist Michael Bruce, were one step up from garage rock. But they knew what they were doing. Danny Fields, manager of Detroit's Stooges, watched the group ready itself for a show with his own act, which was by then faltering under drugs and discouragement: "I'm thinking, 'These Alice Cooper guys are not as good as this band, but they're pros.'"[36]

Mainstream reporters called it sick, decadent, and an impossible new low for rock music. The Alice Cooper band was happy to play the part. "Shep Gordon was very shrewd," bassist Dennis Dunaway conceded, looking back. "He knew how to make negative things into positive things. So, over and over we would do things that would get negative press and use it to our advantage."[37] In 1969 they had opened for Led Zeppelin at the Whisky a Go Go club in Los Angeles; four years later Alice Cooper was raking in more concert money than Zeppelin and likewise traveling in their own luxury aircraft, and opening acts included Canned Heat and Steppenwolf. "The timing was right and that was the key," drummer Neal Smith added. "I think a big part was the element of the band coming out of the Vietnam era; there were lots of times when music is exciting but I think in turbulent times it is more so."[38] They were notorious enough that the public was projecting their own notions of degeneracy on the group that went well beyond anything Shep Gordon or the members might have sanctioned. There was the rumored "gross-out" contest with Frank Zappa, wherein Zappa took an early lead by barfing/defecating onstage until the Alice Cooper vocalist made a last-minute coup by eating the whole mess; there was the rumored torturing/killing of kittens or puppies on-stage before the group's opening number. "It's not a bad idea, but I didn't think of it,"[39] Furnier smirked, to another deluge of copy.

Again, the garish performances and costumes were all a big gimmick, and the rock establishment was torn between calling Alice Cooper out for their exploitation or admiring them for pulling it off. But the typical fan didn't care. "We affect the little teenage boys between the ages of twelve and fifteen more than anybody," Furnier, increasingly identified as Alice himself, told a reporter. "They consider us heroes of our time for some reason."[40] And like the other arena rockers, Alice Cooper's most enthusiastic following was not in the sophisticated big cities but in the sticks. "We were climbing the charts all through the heartland of the USA," said Smith. "Unfortunately and unbelievably we were still not able to crack the Big Apple on the East Coast or LA on the West Coast."[41] Transvestitism and necrophilia were so spectacularly degenerate as to force the urban hipsters into a state of studied blaséness, but middle Americans had less interest in looking jaded. The people there wanted more than anybody to see firsthand what this rock 'n' roll freak show was all about. "It was in the industrial towns of the Midwest where the action was most intense,"[42] Dunaway remembered. "We were going anywhere we could get a gig, and the Detroit area and the Midwest liked us a lot better than the rest of the country did."[43]

In a sense, the infamy of Alice Cooper's music and shows was taken as an accurate indictment of the very culture that produced it. It was a kind of rock counterpart to the stomach-turning sacrileges of 1974's biggest movie, *The Exorcist*: by displaying the worst conceivable visions of horror and vulgarity, the shock-rock singer and the scary film each affirmed the conservatism of the audiences most disturbed by them, even as they'd paid for the privilege. Alice/Vincent was even photographed wearing an *Exorcist* T-shirt. At many gigs, the musicians were pelted with eggs, darts, and firecrackers, in a cere-monious cleansing whereby punters could both punish what in their eyes was a bunch of indecent pervert creep faggots and still enjoy their high-decibel haunted house act. The same concerts often concluded with a piped-in recording of Irving Berlin's "God Bless America," sung by the wholesome 1940s contralto Kate Smith. With Alice Cooper, the rock generation had called its own bluff. If the straights had long complained that their kids' entertainment was shallow, immoral, and catering to the worst instincts of alienated adolescents, they would then get entertainment that epitomized those very vices. The tail of the Alice Cooper tour plane was decorated with a dollar sign—naturally, they were promoting their new *Billion Dollar Babies* album. After they'd finished outraging guardians of morality in the United Kingdom, Charles Shaar Murray of *New Musical Express* opined, "Who won the last American election? It wasn't Alice Cooper, but it might as well have been."[44] Richard M. Nixon, the actual winner, was not available for comment.

One indication of how deeply America had come to terms with at least the tamer versions of rock was that whereas Nixon himself had gritted his teeth through a White House meeting with Elvis Presley in December 1970, Nixon's successor, Gerald Ford, was pleasant and accommodating when ex-Beatle George Harrison visited the Oval Office four years later. Elvis had sought Nixon for certification as an honorary federal narcotics officer, despite his own growing addiction to pharmaceuticals, but Harrison was invited at the behest of Ford's son Jack, a university student. Elvis came alone, but Harrison's entourage included members of his current touring band, among them Indian sitarist Ravi Shankar and a spectacularly Afroed keyboardist, Billy Preston. Between the two encounters, at least some US politicians must have recognized that despite its outlandishness the youth culture was here to stay and could not be neglected as a source of potential support. Even as it was provoking and perturbing as never before, the more moderate exemplars of rock 'n' roll had gained a foothold in the corridors of power.

Around the period of Alice Cooper's sickest successes, yet another Detroit-rooted musician was riffing through Tucson, Albuquerque, Roanoke, and Portland with his own unusual act. Ted Nugent was not exactly a shock rocker; he wasn't particularly rewarded by the newspapers when he performed in a loincloth or an Indian headdress, or when he came onstage swinging from a vine or sitting on a buffalo. But Nugent's stunts were slowly making his name across the same midwestern, middle-market turf as all the other guitar-based bands, and he was shrewd enough to understand that he needed a visual hook to stand out among a lot of rivals doing essentially the same cranked-up, sped-up blues as he was. Nugent also played at a screaming, high-decibel register that made its presence known through sheer loudness. For all his showmanship, he was a superior electric guitar player in an era when any commercial rock band had to have at least one competent six-string soloist just to be taken seriously; hence his sets made plenty of space for when he wailed away on his own, his shirtless torso arched back in an orgasm of sustain and feedback. Even his choice of a semi-acoustic Gibson Byrdland instrument stood out from all the solid-body Les Pauls, Stratocasters, Explorers, and Firebirds of his peers. By the time of the first record under his own name, 1975's *Ted Nugent*, the liner notes could counsel "So turn it up, New York and Los Angeles, and discover Ted Nugent—the energy source that the heartland has been using all along."[45]

Nugent had grown up in Detroit, the second son of a former US Army ordnance officer turned steel company staffer, and he once earned a teenage gig opening for Motown princesses the Supremes at Cobo Hall. He drank deep from the African American influences of Howlin' Wolf, Jimmy Reed, and Chuck Berry but was dismayed by the 1967 riots. "I was behind the counter of the Capital School of Music, on Grand River, with a shotgun," he remembered. "It was a heartbreaker, 'cause I saw my beloved birth city of Detroit goin' up in flames at the hands of idiots."[46] Nugent's industry entry came with the Amboy Dukes, whose druggy 1968 hit "Journey to the Center of the Mind" put them firmly in the hippie camp, and the group did benefit shows for the MC5's manager, John Sinclair, jailed on a marijuana charge. But personnel turnover gradually sapped their drawing power until Nugent himself was the mainstay, and it was then he staked his claim as an independent artist. "I was on the road constantly between 1967 and '75," he said later, "playing 250 to 300 nights a year. You discover connections between the audience and your guitar."[47] Bolstered by his constant touring, *Ted Nugent* moved respectable numbers for the Epic label, and, sharing singing duties with Derek St. Holmes as the leader of his own quartet, Nugent was now selling himself as the Motor City Madman.

Perhaps the maddest quality about him was not his waist-length hair, nor his athletic leaps and runs from his stage risers, his rapid-fire auctioneer-like spiels between songs, or his literally deafening concert volumes, but his avoidance of drugs and alcohol (though not sex) in the rock world of the 1970s. Nugent was an outdoor enthusiast, a trophy game hunter and a gun buff during a time when rock stars were more usually found reclining stoned in a Bel Air hideaway while consulting a Ouija board and disdaining violent physical confrontation, or even strenuous physical exertion, of any kind. "They all thought it was a party," he recalled of being asked to hang with some other celebs back in the day. "I thought it was just a puking, drooling, stinky embarrassment. . . . I mean, literally their heads dropping into giant mounds of cocaine. It was heartbreaking."[48] This uprightness baffled some of his fellow rockers working the halls and festivals alongside him—he supposedly once shit on someone's pile of blow backstage—but cost him few listeners, most of whom were too taken with the indestructible locker-room leer of his early classics with the St. Holmes band: "Free for All," "Cat Scratch Fever," "Yank Me Crank Me," "Dog Eat Dog," "Wang Dang Sweet Poontang," "Just What the Doctor Ordered," "Stranglehold" ("That song has kept America moist for years," he bragged),[49] and the antigovernment tirade of "Stormtroopin'." And Nugent took the Steve Marriott prototype of audience interaction into the territory of full-scale demagoguery, ordering any unlikely concertgoers who wanted to "get mellow" to "*turn around and get the fuck outta here! Do you hear me?*" He was a rock 'n' roll preacher threatening hellfire and brimstone. "If somebody else was in the spotlight, Ted would run and get in it,"[50] St. Holmes noted.

The Nugent persona worked on the punters far more than the reviewers, who seldom saw past his shtick. "*Creem* magazine and most of its so-called writers provided me with constant fortification to my concrete understanding of how transparent, criminal and chimplike the hippie lifestyle truly is," he said in tribute to the Detroit rock publication. "Fuck *Creem* magazine and the stinky, filthy, irresponsible pukes who ran it. Drive safely."[51] Nugent was reaching a hitherto unacknowledged audience that—perhaps to his surprise no less than his critics'—seemed indifferent to what was not yet upheld or derided as political correctness. "I think most of them have a basic knowledge and grip and focus of their talents," he said, assessing his fans in a 1979 *Rolling Stone* profile, "and I believe the reason they can go to the gigs is they have jobs. There's guys out there in pickup trucks who talk four-wheel drive with me, guys out there with amplifiers and guitars who talk music with me, and there's guys out there with big grins on their faces who talk pussy with me."[52]

One subject that did not come up with Nugent and the young men who came to his shows, and to those of his arena rock colleagues, was the looming threat of conscription into the US military. That was because the draft had ended in January 1973, when the Selective Service System announced that no further call-up of males born in the 1950s would be implemented. As America's armed deployment on Vietnamese soil wound down, and as American leaders courted the burgeoning youth electorate (voting age had been lowered from twenty-one to eighteen in 1971), an all-volunteer force became both militarily feasible and politically attractive. It was Richard Nixon, indeed, who had first pledged to end the draft during his 1968 presidential campaign. The upshot was that from 1973 onward, matters of war and peace were less urgent in the minds of rock 'n' roll listeners. For the males, the martial onslaught of a recital by Ted Nugent or other very loud guitar players may have become a substitute for the camaraderie and tests of endurance they were no longer obliged to have in uniform: violent sensory overloads could be a lot cooler when they carried no actual threat of sudden death by enemy fire.

Ironically, many of the loud guitar players who were stepping up to create those overloads had themselves been potential draftees. Born in the late 1940s, the generation of American rock 'n' rollers who began their careers in the wake of the British Invasion (unlike the Englishmen in Humble Pie or the Canadians in Bachman-Turner Overdrive) were required to register at their local Selective Service boards and, if necessary, show legitimate cause for their ineligibility. Wanting to play music and attract girls was not a sufficient excuse not to do so. Steve Tyler of Aerosmith had been ruled unfit due to the drug misdemeanors he'd already racked up, and Joe Perry was declared 4-F after a psychologist, to whom he'd been sent by his concerned parents, contacted local draft officials. In 1967 Dennis Dunaway and Vincent Furnier of the just-formed Alice Cooper band reported to their Selective Service office in Phoenix. Dunaway turned out to have an undetected hernia, but Furnier's status was iffier. "Looking back, it was a funny thing," he later wrote. "I probably would have enlisted in the Army eventually. I wasn't antiwar at all. I wasn't into the peace-and-love movement of the day. I wasn't a protester. I wasn't a conscientious objector. I had no bones about going into the Army and fighting for my country. It's just that I looked so freaky at the time and I didn't want to go into the Army right then because I was in a rock 'n' roll group."[53] Vincent Furnier eventually went to the back of the line in the newly instituted draft lottery, and the future Alice Cooper never had to go to war.

Ted Nugent had a more complicated story. In a 1977 account, which later came back to haunt him, he told the pro-drug magazine *High Times* that in 1967 he had gone down to his own draft board after deliberately making himself act, look, and smell as unmilitary as possible. Nugent outlined his scheme to *High Times*: he stopped bathing, shaving, eating properly, or bothering to use a toilet for several days before his examination, and even took drugs just prior to the appointment. "See, I approached the whole thing like, Ted Nugent, cool hard-workin' dude, is gonna wreak havoc on these imbeciles in the armed forces. I'm gonna play their own game, and I'm gonna destroy 'em. Now my whole body is crusted in poop and piss," he stated. It worked. "And in the mail I got this big juicy 4-F. They'd call dead people before they'd call my ass."[54] In time Nugent took unusual pains to claim the *High Times* interview was conducted as his joke on its contemptible hippie doper readership, conceding only that he did get a draft deferment through enrollment in a Michigan college. "I never shit my pants. I never pissed my pants; I never did anything to get out of the draft."[55] As a strong supporter of the US military, he later explained why he hadn't voluntarily joined the fight against America's enemies in Vietnam: "I didn't know what Communism was," he admitted. "I was not interested in abandoning this intense, high-velocity guitar jihad."[56]

The end of the US draft in the early 1970s seemed part of a transition in rock—or anyway, it came to be one in the minds of its self-appointed historians. Since 1969's Woodstock festival, Mark Crispin Miller concluded in 1977, "More and more records came out, and concerts went on, much amplified, but rock had lost the keen joy of something fresh and illicit."[57] "After all the ideals had been exploded in the late sixties," echoed Gary Herman in 1982's *Rock 'n' Roll Babylon*, "rock remained simply and solely an entertainment, and performances—once they had gravitated towards the mass arena—sought justification in outrageousness."[58] The same year, Canadian critic Peter Goddard took a comparable view: "For most of the older generation, rock mirrored a concern: brand new emotions and potential revolutions. The next generation has tried to pick up this cue. It's tried to make rock central to its life, buying far more records than the first did. Yet all the while, it's sensed that the music . . . was there for fun, nothing more or less. Simply put, the second generation needs the sound the way the first needed the words."[59]

Yet the arena rock that had been flourishing for years by the time of those assessments may have represented a social movement just as idealistic and just as revolutionary as the antiwar protests and student demonstrations—it was the ideals and the revolutions that had been transformed, not the audience's emotional connection to the music. Now, the connection was growing not on the campuses of Berkeley or Columbia, the grassy hills of Woodstock, or the Washington Mall but in the record shops of Main Street and the hockey rinks of Anytown, USA. Now the music was not just acoustic laments and jeremiads against the militarist Establishment but 100-watt battle cries of weekend warriors. Now the music's heroes were not solitary troubadours or teams of global superstars but the twenty-two-year-old freaks next door. Emotional connections to idealistic and revolutionary music were growing elsewhere, too, only not exactly in Anytown, and the music was not exactly rock 'n' roll.

4
Workin' Man Blues

> I dont see how a city no bigger than New York can hold enough people
> to take the money away from us country suckers. Work like hell all day
> every day, send them your money and get a little piece of paper back,
> Your account closed at 20.62. . . . Well, I'm done with them. They've
> sucked me in for the last time.
>
> **William Faulkner, *The Sound and the Fury***

All through the 1960s and 1970s, a parallel change in American values and demographics was occurring alongside the more contentious upheavals of youth, race, politics, and morality that dominated the headlines. This change was marked less by sudden episodes of unrest than by gradual shifts in economics and population, and by an emerging public awareness of styles once confined to a regional subculture but which were becoming current, and even welcome, across the nation. *Time* magazine, still a media barometer of American trends in the era, published a 1971 cover announcing "Dixie Whistles a Different Tune," as the end of racial segregation and a broad migration of people and businesses appeared to be bringing the country's erstwhile backwater to a new position at the forefront of US commerce and customs.

In reality a variety of factors were at play. Certainly the civil rights advances that came into effect under the administration of Lyndon Johnson during the 1960s had placed the US South on equal terms, at least legally, with the rest of the country; it was no longer known to northerners primarily as the home of Jim Crow and the Ku Klux Klan. But this gave Republican politicians an opportunity to wrest support from the traditionally Democratic white electorate in the old Confederate states, emphasizing the party's law-and-order principles to voters troubled by Johnson's backing of what were seen as mostly Black interests. To realize the advantages of the so-called southern strategy, the GOP under Richard Nixon began to focus on the next generations of Dixie—the middle-class, professional, suburban descendants of hillbillies and sharecroppers who still retained some of their ancestors' conservative views.

Takin' Care of Business. George Case, Oxford University Press (2021). © George Case.
DOI: 10.1093/oso/9780197548813.003.0005

More widely, the massive federal investment in agriculture, infrastructure, and energy from Franklin Roosevelt's New Deal onward had brought jobs and homes to the southern and western ranges of the United States in unprecedented numbers. Social Security, another New Deal advance, allowed many elderly northerners to spend their retirements in Florida, Arizona, or Texas. Even the increased consumer popularity of air conditioning made the Deep South and the desert states, long suffering under unbearably hot summers, habitable and productive at climate levels comparable to those of the North and the Midwest. And the expansion of the defense and aerospace industries during World War II and the Cold War largely benefited the South, as manufacturing plants, research centers, and Army, Air Force, and Navy bases sprang up across the lower latitudes of the nation—by some measures, the military-industrial complex funded the biggest employers in Louisiana, Georgia, Tennessee, New Mexico, and other jurisdictions. The Sun Belt could also be called the Gun Belt. For all these reasons, the old economy of sleepy small towns and poor family farms was being modernized within the life of a single generation.

By 1976, when Georgian Jimmy Carter became US president, the South was in the midst of a genuine economic and social resurgence. The rise was all the more apparent when compared to the crises of crime, strikes, manufacturing decline, and racial conflict over desegregationist school busing decrees that struck New York, Boston, Philadelphia, and Detroit throughout the decade. In films and on television, the South and West were represented by the soap-opera intrigues of *Dallas* and the good-ol'-boy vehicular action of *Smokey and the Bandit*, *The Dukes of Hazzard*, and *Convoy*; sports fans loved the championship plays of "America's team," the Dallas Cowboys of the increasingly popular National Football League (along with their sexy cheerleading squad), in addition to the much-publicized daredevil stunts of Montanan Evel Knievel. But the most audible sign of the South's newfound national cachet was the exploding success of country music.

While folk, bluegrass, honky-tonk, western swing, and other sounds of rural white America had been commercially recorded and retailed long before the advent of rock 'n' roll, it was the newer genre that had come to dominate the industry. Country artists still sold and performed widely, but they never matched the attention or revenue drawn by Elvis Presley, the Beatles, and those who came after them. Trade papers tracked country music sales and jukebox requests under charts kept separate from pop or rhythm & blues; only occasionally had singles by Patsy Cline ("She's Got You"), Marty Robbins ("El Paso"), Eddy Arnold ("Make the World Go Away"), or Jim Reeves ("He'll Have to Go") "crossed over" into mainstream acceptance. Under the talents of guitarist-producer Chet Atkins, a smoother, pop-oriented country style came to be associated with Atkins's base at RCA Studios in Nashville, Tennessee, just as rock was becoming more experimental and perhaps even subversive. By the late 1960s, country was due for its own renaissance.

Until that time the influences between rock and country music had mostly gone in one direction. The Byrds, the Flying Burrito Brothers, the Band, and other rock artists could afford to appropriate country motifs into their own styles, but few established country performers wanted to be associated with the sounds and looks of long-haired, dope-smoking Californians or Englishmen. Economically, country was on the defensive, protecting the market share that white southerners like Elvis or Carl Perkins or Jerry Lee Lewis had already cleaved off. Rock 'n' roll stood for youth, novelty, and change; country was the entertainment of the middle-aged and the reactionary. From a business standpoint country may have remained a viable enterprise, but artistically it was stagnating. The "countrypolitan" tones that were Chet Atkins's specialty—polished ballads with only a hint of twang to differentiate them from the middle of the road—were chafing against a generation of singers and songwriters seeking to open up the form for themselves and unwilling to keep pretending that rock 'n' roll didn't exist.

A few nods toward modern issues had come with 1967's "Ode to Billie Joe," Bobbie Gentry's stark song of a young suicide that made it into the Top 40 country charts but hit the peak of the pop ranking, and the following year's "Harper Valley PTA" by Jeannie Riley (written by Tom T. Hall), a catchy crossover hit challenging small-town hypocrisy. The underrated country singer Henson Cargill also scored in 1968 with two singles of social consciousness recorded in Nashville, "Skip a Rope" and "None of My Business." Stirrings of dissent were audible around Music Row, the city's center of studios, instrument shops, and production offices.

But the key player behind country's transformation was Johnny Cash. Raised by poor Arkansan farmers in the depths of the Great Depression, Cash had already been tied to the first wave of rock 'n' roll, briefly sitting in with Presley, Perkins, and Lewis at an impromptu recording session at Memphis's Sun Records in 1956. Though the four men had similar geographical and musical roots, Cash was the one whose efforts had mostly stayed confined to the country charts. His songs "I Walk the Line" and "Ring of Fire" were among the few to have reached a broader audience outside the core. Cash's personal life, however, was as reckless as any rock 'n' roller's, as he struggled with a debilitating addiction to amphetamines and was subjected to a pot bust in 1966. Stories of his unreliability, criminal infractions, and self-destructiveness, were widely reported, and he was also an outspoken advocate for social causes such as the problems of the Native American community. Cash's was not the public image country music normally tried to sell, but it was well poised for acceptance by the rock audience. When he collaborated with Bob Dylan on Dylan's 1969 album *Nashville Skyline*, his credibility helped Dylan as much as Dylan's helped his. At last the really significant crossover, between not country and pop but country and rock, had been made.

Johnny Cash featured Dylan as a guest on his ABC television show, which debuted in 1969, and he subsequently introduced other appearances by certified rockers, including Neil Young and Creedence Clearwater Revival. Cash pushed more boundaries by bringing on antiwar stalwart Pete Seeger. "They said, 'Who do you want for your guests?' and I thought I'd check 'em out," the singer looked back. "I said—the first name I gave 'em was Pete Seeger. Said, 'I want Pete Seeger—he's a good American folk singer and writer and I wanna work with him.'"[1] Johnny Cash was already known as the Man in Black for his unvarying, uncompromising onstage attire, and his song "The Man in Black" explained his sartorial choice in somber antiwar poetry. He also put out the remarkable live albums *At Folsom Prison* (1968) and *At San Quentin* (1969), each recorded at the eponymous jails and further linking him to the tide of activist politics sweeping other areas of society (among his other positions, the singer took a stand for prison reform). It was at the San Quentin performance where photographer Jim Marshall, whose subjects had numbered Jimi Hendrix, Janis Joplin, and the Beatles, captured the indelible shot of an angry Cash giving the finger to the camera—accounts differ as to whether Cash was annoyed with Marshall or with the film crew covering his show, or whether he was giving a message to San Quentin's warden, but the widely seen fuck-you photo was certainly like no publicity still ever put out by Jim Reeves or Eddy Arnold, or for that matter by Jimi Hendrix, Janis Joplin, or the Beatles. As much as his music was fixed in an acoustic, boom-chicka-boom flatpicking format, his attitude made Johnny Cash an honorary rock star.

There was more going on, though, than just the phenomenon of country music becoming slightly more hip with young people outside of the US South. Country was beginning its own boom, the same way rock 'n' roll had taken off with the Beatles' arrival a few years earlier. There had been eighty-one all-country American radio stations in 1961; in 1974 the number of country broadcasters exceeded a thousand. To some extent this was a consequence of the same demographic figures that had affected so much else in the entire culture: more college students, more cars, more crime, more consumers. In another way, country's rising popularity was the silent majority's way of asserting its place in the shifting entertainment landscape. It was one thing to be granted a measure of acceptance within the rock community, but it was something else when country began to declare a defiance against rock itself. Such was the case with Merle Haggard's huge crossover hit of 1969, "Okie from Muskogee."

Until that year, Haggard was known as a steadily working singer who'd placed several songs on or atop the country sales polls. With his backup band the Strangers, he was riding a tour bus through Oklahoma, and his drummer Eddie Burris joked about a road sign: "I bet they don't smoke marijuana in Muskogee," whereupon a series of semi-comic lines were traded back and forth and written down. Like Johnny Cash, Merle Haggard was a contrary man who resisted the groomed polyester elements of his genre; a convicted petty criminal in his youth, he recorded in the studios of Bakersfield, California, and his music had a sharper, bluesier edge than most of what came out of Nashville. Like the Beatles, he was signed to the Capitol label. But for all its tongue-in-cheek origins, "Okie from Muskogee" was heard by millions of listeners as an unapologetic statement on behalf of respect, Old Glory, manliness, and football and against the current fashions for pot, LSD, rebellion, flag burning, long hair, sandals, and the hippies out in San Francisco.

The song instantly propelled Haggard to the front lines of the national divides over music and politics. "Some of the hippies have good minds," Haggard told a trade journal in 1970, "but I don't believe in filth and some of the other things they seem to represent sometimes."[2] He eventually elaborated, "I felt the kids who were bitching about things didn't know any more about it than I did. But that's the way I felt in 1969."[3] Fans embraced him for standing up for old-fashioned values (California governor Ronald Reagan later pardoned his criminal record and Richard Nixon invited him to play at the White House), while the counterculture afforded him a grudging admiration for being so resolutely uncool. His name alone sounded like a literalized Dorothea Lange photo, conveying the tired despair of the rural poor. He even performed his hit on the Smothers Brothers comedy television show, a liberal favorite of 1969, after being introduced as "equal time to the other side," countering the Smothers' usual guests. Merle Haggard himself was far from a country-club Republican and was himself not averse to marijuana and other hard-living indulgences, but "Okie from Muskogee" became an anthem for a sector of the population beginning to argue back on the airwaves and record players of the United States.

Haggard's other material from this period, sung in his distinctively rugged, weary inflections, were likewise paeans to the struggling farmers and factory hands of his own Dust Bowl ancestry: "Hungry Eyes," "Workin' Man Blues," "Branded Man." He went on to achieve a long series of follow-up hits that explored the same themes of patriotism and proletarian pride, including "The

Fighting Side of Me" (1970), "I Wonder If They Ever Think of Me" (1973), and "If We Make It Through December" (1973), although by 1981's "Are the Good Times Really Over" he was sounding a note of resignation over American decline, to the extent of citing Vietnam, Watergate, and Nixon as contributing causes. Born in 1937, he seemed to speak for the parents—or the older, poorer, midwestern cousins—of the Rust Belt teenagers flocking to Aerosmith, Ted Nugent, or, God help them, Alice Cooper. These were the wage earners and bill payers of the agricultural and industrial economies, the mostly unnoticed backbone that underlay the media business capitalizing on the bottomless wants of the baby boomers. They were not trendy. They were not socially progressive. They were not violently opposed to every single plank of the liberal agenda, but the layoffs, gas shortages, and inflation that hit them directly in their wallets dampened much of their enthusiasm. In a pluralistic society more and more defined by tastes in music or television as much as by taste in party or regional allegiance, they needed someone to represent their own identity. Often called "the poet of the working man," Merle Haggard made the cover of *Time* in 1974, in another South-surveying cover story, "Songs of Love, Loyalty, and Doubt: Country Music."

In his records about employment and unemployment, work and welfare, Haggard was really carrying on a tradition. More than any other brand of popular music, country had always addressed the subject of jobs. Golden oldies like Bill Monroe's "John Henry" (1954), Tennessee Ernie Ford's "Sixteen Tons" (1955), and Dave Dudley's "Six Days On the Road" (1963) vied with Loretta Lynn's "Coal Miner's Daughter" (1970) and Haggard's "A Workin' Man Can't Get Nowhere Today" (1977) as unadulterated accounts of people who had really known hard physical labor—at a time when more Americans were moving to white-collar occupations in offices and stores and some futurists were predicting an eventual technocratic Eden of endless leisure and affluence. As John Fogerty had suggested in CCR's "Don't Look Now," there was a sizeable category of citizens largely invisible to the protesters but whose daily toil was what enabled their protests in the first place. Whatever else it may have been, country music was a corrective to the suburban vistas of automation and self-realization that formed the assumptions behind so much of the counterculture's rhetoric.

Female country performers were themselves breaking new ground, not so much in aligning the music with the rock market as in stiffening the resolve of those refusing to partake of it. Tammy Wynette's ornery single "Stand by Your Man" (1968) was to the new feminists what "Okie from Muskogee" was to campus protesters—an earthbound, unashamed diatribe 180 degrees away from prevailing liberal principles. The song, graced by session man

Pete Drake's yearning pedal steel guitar, became a no. 1 *Billboard* country hit and crossed over into the pop charts as well, despite or because of its lyrics (cowritten by Wynette and producer Billy Sherrill) imploring for marital loyalty and forgiveness in the face of male partners' wayward ways. Famously invoked in 1992 by then-prospective first lady Hillary Clinton as something she sure wasn't going to do, "Stand by Your Man" was delivered in Wynette's curled-lip Mississippi accent to epitomize the outlook of proud, long-suffering housewives and girlfriends throughout the heartland, who would never let any fancy New York or California women's libbers define their spousal roles. Wynette's "D-I-V-O-R-C-E," "I'll See Him Through," and "He's Still My Man" and several songs by the scrappy Loretta Lynn, including "Fist City" "Don't Come Home a-Drinkin' (With Lovin' on Your Mind)" and "The Pill," also expressed the sexual politics of beauty salons, trailer parks, and bowling alleys throughout small-town USA in honest and sympathetic language, when those places were often derided in the non-country pop culture: Robert Altman's 1975 film *Nashville*, widely praised by coastal critics for its caustic satire of the city's music industry, depicted a Wynette-like singer as an embodiment of rural white tackiness. Tammy Wynette and Loretta Lynn were major stars in Nashville, but as both celebrities and ordinary people, country's women were a standard joke to outsiders.

Dolly Parton was another such punchline, until she started laughing back to claim her own defiant status during the 1970s: the big-haired, big-busted symbol of old-time southern womanhood, apparently unmoved by the era's feminist fashions. In fact, she was a trailblazer in writing much of her own material and in capturing the hard realities of marriage, courtship, and family life among traditionally impoverished and vulnerable people, with her autobiographical "Coat of Many Colors" (1971), the album cut "Love Isn't Free" (1972), and the poignant "Jolene" (1973). As the fourth child in a family of twelve kids raised in eastern Tennessee, her country stardom—which eventually crossed over to pop and mainstream TV and movie roles—was almost a literal rags-to-riches tale, whereby her extravagant clothes, wigs, and makeup were easily accepted by an audience that knew the dirt-poor history behind them, and who may have known it firsthand themselves. Dolly had earned the right to live and look like a country queen or, to some wags, a "backwoods Barbie." "Up until I was about eleven or twelve," she recollected to an interviewer, "we just farmed. We all had to work in the fields and we all had a job to do. When you're just farmin' and that's the only income you have, and you have twelve children, well, then you don't really have too much."[4]

Other artists were now changing country from within. Songwriters across mediums had been deeply affected by the innovations of Bob Dylan in bringing personal sensibilities and rich literary allusions to once formulaic lyrical realms. Kris Kristofferson, a young ex-Army helicopter pilot and Rhodes scholar, arrived in Nashville in 1965 and began pitching his intimate, lived-in material around the country music capital, to little avail until his 1970 debut album coincided with a rush of admirers covering his songs for themselves—everyone from rocker Janis Joplin with "Me and Bobby McGee" to countrypolitan Ray Price with "For the Good Times." Within a few months he had appeared at both the happening Troubadour venue in Los Angeles and on Johnny Cash's television program, taped in Nashville. Released by the Monument label, *Kristofferson* itself displayed the emotional depth and naked honesty that would never have been heard before the drug and sexual revolutions, introducing the long-lived ballads "Help Me Make It through the Night" and "Sunday Mornin' Comin' Down." Kristofferson was definitely a country artist, but he had long hair and grew a beard, went on to be a leading man in Hollywood movies, and proclaimed a leftish political viewpoint once unthinkable in his field. By the early part of the decade, he was being celebrated by the mainstream press as embodying "The New Nashville Sound."

It wasn't so much that country had evolved to resemble rock, or even to directly compete with it. Rather, it was that both rock and country fans could reach across the record bins or the ticket booths to buy each other's products without shame or embarrassment. There was also an intangible advantage country artists such as Johnny Cash and Merle Haggard could claim over younger singer-songwriters like Neil Young, Joni Mitchell, Jackson Browne, Leonard Cohen, and Bob Dylan himself: the quality, ever more valuable in late twentieth-century America's clogged media channels, of perceived authenticity. The very facts that country attracted a smaller segment of the purchasing public, that its corporate headquarters sat in Tennessee rather than London, Los Angeles, or New York, and that its earliest examples came from a time before television and electric guitars were what earned it its newfound reputation. It was the same difference that got people appreciating Muddy Waters and Albert King more than Canned Heat or Edgar Winter, the suspicion that certain acts had really lived the experiences they sang about, while others were only copying the form (and diluting it) for fun and profit. Among the record-buying cognoscenti, a growing sect of educated, middle-class purists heard in country music a connection to down-home reality that bigger stars of other styles could never replicate.

Another of the new breed was Waylon Jennings. Jennings had been but one of many country singer-guitarists playing barrooms and theaters across California, Texas, and the Deep South—he had been a touring accompanist for Buddy Holly and just missed joining the rock 'n' roll pioneer on his fatal airplane flight in February 1959—until he too began to buck the conventions of the business. Legendary groupie Pamela Des Barres recounted how her 1970 affair with Jennings, gigging at the Palomino Club in Los Angeles, may have inspired him. Glancing at the rock star posters in her bedroom, he asked Des Barres, "Do you really like all this long ha'r and everythang?"[5] At their next encounter, she wrote, "He was considerably shaggier, hipper, and hornier than the last time I had seen him."[6] Jennings was another artist with an appetite for amphetamines and alcohol, despite the anti-drug lectures he received from RCA's Chet Atkins. Into the new decade, he began to sport a beard, jeans, and leather vests. At shows in San Francisco, he'd attracted the admiration and security muscle of the local Hells Angels; he even opened for the Grateful Dead. Jennings's albums *Ladies Love Outlaws* (1972) and *Honky Tonk Heroes* (1973) marked a clear break with the approved Nashville sound and look. When a disc jockey contacted Hazel Smith, the Nashville publicist for Jennings's recent producer, Tompall Glaser, and asked for a summary of the two men's style, Smith skimmed a dictionary to find a quick response. "I decided to look up the word *outlaw*," she remembered. "I don't know why I did. . . . But what these guys were doing, the music, was certainly different than what had ever been done in this hillbilly town."[7]

The description stuck. By early 1974 the influential *Country Music* magazine was running articles titled "In Defense of the Telecaster Cowboy Outlaws," naming Waylon Jennings, Kris Kristofferson, Tompall Glaser, songwriter Billy Joe Shaver, and others as part of the new trend. For fans, "outlaw country" was a convenient shorthand for performers from a stereotypically straight medium daring to sing and live like the musicians who had hitherto outsold and outpartied them, but there was more to the outlaws than any superficial displays of hippie chic. The point was not to be like wasted rock stars but to enjoy some of the rock stars' creative autonomy—the strictures of Nashville had long meant acts like Waylon Jennings were required to submit to producers' and record companies' dictates of whose songs to record, with what lineup of studio session men and which instrumental backing, and when and where to give concerts. No more, said the outlaws. By the mid-1970s they were commanding more authority in charting their own professional pathways, just as successful rock players had demanded and won for themselves. Indeed, their records were given serious consideration in *Rolling Stone* and other rock-friendly outlets, not because of the music but because of the kindred musical spirit that went into it. Chet Flippo, a *Rolling Stone* writer who had caught on to the fresh clout of Jennings and his peers, later put the outlaws in perspective: "Country artists gained control over their own record sessions, their own booking, their record production, everything else related to their own careers, including the right to make their own mistakes.... It had nothing to do with long hair or wearing black leather or smoking dope or any other such trivial sideshow issues. It was actually a fairly sober attempt at gaining self-determination and independence."[8]

In the larger scheme of things, the travails of full-time entertainers seeking artistic fulfillment were not that important, no matter what kind of entertainment they were purveying. Film directors, actors, and rock and jazz musicians had long been participating in familiar narratives of the genius creator up against the soulless corporate hacks who tried to straitjacket their expressive selves. And the rush to get on the outlaw bandwagon, as shown by the record companies' ads and the music writers' articles, soon attracted some skepticism. Were the outlaws real, or just a clever selling point? "It's romantic to call someone an outlaw," said Waylon Jennings. "And in this country, romance sells. If you're in the record business and you don't realize the power of promotion, you'd better go back to the farm and start milking cows."[9] In 1976, an unnamed musician was quoted in the American political biweekly *New Times*: "As people feel more and more trapped in their lives in this country, with their dull lifeless jobs, boring family lives and hopeless inflation, the music industry tantalizes them with these images of fake rebels to look at."[10] As had happened so often in the past, and would happen so often into the future, capitalism reaped the rewards of cool.

But the outlaws, who by some definitions would also include Johnny Cash and Merle Haggard as well as lesser-known mavericks David Allan Coe and Townes Van Zandt, lent a genuine political edge to a kind of music that had always seemed to stand for the status quo. Much of that edge at first implied a budding liberalism in the conservative heartland—the acceptance or endorsement of drugs, promiscuity, and even interracial romance in Haggard's "Irma Jackson," and Jennings's "Black Rose," written by Billy Joe Shaver—but the politics could also veer toward the populism of Haggard's "Okie from Muskogee" and other songs. Attempting to shore up support as he became more entangled in Watergate in 1974, Richard Nixon commended the country demographic when he appeared at the Grand Ole Opry: "As we all know, country music radiates a love of this nation. Patriotism.... It's good for Americans to hear it. We come away better having heard it."[11] Later, Johnny Paycheck's 1977 no.1 hit, a version of Coe's "Take This Job and Shove It," made perhaps the bluntest announcement of class frustration country had yet produced. The subgenre of trucker and CB-radio tunes (Haggard's "White Line Fever," C. W. McCall's "Convoy," Jerry Reed's "East Bound and Down," for example) further highlighted the honest virtues of regular working men, often as they evaded the government power represented by the "Smokeys" or State Troopers. This wasn't really a matter of left versus right but of complacent versus cantankerous. Starting with the outlaws, and egged on by Richard Nixon, country music and its audience were learning not to be complacent.

The greatest of the outlaws, of course, was Willie Nelson. Willie had more than paid his dues in Nashville, having composed at least three country classics in the widely covered "Funny How Time Slips Away" and "Night Life," on top of Patsy Cline's "Crazy." But he had struggled to make his own name as a performer and RCA recording artist, and by 1971 he had returned to his native Texas, shedding his old suits and hairstyle along the way. "I remember thinking, 'Fuck coats and ties! Let's get comfortable,'"[12] he recalled. Signed to a new label at CBS, he made what could be counted as country's first concept album, *Red Headed Stranger*, in 1975. With its haunting old-West storyline and simple, sparse acoustic signature, and with luminous tracks, including a cover of Roy Acuff's "Blue Eyes Crying in the Rain" and the original guitar in-strumental "Bandera," the record was a big seller and made Nelson a national star in his own right.

Yet Willie Nelson was not just an outlaw. "Along with Kris Kristofferson and Merle Haggard, Waylon and I were being put in another category outside the box of straight-ahead country," he reflected in his autobiography, *It's A Long Story*. "The labels were many, from 'progressive country' to 'outlaw country' to 'renegade rock.' Critics struggled to find the right words, and for my money, they never did. I would have preferred no label at all."[13] Willie came to embody the spirit of country music itself, replacing the worn image of the cowboy-hatted, bolo-tied Grand Ole Opry square with that of a bearded, braided dude in T-shirt and jeans. Aside from his music, which secured the place of western ballads and swing in the Great American Songbook—*Stardust*, his 1978 album of jazz standards, was a savory blend of Manhattan cocktail and Lone Star sagebrush—his easygoing demeanor and appearance recast country as a libertarian idiom, arguing against its Nixon-era law-and-order associations. The Cosmic Cowboy played for President Jimmy Carter and later admitted he had smoked a joint on the roof of the White House. Never again could the category of country be glibly dismissed as a backward, repressed, hopelessly unfashionable regional laughing stock. By extension, thanks to Willie Nelson, never again could the constituency of country listeners be written off in the same manner.

Like Johnny Cash, Willie was an indispensable bridge between the rock and country masses. Trying to put the outlaws into a bigger context, Willie theo-rized, "The word 'progressive' has been used a lot in relation to our music. But I really think it's the *listener* who is progressive. If someone can listen to a guy with long hair and a bandanna sing country songs and not criticize him for the way he looks, that's progressive."[14] In 1973 he staged his first annual "picnic" at a ranch near Dripping Springs, Texas, outside the state capital (and progressive oasis) of Austin. The picnics were planned and executed in emulation of previous rock festivals in Woodstock, Atlanta, and the Isle of Wight—and suffered the same problems of security, organization, and finance—but the assembled performers brought together two publics hitherto assumed to be mutually exclusive. Yearly Fourth of July Picnics followed at various locations in Texas and elsewhere, headlined by Willie and featuring a diverse set of attractions, ranging from ones firmly in the country camp (Tom T. Hall, Roger Miller, George Jones) to those decidedly outside of it (the Grateful Dead, the Pointer Sisters). "It's something everybody wanted," Willie told reporters after the first event. "It was all about everybody coming together to listen to music—country, rock, blues, gospel, jazz—everything."[15] In 1976, though, some locals at the picnic's site of Gonzales, Texas, weren't happy about it. "To allow this invasion is to invite the anti-American, anti-Christian hippie subculture right into our homes,"[16] a spokesman complained. The picnics were an early portent of how both protest and reaction might temporarily unite under—or devolve into—pure entertainment, as young potheads partied to the sound of fiddles and dobros, while bourbon-sipping Tennesseans joined in an indulgent communal vibe.

Previously issued RCA songs by Willie Nelson, Waylon Jennings, Tompall Glaser, and Jennings's wife, Jessi Colter (rockabilly great Duane Eddy's ex), were compiled on 1976's *Wanted: The Outlaws*, which codified the outlaw country movement to widespread popularity and became the first platinum country album, with sales of over a million copies. Again, it was not just the material itself, which had a raucous Waylon-Willie duet in "Good-Hearted Woman" and Nelson's slyly autobiographical "Me and Paul," but the entire package that redefined the values country music and its audience represented. Outlaws from American history (the album was designed as a wanted poster) were romanticized as gun-toting Robin Hoods like Jesse James, Pretty Boy Floyd, and Bonnie and Clyde, who lived and died on the wrong side of authorities like sheriffs and bankers but were beloved by the common folks. In the same way, Nelson, Jennings, and their friends were now revered as original personalities freed from the cookie-cutter imperatives of Nashville and showbiz generally. Given the personal habits and beliefs of the outlaws— Jennings went through a coke bust and battled with substance abuse for the rest of his career, and Nelson gradually became known as a champion of cannabis legalization—no one still thought rock 'n' roll and its followers had the lock on nonconformity.

Predictably, however, nonconformity in time became another type of fashion. As early as 1978, Waylon Jennings put out "Don't You Think This Outlaw Bit's Done Got out of Hand," teasing the very persona that had made him rich, famous, and self-destructive. "Country music is slow to change," he opined. "The folks in Nashville thought Willie and me were just plain crazy when we turned away from what everybody else was doing. Then when what we did succeeded, suddenly everybody became an outlaw."[17] He was enlisted to sing the theme song for *The Dukes of Hazzard*; Willie Nelson was featured in *The Electric Horseman* with Jane Fonda and Robert Redford and a string of other movies and television spots. Kris Kristofferson costarred with Barbara Streisand in a 1976 remake of the show business fable *A Star Is Born* and in films by Martin Scorsese (*Alice Doesn't Live Here Anymore*) and Sam Peckinpah (*Pat Garrett and Billy the Kid*, with a cameo by Bob Dylan). Willie, Waylon, Kristofferson, and Johnny Cash formed the popular country supergroup the Highwaymen in the 1980s, trading on their now certified legendary status in Nashville, Austin, and the rest of the United States.

And as social conservatism revived in America through the late 1970s, some country music grew more blatant in its biases: marginal player Vernon Oxford made the country charts with 1976's "Redneck! (The Redneck National Anthem)" and "Redneck Roots" the next year. In 1981 Barbara Mandrell sang a virtual traditionalist manifesto with her biggest hit, "I Was Country When Country Wasn't Cool," responding to the wave of slick urban cowboys gravitating to tony nightclubs in Dallas and Houston. Now country was not just something you listened to but something you were.

During the outlaws' heyday, rock 'n' roll was too big and still too bad to be politicized like that—yet. Rock 'n' roll music was too loud and aggressive, except, perhaps, when the musicians admired country. Its lyrics were too rebellious, except, maybe, when the lyricists shared country's proud ideals of work, homeland, and personal honor. Its parties were too wild, unless the partiers had country's affinity for pills, whiskey, and women. And rock 'n' roll's mass international appeal was too wide, other than when its native land was, of all places, the US South.

5

Swamp Music

> Freebooters, armed and drunk—a legion of gamblers, brawlers, and whorehoppers. Blowing into town in a junk Model-A with bald tires, no muffler and one headlight . . . looking for quick work, with no questions asked and preferably no tax deductions. Just get the cash, fill up at a cut-rate gas station and hit the road, with a pint on the seat and Eddy Arnold on the radio moaning good back-country tunes about home sweet home, that Bluegrass sweetheart still waitin, and roses on Mama's grave.
>
> **Hunter S. Thompson,** *Hell's Angels*

The three-chord D, C add 9, and G introduction should be about as instantly recognizable to most Americans today as the opening notes of their national anthem; likewise, the mournful slide guitar descant over piano and organ is no less immediately transporting than "America the Beautiful." Each of the two songs is pushing fifty years old. The lyrics of both were composed and vocalized by a young man with an intense devotion to his family and his roots, who within a few years would come to his end by the very means and on the very soil of which he had sung. Each piece of music, once so identified with a specialized locality and way of life, is now emblematic of an entire ethnic and economic population residing across the United States. It is probable that, no matter what time or occasion, at this very moment, "Sweet Home Alabama" and "Free Bird," the two most familiar works by Lynyrd Skynyrd, are being heard in numerous car radios, bars, airports, and shopping malls at numerous points around North America.

In their prime of the 1970s, Skynyrd were the biggest band of the emerging genre quickly reduced to the label "southern rock." The term is unintentionally ironic, since the essence of rock 'n' roll comes from rhythms, progressions, and verses first crafted in the former Confederacy, where the musical traditions of Blacks and whites were among the very few social exchanges that freely passed between the two populations. All rock is southern rock. European

Takin' Care of Business. George Case, Oxford University Press (2021). © George Case.
DOI: 10.1093/oso/9780197548813.003.0006

instruments played by African slaves; Appalachian intervals strummed over a Ghanaian cadence; Scottish and Irish ballads adapted by Cajuns and Creoles; the rhymes of the cotton field and the Mississippi River repeated and revised in nearby churches and saloons; Tupelo; New Orleans; Memphis; Macon; the Delta; the blues. Anyone who plays rock 'n' roll is taking a symbolic journey to one clearly defined territory. Lynyrd Skynyrd and their southern contemporaries were put inside an arbitrary category that really included a lot of artists who didn't care to admit it.

The reason for this is the fruitful era from the early 1960s onward, when young people's popular music expanded to a national and international language that far transcended its regional origins. Rock 'n' roll was taken up by distinctly non-southern performers who might have grown up in the suburbs of Los Angeles, like the Beach Boys, or small-town Minnesota, like Bob Dylan, or bustling Detroit, like the Motown acts. Then came the British Invasion, propelling rock further ahead through Scouse- and Cockney-accented musicians who had only known America through records and films. Psychedelic Californian groups at the Monterey Festival might have come from another universe than the one that had produced Jerry Lee Lewis or Little Richard. And even if all of their material derived from styles that initially developed around Louisiana, Tennessee, or Georgia, there were several crucial years when the social character of the actual US South—its bigoted cops and backward politicians, its Baptist ministers and Beatle-burning bonfires, its color bars and cornpone culture—was an embarrassment to most of the people playing its music. Perhaps in the same way that the British acts had a novel appeal in North America through being rock 'n' rollers from a country typically associated with aristocracy, tea, and stiff upper lips, the southern bands started off as curiosities: dope-smoking long-haired electric guitar players from a landscape more famous for its crew-cuts, moonshine, and banjos.

Over time, Skynyrd and their neighbors would change rock itself. When some rock 'n' roll acts paid tribute to country music's orchestration and song structures, country returned the compliment by taking on some of rock's experimental boldness. Then rock replied again by lifting some of country's lyrical ethos: the melancholy, the fealty to past and property, the penchant for alcohol, and the mistrust of official authority. If country had tacked leftward with the outlaws—fitfully, but leftward nevertheless—some strains of rock would start swinging ever so slightly to the right. In the early 1970s such an inclination would have been hard to perceive, by either conservatives or liberals. Today it is unmissable. The southern rock bands were not political, but just by unapologetically declaring their backgrounds at a time when those backgrounds were the music's most retrograde, they were making a political statement.

That statement, insofar as it could be called one, was first articulated by the Allman Brothers. By the end of the 1960s, the strongest and most commercial music coming from the American South had been the hard soul of James Brown, Aretha Franklin, Otis Redding, and Wilson Pickett, until Georgian Phil Walden of the newly formed Capricorn Records (a subsidiary of Atlantic) sought to tap into the bigger national audience of rock fans—namely, young white people. He picked out slide guitar virtuoso Duane Allman from his gig doing sessions at Alabama's Muscle Shoals studios, and within a few months a band formed around Duane and his younger brother Gregory, who played guitar and keyboards and could sing. A first album, *The Allman Brothers Band*, was released in March 1969, but their first big success came with 1971's live record, *At Fillmore East*. Capricorn's base in Macon, Georgia, became the Allmans' center and fixed their connection to the South, even as their popularity with college-age punters radiated out across America. "Everyone in the industry was saying that we'd never make it, we'd never do anything, that Phil Walden should move us to New York or LA," said co-guitarist Dickey Betts. "Of course, none of us would do that, and thankfully, Walden was smart enough to see that would just ruin what we had."[1] "We elected to stay down South and do it from there rather than going where all the damn competition was,"[2] Gregg Allman concurred.

Yet for all their mass appeal, the Allman Brothers Band did not play the routine hard rock, or country rock, or even straight blues rock of the era. Instead, they offered a striking fusion of jazz, soul, and blues that easily matched the high musical chops of their international competitors while staying uniquely grounded in its southern roots. When so many white bands were affecting a southern sound (the Rolling Stones' "Honky Tonk Women," the Band's "Up on Cripple Creek," CCR's "Born on the Bayou," for example), at last a band of born-and-bred southerners were showing how it was really done. "The first stuff you hear is so important, man," Duane reflected in a 1971 interview. "Like Hank Williams—I love it. The rhythm of it is basically cut and dried, like rock 'n' roll. It's good ol' foot-stompin' stuff!"[3] Gregg Allman's organ tone added a churchy dignity to "Whipping Post" and "It's Not My Cross to Bear," something that entirely guitar-playing acts never had, while the sumptuously meshed soloing of Duane and Dickey Betts defied the conventional lead-rhythm dynamic that was then prevalent. "The ideas for playing harmony lines came both from the fiddles of Western swing music, which I had heard a lot of growing up, and the jazz horns of Miles Davis and John Coltrane,"[4] Betts explained. The Allman Brothers were heavy, but they were not heavy metal.

Gregg and Duane's expressiveness on vocals and guitars further lent the original sextet a personal gravitas that most rock, built around themes of youthful passion or provocation, rarely suggested. The moods of "Midnight Rider" and "Melissa," the tasty instrumental "In Memory of Elizabeth Reed," and the molten Elmore James cover "One Way Out" were older and wiser than many songs by people the same age as the Allmans; perhaps it had something to do with their growing up fatherless after US Army lieutenant Willis Turner Allman was murdered by a stranger on a Tennessee dirt road in 1949, when his two sons were just toddlers. A thousand twentysomething rock 'n' rollers might strive to sing of pain and suffering far beyond their years, but the Allmans' pain didn't seem like such a pose. The band knew more tragedy when Duane perished in a motorcycle accident in 1971 and bassist Berry Oakley died in a similar crash the next year. Hard drugs were also part of the Allmans' scene. Duane had only recently quit heroin before his fatal ride, and Oakley had been using on the day of his death. Continuing with a roster of surviving and new players, the Allman Brothers' "Ramblin' Man" from 1973 (sung by Betts) became their most well-known single, a country-tinged travelogue of Georgia, Nashville, and New Orleans that also eulogized the Allmans' lost parent, who really had wound up at the wrong end of a gun. "We knew it was a good song but it didn't sound like us," admitted drummer Butch Trucks. "We went to the studio to do a demo to send to Merle Haggard or someone."[5] The blues in the Allmans' sound had been earned the hard way.

For casual followers, the Allman Brothers Band forced a reconsideration of southern stereotypes just by the fact that the group's lineup, over numerous personnel changes, was consistently interracial. It was Duane's decision to build the ensemble around dual percussionists, because, as he told new recruit Johnie Lee "Jaimoe" Johnson, "James Brown and Otis Redding have two."[6] With Mississippi-born Jaimoe sharing drum duties with Trucks, the image of the Allmans instantly deflected any potential suspicions of old-fashioned white southern bigotry—Jaimoe was Black, as was Berry Oakley's replacement Lamar Williams, a Vietnam veteran. In those days many white acts featured occasional Black sitters-in, but not often were bands as harmoniously integrated as the Allmans; only Sly and the Family Stone, Santana, Pacific Gas & Electric, and the Jimi Hendrix Experience (none of them from the US South) featured Black and white musicians alongside each other under the same cohesive identity. This took some balls. "Having Jaimoe in the band was a very big issue in 1969 in the Deep South," confirmed Allman road crew member Kim Payne, "where segregation was still pretty strict. . . . The long hair was enough to start shit in most places, but Jaimoe . . . that was enough to spark the gasoline."[7] Gregg Allman also recounted, "Our family thing only grew stronger, and that included dealing with the perennial redneck questions: 'Who them hippie boys and who's the nigger in the band?' We dealt with that second question quite a bit. . . . But Jaimoe was one of us and we weren't going to change that for nobody."[8] The implications of Jaimoe's, and later Williams's, secure places in the Allman Brothers Band changed what it meant to be a young white southern American in the early 1970s, for both outsiders and southerners themselves.

In this post–civil rights period, the South struggled to shed the stigma for which it was known around the United States and the rest of the world. The ugly scenes of Black students escorted by armed guards to forcibly desegregated schools, of white police with fire hoses and attack dogs menacing peaceful protesters, of white onlookers jeering Black sitters-in at lunch counters, had been seared into the popular imagination. The conclusion of *Easy Rider* had showed the cool Californian antiheroes gunned down by vicious Louisianan hayseeds. Now here was a rock 'n' roll band of hairy white potheads, sharing their stage and studio with an African American drummer, *and they were all from the South.* "This multiracial outfit of hippies and rednecks created a soundtrack that relieved young southerners of the weightiness of their guilt, fear, and economic insecurities," wrote North Carolinian Mark Kemp, a future *Rolling Stone* editor, in his memoir *Dixie Lullaby: A Story of Music, Race, and New Beginnings in a New South*: "The family legacies of racism, the drudgeries of a rural, working-class existence . . . There were skeletons in the closet of the entire South, a truth that simultaneously fascinated and terrified me. . . . I had no words for all of it. So I let the Allman Brothers Band hold it for me for a while."[9] After the Allmans, white people growing up in Dixie had a convenient denial for those who automatically equated their culture with racial prejudice.

The culmination of the Allman Brothers Band's rehabilitating the South came in 1975, when they were already a major draw across the country, complete with private tour jet and abundant cocaine provisions. On November 25, the group performed a benefit concert for Georgia governor Jimmy Carter, then just beginning a long-shot run for the US presidency. Carter was his state's first post-segregationist leader, and he held progressive views on race and drugs; the $40,000 raised by the Allmans' show was enough to keep him in the campaign. "He was a really nice guy, and he was really hip to music," Gregg Allman remembered of Carter. "If you ask me, he wasn't nothing but a hippie who had to get a haircut. His mind was young and wide open."[10] For some Americans, at least, Carter's ascendancy denoted a "New South" that had finally risen above its legacy of ignorance and division, and the rock music of the Allman Brothers Band had played a crucial role in his political career. Though his single term was hardly a success on either the domestic or foreign fronts, Jimmy Carter seemed to prove that his region and his public had moved beyond their dark histories.

As the Allmans had grown in popularity, especially after *At Fillmore East*, record companies began to hunt through the group's homeland to sign comparable acts—just as they already had done in Britain after the Beatles and San Francisco after the Monterey Pop Festival, and would again in Seattle after Nirvana. Among the hunters was Al Kooper, a keyboardist, guitarist, and industry insider who'd played on Dylan's *Highway 61 Revisited* and *Blonde on Blonde*, among other stars' music, and who'd started his own MCA-affiliated record label, Sounds of the South. In an Atlanta nightclub in 1972, he discovered a band managed by Alan Walden, the brother of Capricorn Records' Phil Walden, the company to which the Allmans were contracted. Kooper was impressed with the group, at that moment consisting of five young guys, three of them from Jacksonville, Florida, and all clearly driven hard by their frontman. That frontman was Ronnie Van Zant, and the band—*his* band— was Lynyrd Skynyrd.

Between 1973 and 1975, Skynyrd released three successful albums, *Pronounced Leh-nerd Skin-nerd*, *Second Helping*, and *Nuthin' Fancy*, under Kooper's production, and managed a fluctuating membership built around singer Van Zant and guitarists Allen Collins and Gary Rossington. Two more well-received records, *Gimme Back My Bullets* and *Street Survivors*, came out in 1976 and 1977, while the group regularly toured the United States and Europe and ventured as far afield as Japan. They had valuable exposure opening for the Who on an early American circuit and for the Rolling Stones at a festival show in Britain in 1976. But their most appreciative audiences were always found in the US heartland, where their unique hard rock honky-tonk became the voice of several generations of working-class white kids: proud, loud, and unpretentious. This voice has resounded several decades after the band's plane crashed into a Mississippi swamp in 1977, killing Ronnie Van Zant and two other performers from the act, along with their road manager and both aircraft pilots. The endurance of Lynyrd Skynyrd's music and mystique represents a crucial element in the transformation of US politics and pop culture of the last fifty years.

If the Allman Brothers Band had demonstrated that southerners could fit into the counterculture of the late 1960s and early 1970s, Lynyrd Skynyrd forced the counterculture to adapt to the South. They too were hirsute rockers who partied hard and weren't afraid to challenge prevailing authority—the band was named after Van Zant and Rossington's gym teacher at Robert E. Lee High School, a hardass called Leonard Skinner who hated pot-smoking long-haired boys—and had eagerly caught the earliest appearances by the Allmans around the Florida panhandle. But Skynyrd played a tougher, tighter rock that had little of the Allmans' improvisatory jazz or soul affectations, and they did not have any African American personnel. Like Creedence Clearwater Revival, Steppenwolf, or Grand Funk Railroad, Skynyrd seemed to connect with a sector of the baby boom market that was not quite hippies and not exactly protesters—rebellious young people whose rebellion stood against both more and less than whatever was being denounced on coastal campuses or at marches on Washington, DC. In some ways, Skynyrd's public was indistinguishable from the fans of every other pop personality; you could be into Skynyrd just as much as you were into the Allmans, Alice Cooper, Cat Stevens, Humble Pie, or Pink Floyd or the late Jimi Hendrix. In other ways, however, Skynyrd brought out a quality of regional, economic, and even racial solidarity hitherto mostly dormant in their generation. Tens of millions of listeners around the world shared a taste for some variety of rock 'n' roll or another. Lynyrd Skynyrd's rock 'n' roll was an indication of how eclectic that variety had become.

Ronnie Van Zant, Allen Collins, and Gary Rossington had grown up influenced by the Rolling Stones, the Yardbirds, the Animals, Them, Free, and other British Invasion blues-based bands. The guitar players were also impressed by Hendrix, Eric Clapton, and the first works of Led Zeppelin. But Van Zant had a fondness for the unadorned Americana of CCR and the bleak, blunt poetry of Merle Haggard, and he affected the yodeling, yee-haw vocal accents of country casualties Jimmie Rodgers and Hank Williams. Unusually for rock 'n' roll groups, stage and studio assemblies of Lynyrd Skynyrd sometimes featured no less than three electric guitarists—Collins and Rossington were first joined by Ed King, once of the Strawberry Alarm Clock, and later by Steve Gaines, who perished in the '77 crash—which gave the group a stinging set of tones and made for a layered and very finely arranged soloing more elaborate than even that of Duane Allman and Dickey Betts in the Allman Brothers. Rossington and Collins, as well, were prone to squawky, high-pitched lead breaks that sounded almost like distorted banjos or fiddles: many of their bends alluded to pure bluegrass or country techniques as much as the liquid moan of Clapton or Free six-stringer Paul Kossoff, and the duo often picked acoustic-style open chords on their amplified instruments, rather than the more typical barres. As with the Allmans, Skynyrd featured a full-time pianist and organist in the group—usually Billy Powell, but some keyboard parts were played by Al Kooper himself—imbuing the songs with either a sacred, hymnal undertone or a rollicking ragtime bounce. Whereas the Band or the Flying Burrito Brothers were often summed up as country rock, Lynyrd Skynyrd invented a subgenre that might have been termed country metal (one of Skynyrd's last gigs was at Willie Nelson's 1977 Picnic in Tulsa, Oklahoma). Reviewing 1975's *Nuthin' Fancy*, *Rolling Stone* characterized the band as "Creedence with firepower."[11]

And like Creedence Clearwater Revival, Skynyrd disdained the diva poses that singled out members of other acts. No one in the band was a cover boy; Ronnie Van Zant in particular was an average-looking dude, short in stature with thinning hair and a paunch, who had an arm tattoo depicting an eagle over an American flag above his father's name, Lacy (in an era when skin ink was still associated with jailhouses and garages rather than being the requisite hipster accessories of today). The rest of the players were themselves just scrawny southern white folks who scarcely stood out from any of the spectators at their concerts, though with extremely long hair that had earned them the wrath of coach Leonard Skinner and others his age. Publicity photos made the hangdog-eyed Allen Collins appear totally stoned, which was not all that inaccurate. Van Zant and bassist Leon Wilkeson wore cowboy or other hats for their gigs.

Ronnie Van Zant, of course, was Lynyrd Skynyrd's certified leader. He didn't really play guitar or any other instrument, but he directed the musicians, was a stickler for rehearsal and performance discipline, and wrote almost all of Skynyrd's lyrics. "He definitely kept a handle on things, and if you got out of line or if you got lazy, he'd be right there in your shit,"[12] recalled Ed King. "Ronnie wrote most of his lyrics either driving around Jacksonville checking out different neighborhoods—especially poor ones, black or white—or in the shower," Gary Rossington remembered. "Many times when we were on the road, he'd end up running into my room . . . saying, 'Check this out. Write some music to that real quick.'"[13] Van Zant was the eldest son of a truck driver who reportedly named his boy after actor Ronald Reagan (not yet a politician when Ronnie was born in 1948), and he grew up in a hardscrabble Jacksonville district he described as "Shantytown." As an adult in a working rock 'n' roll group, he became equally known for his forthright decency and generosity when sober and violent mean streak when drunk. "He was an outstanding bandleader, but towards the end of the time that I was in the group, he drank way too much," King said of him. "And when he drank, he was a totally different person. It runs in his family."[14] The splendidly southern-named Artimus Pyle, who drummed for Skynyrd from 1975 on, backed up the memory. "I loved and respected Ronnie Van Zant. . . . But I have seen the man turn into the devil right in front of me and hurt people."[15]

Drinking, in fact, was a Lynyrd Skynyrd trademark. The members had numerous alcohol-fueled altercations while traveling together, and Van Zant accumulated a long list of arrests for drunken brawling. One scrap on a European tour resulted in bad gashes to Rossington's hands, administered with a broken bottle by Van Zant, stemming from a dispute over pronunciation of the word "schnapps." "If they couldn't find anyone to fight, they'd fight each other,"[16] Al Kooper recounted. Their music, too, celebrated booze during the years when the indulgences most rock promoted, subtly or not, were the hippie trips of cannabis and LSD (the Allman Brothers' logo was a stylized mushroom). Numerous Skynyrd tunes refer to the old-fashioned vice of liquor: "Poison Whiskey," "Whiskey Rock-a-Roller," "Don't Ask Me No Questions," "Trust," "Saturday Night Special," and "You Got That Right," while "That Smell" and "The Needle and the Spoon" threw in the newer dangers of cocaine, Quaaludes, and heroin. A familiar Lynyrd Skynyrd T-shirt and poster graphic borrowed the label design of Jack Daniel's whiskey. By highlighting, even critically, a legal substance used and abused for centuries, rather than illegal substances identified with youthful dissent, Skynyrd had taken a lyrical stand on the side of tradition.

Van Zant's verses further evoked, and extended, the resigned temperament of the Allman Brothers. This again was a marked departure from the shock rock of Alice Cooper and his ilk, or the hey-people-let's-change-the-world spirit of a lot of Lynyrd Skynyrd's predecessors and peers. The debut album *Pronounced Leh-nerd Skin-nerd* alone had three songs of reflective sorrow that seemed inextricable from their low-born southern provenance: "Tuesday's Gone," "Simple Man," and the epic "Free Bird." "Simple Man," a slowly building power ballad in A minor, presented the sage motherly advice of humility and faith immediately recognizable to its audience, even if its inclusion on the record was at first vetoed by Al Kooper. "Ronnie took Kooper out to the parking lot, opened the door to Kooper's Bentley, and said, 'Get in,'" Ed King reminisced. "Ronnie shut the door and said, 'When we're done cuttin' it, we'll call you.' We cut the whole tune without him. When a band knows what it wants to do, it has to go with its heart and not listen to people on the outside."[17] A Skynyrd anthem from before its official release, "Free Bird" originated with Allen Collins and was stretched out at gigs to give Van Zant a rest from singing duties; its opening line, asking if a lover would be remembered when he was gone, was an actual query from Collins's then-girlfriend and later wife, Kathy Johns. "Free Bird" was not about chasing girls but leaving one, with Billy Powell's delicate piano filigrees adding a bittersweet majesty to Collins's chords, making the song an FM and concert classic comparable to Led Zeppelin's equally grandiose "Stairway to Heaven." Subsequent Skynyrd cuts, like "All I Can Do Is Write about It," "Every Mother's Son," and a cover of Merle Haggard's "Honky Tonk Night Time Man," likewise sounded a denim fatalism that stood out in the mid-1970s but which would become a standard theme of rock in later decades. The trains and buses that were staple images of the blues also rode through Van Zant's lines, in "Tuesday's Gone," "Railroad Song," "Whiskey Rock-a-Roller," and "Roll Gypsy Roll." For music primarily aimed at youth, Lynyrd Skynyrd songs offered a sort of vicarious jadedness many youthful listeners sought to know for themselves.

Skynyrd's other nod to tradition, though, was not as simple as acknowledging the perils of drinking cold whiskey or the simple values of following your heart and no one else. Part of the marketing strategy constructed around the band was a deliberate exploitation of their southern origins, a ploy the members disliked—"We always considered ourselves just a band from the South, not really a Southern rock band,"[18] Rossington said—but were in no position to overrule. Once they were signed to MCA through Al Kooper's Sounds of the South and with their first two albums selling strongly, Lynyrd Skynyrd concerts were performed in front of a Confederate flag, and some sets began with a rocked-up instrumental version of the Old South minstrel standard "Dixie." In the immediate post–civil rights years, it was difficult to place these devices on a political spectrum. They might have indicated brazen support for the slaveholding and segregationist racial order that had long defined Lynyrd Skynyrd's home territory of the former Confederate States of America, but then again, the group was a bunch of shaggy boys who played loud rock music for hopheads around the United States and the world. When conjuring a personification of southern racism in 1974, Birmingham public safety commissioner Bull Connor and Alabama governor George Wallace came to mind long before Ronnie Van Zant and his buddies.

But in 1975, at a performance in Tuscaloosa, George Wallace himself conferred upon all Skynyrd players certification as honorary lieutenant colonels in the Alabama State Militia. Wallace by that time was in his second of three terms as Alabama governor and was infamous for his pro-segregationist stance in the early 1960s, a position he did not renounce until later in the 1970s. In some accounts, Ronnie Van Zant dismissed the Wallace honor as a "bullshit gimmick thing,"[19] probably meant to boost Wallace's standing with young voters more than Skynyrd's with middle-aged whites, but Ed King admitted, "Ronnie was a big fan of George Wallace. He totally supported him. We all did. We respected the way Wallace stood up for the South. Anyone who tells you any differently is lying."[20]

The official line on Skynyrd's racial attitudes, maintained by an extensive community of southern and non-southern fans as well as surviving and substitute members (Ronnie Van Zant's brother Johnny has sung for a relaunched Lynyrd Skynyrd since 1987), restates the heritage-not-hate theme advanced by southern whites in debates over Confederate iconography like flags and statues. In this argument, Skynyrd's redneck affectations celebrate a bygone way of life—rural, close-knit, stubbornly independent—rather than any contemporary political affiliation or social plank. Moreover, apologists highlight positive references to African Americans in Skynyrd lyrics like "Swamp Music," which invokes bluesman Son House, and "The Ballad of Curtis Loew," about a fictional front-porch guitar picker. An early hero of the scrappy young boxing buff Ronnie Van Zant was Cassius Clay, later Muhammad Ali. Van Zant himself was equivocal over the onstage display of the Confederate flag: "It was useful at first, but by now it's embarrassing,"[21] he eventually said.

Privately, however, stories from band insiders (including Al Kooper) suggest the musicians were hardly progressive in their views—they had the casual prejudices of their background and generation and were not above uttering anti-Black racial slurs.[22] Certainly there were no people of color in their entourage or their core audiences. Their all-female backup vocal trio of later shows was dubbed the Honkettes, perhaps an oblique play on the common African American epithet for Caucasians. Some of Skynyrd's base may have only been seeking a conditional truce with the Black population they lived alongside, similar to that later expressed on bumper stickers and T-shirts in response to the promotion of Spike Lee's 1992 biopic *Malcolm X*. Over the crossed bars of the Confederate flag, the slogans read, "You Wear Your X, and I'll Wear Mine." Skynyrd's respect for George Wallace was motivated by the same murky mix of offhand, learned white racism and class-based populism that inspired all the governor's backers in those years (he ran for the US presidency as an independent in 1968 and as a Democrat in 1972 and 1976, despite being paralyzed in an assassination attempt in 1972). "To Ronnie, Wallace was not just a man who wouldn't let Blacks into college, he was a man who spoke for poor, uneducated people who didn't have a voice,"[23] Ed King explained long after Van Zant's death. "Of course I don't agree with everything Wallace says," Van Zant stated in a 1970s interview. "I don't like what he says about colored people. . . . We're Southern rebels, but more than that, we know the difference between right and wrong."[24]

Other Lynyrd Skynyrd material offers more political ambiguity. "Saturday Night Special," from 1975's *Nuthin' Fancy*, took on the indiscriminate use of cheap handguns and a general proliferation of violence—hardly messages to endear them to a crowd of rifle-toting southern crackers. Cowritten by Van Zant and Ed King, the song was featured in the soundtrack of Burt Reynolds' 1974 prison film *The Longest Yard* and in the 1978 labor drama *Blue Collar*. Skynyrd members including Van Zant owned and used guns, and "Saturday Night Special" was not advocating mandated firearms restriction so much as responsible use of accurate weapons ("Saturday night special" denotes an inexpensive, poor-quality gun purchased for a holdup or other crime). "Gimme Back My Bullets," conversely, didn't literally ask for more ammunition but for the kind of success an industrious professional musician had already known and felt he still deserved (typographic "bullets" were how the trade paper *Billboard* denoted fast-selling records). "Workin' for MCA" was the most convincing of the rock subgenre of artist complaints against corporate power, with its extra dimension of Yankee slickers ripping off hard-luck southerners. An early B-side, "Mr. Banker," was a poor man's plea for a rich man's charity, set to a slow blues, while "Things Goin' On" hinted at the money and lives wasted on the space race and in Vietnam, and "All I Can Do Is Write about It" was a subtle call for environmental awareness. Within the Skynyrd discography, such songs belie the convenient label of "redneck rock" often stuck on them.

But then there's "Sweet Home Alabama." The one Skynyrd track to rival the airplay and influence of "Free Bird," the opening number from 1974's *Second Helping* became a hit single at the time and a permanent source of controversy ever since. This was the most incendiary of all the southern postures taken by the act—an upbeat ode to the state most tarnished by violent white hostility to Blacks and Black civil rights—despite its simple construction and off-the-cuff origins. Composed by Gary Rossington around three major chords, embellished by Ed King's banjo-like fills and Billy Powell's barrelhouse piano, " 'Sweet Home' was a classic the minute we wrote it,"[25] King said. "We used to travel through Alabama a lot and get onto back roads and just marvel at how pretty it all was and how nice the people were," Rossington recalled. "And Neil Young was, and still is, one of our favorite artists, so when he came out with 'Southern Man' and 'Alabama,' criticizing the South, we said 'Well, what does he know? He's from Canada.' "[26] The Young tunes that irked Skynyrd had been issued as album cuts on 1970's *After the Gold Rush* ("Southern Man") and 1972's *Harvest* ("Alabama"); both numbers took aim at the state and the region's brutal backwardness in race relations. To Ronnie Van Zant and the other members, though, they were all too typical of the sanctimonious and patronizing consideration the South had long been given by outsiders—in this case, an outsider not even from America.

Van Zant's lyrics to "Sweet Home Alabama" have become a mine of meaning, rationalization, and evasion for over four decades. Beginning with a quote from CCR's "Proud Mary," the verses mention family, blue skies, the musicians of Muscle Shoals, and old Mister Neil Young's criticisms, but the most contentious lines acknowledge the flashpoint city of Birmingham (Alabama's state capital is Montgomery) and the unnamed but unmistakable governor, George Wallace. The reactionary politician is ceremoniously booed by the band, but in the next line Van Zant points out the current Washington scandal of Watergate and asks the listener if he has any private regrets that might be just as reactionary or just as scandalous. Are *you* confident you could never be labeled a social regressive by a hippie folk-rock star? How much better, really, are *your* personal values than the president's, the governor's, or an ordinary Alabaman's?

Reactions to "Sweet Home Alabama" were as varied as those of the people who inspired and contributed to it. "It was basically a joke song," Rossington avowed. "We were told by some people to take out the parts about Neil Young and George Wallace, but we said, 'Hey, it's just a song, and we're going to record it the way we wrote it.'"[27] In his memoirs, Neil Young admitted, "My own song 'Alabama' richly deserved the shot Lynyrd Skynyrd gave me with their great record. I don't like the words when I listen to it today. They are accusatory and condescending, not fully thought out, and too easy to misconstrue."[28] But backup singer Merry Clayton, whose unearthly howl had earlier electrified the Rolling Stones' "Gimme Shelter," said that she and Clydie King each provided vocal accompaniment to the Skynyrd track with great reluctance as African Americans. "[Alabama's] not sweet home to black people!" she noted. "It's not sweet home at all. . . . If you listen to it we're all singing through our teeth, like we're really angry. That's how we got through the recording."[29] Clayton elsewhere described "Sweet Home Alabama" as "a song that will live in infamy."[30]

For white southerners, the Lynyrd Skynyrd song offered just the right blend of contrition (*Boo, boo, boo*) and contrariness (*Tell me true*) to stand as a declaration of their qualified allegiances: no to historic racism and discrimination, but yes to kinship and local roots. In the long run, "Sweet Home Alabama" was an early anticipation of how shame has limited potential as a political impetus. If enough people are told for long enough that they should feel guilty about who they are or where they come from, then inevitably some of them will resist by claiming to feel proud. Other groups had nullified the supposed inferiorities of their race or their sexuality this way; "Sweet Home Alabama" gave poor whites a parallel boost. In 1974 few thought the catchy rock number, which became a Top Ten success across the country, constituted any kind of backlash against civil rights, but over the years it has been saddled by both friends and foes with a reputation as a marker of racial identity the instant its twangy first notes are sounded—which, perhaps, says more about America than Lynyrd Skynyrd. Ronnie Van Zant's spoken request to *Turn it up* over the opening bars, originally a simple demand to the musicians in his charge, is today echoed by concertgoers who may mean many other things besides boosting decibel levels. Whatever they intend to say, "Sweet Home Alabama" still says it for them.

Moved by, or at any rate coinciding with, the growing fame of Lynyrd Skynyrd, an odd kind of revival was identified in the United States through the 1970s and beyond: "redneck chic." The rise of outlaw country and various other pop entertainments was also a factor, but their combined effects came down to a sanitized version of southern traditions that eliminated the most egregious manifestations of anti-Black bigotry (minstrel shows, segregation, lynching, the Klan) to glorify an ostensibly quaint past (cowboy hats, over- alls, dirt roads, bootleg whiskey, fried chicken, the Confederate flag). What was significant in redneck chic was how much of it was represented through long-haired rock 'n' roll bands—when both long hair and rock 'n' roll were generally equated with liberalism—which further distinguished the positive modern portrayals of the South from the problematic realities behind it. With different appreciations for those portrayals and those realities, record compa- nies and fans could now find numerous "southern rockers" to capitalize on the newer, nicer stereotypes.

Capricorn Records of Macon, Georgia, home of the Allman Brothers Band, had also acquired southern acts including Hydra (from Atlanta), the Marshall Tucker Band (Spartanburg, South Carolina), Wet Willie (Mobile, Alabama), and the Dixie Dregs (Augusta, Georgia). Marshall Tucker won major sales with their self-titled first record in 1975, featuring the perennial jam "Can't You See," while various permutations of the fusion-oriented Dixie Dregs remained a big attraction among serious music buffs for many years; guitarist Steve Morse eventually replaced Ritchie Blackmore in British hard rockers Deep Purple. Al Kooper's Sounds of the South signed Mose Jones, also from Atlanta, and the quirky Elijah, a horn-based funk group from Los Angeles, al- though both were quickly overshadowed by Kooper's other discovery, Lynyrd Skynyrd. Charlie Daniels was a multi-instrumentalist who'd already played with Bob Dylan as a Nashville session man and who worked wicked fiddle bursts into his own material; his 1974 number on Capitol, "The South's Gonna Do It," cited other current southern rockers including the Allmans, Skynyrd, Marshall Tucker, and Wet Willie.

Other artists emerged from across the region, their careers clearly driven by the established names of the Allman Brothers and Lynyrd Skynyrd. Ozark Mountain Daredevils of Springfield, Missouri, made an eponymous first album in 1973 and won their biggest score with 1975's smoothly psychedelic drug saga "Jackie Blue." The Atlanta Rhythm Section's shag-carpet funk of "So Into You" was outtasight in '76. Black Oak Arkansas, from the town and state of those names, put out a debut record in 1971 and took on the personas of a hillbilly Grand Funk Railroad, incorporating banjo, steel guitar, and even washboard into their sound and touring widely (including opening spots for Alice Cooper) with brainless heavy-duty boogies titled "Hot and Nasty," "Hot Rod," "Hey Y'All," "Rebel," "Moonshine Sonata," and the 1973 live album *Raunch 'n' Roll.* Their frontman was the incomparable Jim "Dandy" Mangrum, who wore spandex pants and whose stage patter was drawled in a backwoods accent as thick as barbecued hog; naturally they performed a cover of the 1957 rhythm and blues hit "Jim Dandy to the Rescue." Out of Skynyrd's home of Jacksonville came Molly Hatchet, with two hit albums and a classic single, "Flirtin' with Disaster," in 1978 and 1979. They notably combined the requisite amped-up country guitar runs and southern vocal timbres with record sleeves boasting heroic sword-and-sorcery illustrations by fantasy artist Frank Frazetta. Ronnie and Johnnie Van Zant's middle brother, Donnie, led 38 Special through the 1970s and 1980s, with varying lineups that sometimes included Skynyrd founding bassist Larry Junstrom and backup singer Dale Krantz, the wife of Gary Rossington. The Outlaws, not to be confused with the country movement, were from Tampa and signed to Arista Records in 1974 on the recommendation of Ronnie Van Zant, and they were best known for their 1975 pieces "There Goes Another Love Song" and the finely orchestrated electric bluegrass solos of "Green Grass and High Tides." After their disbandment, guitarist Hughie Thomasson had a stint in a later edition of Lynyrd Skynyrd, as did Rickey Medlocke of Blackfoot, a long-suffering opening act from Gainesville.

Southern rock was defined enough as a style that even artists not from the area could produce music that seemed to fall into the category: the early heavy metal of "Mississippi Queen" called up Louisiana, Vicksburg, and the Cajun Lady herself, despite been performed by Long Island's Mountain in 1970. Fellow New Yorkers Ram Jam achieved a lone grab at rock immortality in 1977, with their blasting cover of a traditional blues sometimes credited to Huddie "Lead Belly" Ledbetter, "Black Betty." Lyrically, Ram Jam's "Black Betty" played with some inflammatory insinuations of its heroine, from Birmingham way down in Alabama and shakin' that thing, all adding up to a gratuitously sexist and racist joke that no actual southerners could have gotten away with; as it was, the song drew complaints from Black groups and has been protested when its martial rhythms are sounded at modern-day sporting events. Classier by far were the Doobie Brothers from Southern California, like the Allman Brothers Band a multiracial, keyboard-based group, who specialized in soulful harmonies and stone grooves. Their popular cuts "South City Midnight Lady," "China Grove," "Listen to the Music," and "Black Water" offered supple pictures of cheap whiskey, the Lone Star state, San Antone, the Mississippi moon, and funky Dixieland. The tight gospel rhythms of the Doobies' great "Jesus Is Just Alright" attracted an unlikely fan base, as reported by guitarist-vocalist Pat Simmons: "That song was always well-received, even in the roughest of biker bars. The heaviest of heavy-duty people would come up to us and say, 'Man, that's great. You really said it, brother.' Redneck bikers everywhere loved it. It was like someone was telling them they were worth the trouble, you know?"[31]

What did southern rock mean? Though all these acts had a wide range of influences, musical configurations, and home bases, their common connection was in their artistic mandates. They were not, for the most part, conveying serious social messages or taking explicit political stands. But coming from the South (or sounding like they did), they thereby continued the Allmans-Skynyrd precedent of denying that there were any automatic social or political obligations that went with their backgrounds. It also mattered that the bands' most prominent individual members, like Duane and Gregg Allman, Ronnie Van Zant, or Jim "Dandy" Mangrum, were represented as heirs not to the southern elite of plantation owners and belles of the ball but to the common working folks of farmers and truck drivers. They were not singing in praise of a distant antebellum wonderland but of a complex modern system in which their status was uncertain and their superiority could no longer be assumed.

The Outlaws, Molly Hatchet, and Black Oak Arkansas made party rock for good ol' southern boys and gals, uncomplicated by burdens of grievance or self-reproach. Their implication was that even the poor and the unsophisticated—even rednecks and white trash—had a right to the catharsis of foot-stompin' rock 'n' roll. In this they stood as a musical retort to the moralism of a long string of white and Black pop records, from the Beatles' "Blackbird" and Bob Dylan's "I Shall Be Released" to Stevie Wonder's "Living for the City" and James Brown's "Say It Loud—I'm Black and I'm Proud," along with a solemn jukebox selection of Sam Cooke's "A Change Is Gonna Come," Barry McGuire's "Eve of Destruction," Janis Ian's "Society's Child," Sly and the Family Stone's "Everyday People," the Youngbloods' "Get Together," Elvis Presley's "In the Ghetto," the Rascals' "People Got to Be Free," Three Dog Night's "Black and White," the Temptations' "Ball of Confusion," Crosby, Stills, Nash & Young's "Ohio," Marvin Gaye's "What's Going On," and many others. Rock may have developed a conscience, but southern rock made a point of not being much troubled by it. Rock fans who were tired of causes or who'd always been indifferent to them found in southern rock a refreshing validation of their compassion fatigue. If they were called intolerant or ignorant because of it, that was a fair price for not being scolded in song yet again.

But the most consistently successful performers to gain prominence with the southern wave were from a state that had its own unique American character: ZZ Top, out of Texas. Formed in Houston in 1969, the enduring trio has outlasted virtually all the bands they began with and remains among the most musically and visually recognizable in rock 'n' roll. Like Texas itself, ZZ Top had an independence from both the northern US and from the southern Black Belt. The vast spaces of their home locale; the mix of white, Black, and Mexican influences in their environment and work; and the growth of Texas within the national economy and culture made the group an emblem of the country's westward and southward expansion. Rock musicians had already worn sideburns, moptops, Afros, tie-dyed T-shirts, makeup, and rebel regalia—now they came wearing Stetsons and cowboy boots.

ZZ Top's trademark Texan look, indeed, became a vital part of their overall aesthetic. From the beginning, longtime manager Bill Ham devised a performance and publicity image around the threesome of Billy Gibbons (guitar and vocals), Dusty Hill (bass and vocals), and Frank Beard (drums) that centered on their Lone Star home and depicted a cartoon vision of Texas life to audiences around the world. They gave shows in front of a Texas state flag and had hay bales, wagon wheels, prop buzzards, and steer skulls onstage; at some performances the desert animals like rattlesnakes and buffalo were not even props but live specimens. "All we did was take what we were and brought it forward," Hill said of their early campaigns. "We obviously had a great amount of pride in being from Texas. It all bloomed out of the seventies. We were bunched up with Southern bands, and there's nothing wrong with that at all. . . . We just wanted to make it clear that we weren't a Southern band. That's more like Georgia, I think. We were a Texas thing."[32] The regional branding of ZZ Top, as it were, was definitely a gimmick, but it was one that worked, just as emphasizing a Texan identity had paid off for Willie Nelson and Waylon Jennings. Added to the cactus-and-coyote insignia was the effectiveness of the band's unchanging lineup, which contrasted with Lynyrd Skynyrd, the Allman Brothers, and many other rock outfits ("Same three guys—same three chords," Billy Gibbons would eventually remind punters), and Ham's insistence on minimal offstage exposure. For the crucial first few years of their career, ZZ Top were only seen when they were gigging, which was almost constantly. They lived on the road and shared or topped bills with everyone from Skynyrd and the Doobie Brothers to Savoy Brown, Santana, and Alice Cooper.

ZZ Top's three-man format also required, or permitted, a far tighter musical cohesion than most blues-based rock groups ever mustered. Unlike some of the four-, five-, or six-piece ensembles active at the same time, Gibbons, Hill, and Beard didn't do wandering I–IV–V jams but instead no-margin-for-error boogies plotted down to the last drum fill, guitar lick, and turnaround, as heard in their great run of Delta- and Chicago-inspired electric riffs, like "Backdoor Love Affair," "Jesus Just Left Chicago," "Heard It on the X," "Nasty Dogs and Funky Kings," and "I'm Bad, I'm Nationwide." Not only did Gibbons have an exceptional blues voice, but his slide and conventional soloing techniques put him among the best of the era's other rock guitarists; he reportedly played with a peso instead of a pick and achieved a brilliantly distinctive crunching, scraping, squealing tone on his Les Pauls. Despite ZZ Top's legitimate blues skills, though, Gibbons's expertise was a somewhat discomfiting cameo of all rock history, as this son of an orchestra conductor and a one-time member of Lyndon Johnson's staff had first accessed the music through his relatively affluent family's African American maid and her daughter. Even in his apprentice band, the Moving Sidewalks, Gibbons had opened for the Jimi Hendrix Experience (another hard rock trio) and had met and learned from Hendrix himself. Hill and Beard's rhythm section, for its part, was a minimalist but impregnable foundation for Gibbons's tangy leads, often veering into full-on funk, as in "Ko Ko Blue," "Waitin' For the Bus," and a cover of Sam and Dave's "I Thank You," cowritten by Isaac Hayes. Hill also shared or took lead vocals on several songs, his clear pitch contrasting nicely with Gibbons's growl.

For all their unassailable prowess at Texas blues, ZZ Top was first and foremost a guy's band. It wasn't just how they played but what they sang about that made their name and secured their base. Unabashed machismo was anticipated by the "cock rock" of the Rolling Stones and other British blues-rock acts, and before that by the blues originators themselves, such as Howlin' Wolf and Muddy Waters, but ZZ Top expressed the twenty-two-year-old working male's perspective with unexampled frankness: they sang of cars ("Chevrolet," "She Loves My Automobile," "I Wanna Drive You Home"), hard partying after a hard day ("Just Got Paid," "Beer Drinkers and Hell Raisers," "Master of Sparks," "Arrested for Driving While Blind"), bordellos ("La Grange," "Mexican Blackbird"), and young women and various body parts or clothing accessories thereof ("Hot, Blue and Righteous," "Francine," "Precious and Grace," "Tush," "Legs," "Pearl Necklace," "Cheap Sunglasses," "Blue Jean Blues," "Fool for Your Stockings," "Tubesteak Boogie"). For a long time male rock 'n' rollers, and male pop artists generally, had striven to appeal to adolescent girls more than any other market; if the girls' brothers or boyfriends bought the records or the tickets too, so much the better, but the songs were largely directed at female sensibilities. The popularity of bruisers like Steppenwolf or bozos like Grand Funk, however, had proved to record companies that they didn't need to aim their product to readers of *Tiger Beat* or *Sixteen*. Young men would shell out to see or hear their favorite rock performers too, but for very different reasons, and so ZZ Top made no effort to woo the ladies. By the mid-1970s, meanwhile, women of all ages were loudly claiming their independence and their refusal to be objectified, and a large sisterhood took to liberated female stars Helen Reddy, Carole King, Carly Simon, and Joni Mitchell. The intersection between them and the purchasers of cock rock was nil. Consciously or not, the lil' ol' band from Texas flattered the masculine instincts—bravado, camaraderie, physical endurance, and plain lust—which feminism was calling obsolete. It was a winning formula that would be widely copied.

This formula was made all the more open with the advent of rock videos and ZZ Top's career resuscitation in the early 1980s. Up to then their popularity had been in a slow descent, while Frank Beard fought a heroin habit and Gibbons temporarily took up residence not in Paris, Texas, but Paris, France. With the songs now formatted into four-minute mini-movies, the cool cars, sexy babes, and Texan backdrops always suggested by the music were manifested in telegenic visual hooks, as in the promotional clips for "Gimme All Your Lovin'," "Got Me under Pressure," "Sleeping Bag," and "Rough Boy." This material given the video treatment, from 1983's *Eliminator* and 1985's *Afterburner*, became the group's biggest hits and was how younger audiences first came to know them. It was all processed through a semi-synthesized makeover by Gibbons, with augmentation by electronic drums and other studio artifices. "The '80s technological advancements . . . made for an interesting challenge," the guitarist explained. "Hey, can a down-and-dirty blues band ever make sounds with this stuff that will work?"[33] You could really see and hear the difference—between the old, bluesy ZZ Top and the techno-MTV edition—yet the "good bros, good times" spirit their back catalog had firmly established was the same. The group had a legacy to uphold and another generation of boys to instruct in the beer-drinking, hell-raising, pearl-necklace-bequeathing ways of manhood.

By then the legacy and lessons of Lynyrd Skynyrd had gone even deeper, even if the original group was not around to parody itself on TV or update its sound with drum machines. Posthumously, they had become central to a continued cult of white southern nationalism that extended well beyond Florida, Georgia, and Alabama, and even outside of the United States. Skynyrd, ZZ Top, and acts as different as Black Oak Arkansas and the Doobie Brothers increasingly found their most committed loyalists among the biker crowd, who loved the music for its combination of hard-hitting dynamics and rugged uprightness, just as they had previously taken to CCR and Steppenwolf. "Jesus Is Just Alright," "Jim Dandy to the Rescue," "La Grange," "Gimme Back My

Bullets," and "Sweet Home Alabama" seemed to celebrate pre-rock values in a rock idiom. They were not teenybopper songs. The artists were not jet-setting millionaires. The lyrics did not call for radical overthrows or for everyone to love everyone else. Rather, they were earthier paeans to the fundamental satisfactions of sex, partying, and not being answerable to other people from other places. To the Hells Angels and other one percenters, Skynyrd and the southern rockers were the house bands of a separatist, self-determining creed taking root across Western societies.

Not that anyone in Lynyrd Skynyrd ever sought the rank. Until its reformation under Johnny Van Zant and a team of survivors and replacements, the remaining Skynyrd family struggled with the lingering effects of their plane crash tragedy. All the Convair's passengers left alive when the aircraft plowed through the Mississippi woods and swampland suffered broken bones, lacerations, and other severe injuries, along with lifelong psychological trauma. "I just had to get used to constant, day-in, day-out pain," Gary Rossington laughed bitterly about latter-day performances with an implanted metal rod in his limb. "With the bar in my arm, I can always tell when it's going to rain."[34]

Others fared worse. Bassist Leon Wilkeson, who'd fleetingly been declared dead in the Convair wreckage, died in 2001 at age forty-nine, from the combined effects of emphysema, cirrhosis of the liver, and an accumulation of painkilling drugs in his system. Allen Collins's wife, Kathy, who had first voiced the query that eventually led off "Free Bird," died while miscarrying the couple's third child, in 1980. Collins himself, whose wistful chord sequence and fiery soloing had made the Skynyrd anthem, was already shattered by the 1977 disaster and then fell to living the alcoholism and self-destruction his late bandmate had sung of in "Poison Whiskey" and "That Smell": "After Allen's wife died, he dove into a bottle and never came out,"[35] said Billy Powell. He ran up numerous arrests for drunk driving, until a final car accident killed a female passenger and left him paralyzed from the waist down in 1986. Not quite four years later, Larkin Allen Collins died of pneumonia, complicated by his paralysis and his broken heart.

Collins's singer and buddy Ronnie Van Zant was already resting in Jacksonville Florida, where he had lain since October 25, 1977. That day, Ronnie's brother Donnie, of 38 Special, and southern rocker Charlie Daniels had sung "Amazing Grace," and country outlaw David Allan Coe's "Another Pretty Country Song" was also heard. Then the simple southern man Ronald Wayne Van Zant was laid to rest, while from a small speaker wafted the quietly dignified music of his favorite songwriter, Merle Haggard, singing "I Take a Lot of Pride in What I Am."

6

British Steel

The tune had been haunting London for weeks past. It was one of
countless similar songs published for the benefit of the proles by a sub-
section of the Music Department. . . . But the woman sang so tunefully
as to turn the dreadful rubbish into an almost pleasant sound. . . . It
struck him as a curious fact that he had never heard a member of the
Party singing alone and spontaneously. It would even have seemed
slightly unorthodox, a dangerous eccentricity, like talking to oneself.
Perhaps it was only when people were somewhere near the starvation
level that they had anything to sing about.

George Orwell, *Nineteen Eighty-Four*

Many of the factors that fueled Americans' turn to populism in the 1970s—
inflation, industrial failure and labor conflict, racial tension, the perceived
corruption or impotence of leadership, the pervasive sense of cultural dislocation—also affected other societies with different histories. And countries
besides the United States were further contending with their own unique
problems, which were if anything more challenging than those of the Western
superpower. During this period, America's partner and ally Great Britain
faced not just high prices and energy shortages but crippling shutdowns of key
industries, a bloody civil war in its province of Northern Ireland, a significant
influx of nonwhite immigrants from former British colonies, the official national emergency of a mandated three-day week in 1974, and the widespread
public service strikes of the "winter of discontent" in 1978–1979. The United
States was in difficulty, but the United Kingdom was in crisis.

All of Britain's predicaments were accentuated by the nation's relatively
small size and high population density, which meant that equivalents of the
social and regional differences spread across North America were compacted
into an area scarcely larger than California or Saskatchewan. There was also
the enduring British class system, far more entrenched than its parallels in
America or Canada, wherein the divides between workers, managers, and

Takin' Care of Business. George Case, Oxford University Press (2021). © George Case.
DOI: 10.1093/oso/9780197548813.003.0007

gentility went back many generations and whereby hereditary titles were still commonly held and awarded. As the former heart of the world's grandest empire, now relegated to second-tier status, and the birthplace of the Industrial Revolution, now sputtering to a close, Britain had a populist tradition that was centuries old. Accordingly, its modern expressions—whether they were received at home or abroad—had a lot of past behind them.

Since 1964, of course, pop music had vastly expanded as an arm of the British entertainment business, and British acts were consistently among the biggest international music stars. Yet the national musical scene had remained remarkably parochial, with a volatile and often unlikely procession of local talent vying for British audiences. In some ways, the London-based music industry served as a farm team for the vast global market: even before the Beatles, but certainly after them, artists who'd first succeeded in the United Kingdom had been compelled to cross the Atlantic and try their luck with the larger and wealthier American buying public. Much of their music was heavily influenced by Americans anyway (as was much British postwar pop culture generally), so it was a natural step to take. But other British performers fared better in their own country, or in western Europe, without ever building a really strong appeal among the Yanks. A snapshot of the British sales charts from the late 1960s and through the 1970s reveals a number of world-famous names and transoceanic hits alongside curiously provincial players whose work never translated well elsewhere. In 1969 the Who's "Pinball Wizard" was below Mary Hopkins's "Goodbye" and Lulu's Eurovision entry "Boom Bang-a-Bang" in the *New Musical Express* singles ranks; a couple of years later Atomic Rooster's "Devil's Answer" was more popular than George Harrison's "Bangla Desh"; in 1975 Roger Whittaker's "The Last Farewell" was rated a bigger seller than David Bowie's "Fame," and so on and so on. Some eminent British rockers—John Lennon being a prime example—exiled themselves to America or elsewhere rather than submit to the tax penalties or career vagaries of their native country. In addition, the British pop environment was not as balkanized by genre (or, some might say, by race) as in the United States, so hard rock and comedy songs, disco and easy listening, country and glitter, were all in direct rivalry for airplay and retail purchase. And as everywhere, from week to week it was usually anonymous one-hit wonders whose material was dominating the established celebrities in millions of listeners' ears.

Given that flux of British pop music and the depth of British class divides, young people's pick of rock 'n' roll records was only one marker of social position, not as immediately revealing as one's accent or the occupations once held by one's grandparents. The children of aristocrats had been thrilled by the surly bohemianism of the Who and the Yardbirds; sons and daughters of lorry drivers and pitmen were entranced by the flouncy pomp of Elton John and Queen; in each case the fans' origins could hardly be disguised by the affectations of the musicians. For other punters, though, their class background was not hidden but emphasized by their preferred pop singers, and that identification would become stronger as the 1970s moved forward and Britain's economic and political indicators sank further into decline.

In its first years of worldwide success, British rock had maintained a conceit of classlessness that had taken hold in Swinging London and reflected the ideal that the old shackles of income and family background were at last obsolete. Backstage, the Animals or Them might show themselves to be hardened products of proletarian Newcastle or Belfast (head Animal Eric Burdon and Them singer Van Morrison were both sons of electrical workers), but in the press and in the clubs, the bands were all celebrated for their revolutionary admission at every strata of mod society. "Overnight it was fashionable to be working class and at art college," remembered the Kinks' Ray Davies from North London, whose father worked as a butcher and a gardener. "None of this was affecting me, because I felt that I had always been what all these silly confused trendies were trying to become."[1] Only as the party wound down and the British public faced the grim realities of the new decade did young people's popular music reassert the distinct social backgrounds of its creators and its constituents. It was Lennon, again, who offered a sample of this, in his stark acoustic "Working Class Hero," from *Plastic Ono Band* (1970). Yet the act whose music best represented the machined, mechanized trauma of working-class reality released their self-titled debut the same year: *Black Sabbath*.

Now lauded in many quarters as the founders of heavy metal, death metal, or doom rock and blamed or credited with launching a wave of occult-themed bands that have been hailing Satan for several decades, Black Sabbath's deeper importance may lie in the socioeconomic roots of its initial lineup. By the time of the quartet's first record, young audiences' appetite for fast and distorted electric white blues had already been noted by the music industry—Iron Butterfly, Vanilla Fudge, Cream, and the landmark launch of Led Zeppelin had demonstrated the niche's commercial viability—and Sabbath were on board early. Their second album of 1970, *Paranoid*, featured the classic title track, which propelled them to some measure of international stardom for the next few years, along with their distinctive horror-movie lyrics and dissonant chord intervals, which complemented the era's widespread fascination with all things demonic. But underneath the topical gimmickry of the songs was an implied rejection of the middle-class idealism that had come before them. Black Sabbath was formed of young dropouts from the historic center of Britain's industrial base, in Birmingham in the English Midlands. As early as 1841, Charles Dickens in *The Old Curiosity Shop* described the region's blighted landscape: "On every side, and far as the eye could see into the heavy distance, tall chimneys, crowding on each other, and presenting that endless repetition of the same dull, ugly form, which is the horror of oppressive dreams, poured out their plague of smoke, obscured the light, and made foul the melancholy air."[2] Over a hundred years later, the same atmosphere informed the moral and spiritual message of Black Sabbath.

Led Zeppelin's Robert Plant and John Bonham had themselves grown up in the Birmingham metropolis, but in the outlying cities of Wolverhampton and Redditch, respectively. Sabbath's Ozzy Osbourne, Tony Iommi, Terry "Geezer" Butler, and Bill Ward, in contrast, were from the core district of Aston. Heavily bombed by the German Luftwaffe during World War II, and reliant on the manufacturing industry, whose competitiveness fell sharply in subsequent years, Aston was not a model of postwar progress or prosperity. "It was an awful, gang-infested, rough part of Birmingham,"[3] recalled guitarist Iommi, whose Italian immigrant parents owned a small shop. "We were completely surrounded by violence and pollution, so that was a big part of our music. We were living our music."[4] "Unless your life's ambition was to work in a factory, killing yourself with all-night shifts on an assembly line, there wasn't much to look forward to, growing up in Aston," echoed singer Osbourne, the son of a toolmaker. "There were just grey skies and corner pubs and sickly looking people who worked like animals on assembly lines. There was a lot of working-class pride, though."[5] Drummer Ward added, "There was a lot of pride, coming from Aston. I sensed that they were prideful people. This was not a rich place at all. Most people were just regular factory workers and they got by and they made do."[6] "They even used to take the piss out of our accents in England," said bassist and chief lyricist Butler. "They slagged us off because we weren't from London or Liverpool or Manchester."[7] As they were raised in such an environment, it was inevitable that the musicians' sludgy and very dark material reflected an impatience or disillusionment with the bright optimism of flower power. "The only flowers anyone saw in Aston were the ones they threw in the hole after you when you croaked it the age of fifty-three 'cos you'd worked yourself to death," Osbourne stated. "I hated those hippy-dippy songs, man."[8]

Among all their allusions to drugs ("Fairies Wear Boots," "Hand of Doom," "Sweet Leaf," "Snowblind") and the Devil ("Black Sabbath," "NIB," "The Wizard," "Electric Funeral"), a number of Sabbath tunes addressed the economic regime they knew firsthand, as in the wealthy politicians who send the poor off to fight and die, in "Wicked World" and their pacifist masterpiece "War Pigs"; in the futility of the daily grind, in "Killing Yourself to Live";

and the drab terrains of urban youth, in "Back Street Kids." Publicity bios mentioned in passing that Osbourne had once worked in a slaughterhouse and done time for burglary, while the teenage Iommi had had the tips of his chording fingers severed in an industrial accident at his job in a sheet metal factory, but overlooked in the stories was the dead-end class strictures they depicted, which had been escaped only through the fortuitous avenue of rock stardom. Of the attempted psychedelia of his and Butler's early group, Rare Breed, Osbourne admitted the act could never have matched its model: "Pink Floyd was music for rich college kids, and we were the exact fucking opposite of that."[9] In 1972 Black Sabbath went on a tour incongruously paired with the prog-rock band Yes. "They hated us, because I'm sure in their minds they were the clever players and we were the working class,"[10] Iommi remembered.

More broadly, the grating sonic signature of the band's live and recorded performances, as well as their terrifying aggression and decibel levels, seemed to speak to the generation growing up in the shadow of mass social and environmental decay as they woke up from the utopian dreams of their elder siblings. Like the unionized mills and factory floors where the punters' parents and grandparents labored, the music was ponderous, angry, physically tough, and technically demanding; Iommi in particular was one of the more virtuosic rock 'n' roll guitarists of his time. In *Rolling Stone*, an unusually appreciative Lester Bangs wrote that Black Sabbath "has concentrated relentlessly on the self-immolating undersides of all the beatific Let's Get Together platitudes of the counter culture,"[11] and in a long essay for *Creem* Bangs admired how Sabbath's "themes are perdition, destruction, and redemption, and their basic search for justice and harmony in a night-world becomes more explicitly social all the time." The critic also pointed out that the porcine metaphors of "War Pigs" harked back to "firebrand rhetoric of agit-prop pamphlets of the Socialist Workers and other parties farther left since the time of the First World War."[12] Even if most fans, and certainly the performers themselves, were too blasted by drugs and distracted by occult trappings to perceive the political implications in Black Sabbath's music, its long-term popularity and influence represented a profound shift in the outlook of the population growing up from the 1970s onward. The economic system in which the artists and the audience lived did not offer boundless opportunities for gratification, and power was not shared fairly by those who ran it. "Our songs had real things behind them, which I think people wanted at the time," Osbourne remarked. "People must have been wanting to hear something real for a change." The vocalist summed up the genre Sabbath established: "Slum rock,"[13] he shrugged.

The domestic and foreign success of Sabbath and Led Zeppelin, at least until the end of the 1970s, inspired a rush of hard rock groups from the United

Kingdom with similar templates and who aspired to a similar penetration of the international market. Like their counterparts in North America, the British bands played loud electric riffs elaborated from old blues lines, delivered by wailing singers, flashy guitar soloists, and feral drummers (more complementary than Yes, a regular stateside opening act for Black Sabbath was Black Oak Arkansas, whose drummer, Tommy Aldridge, later played in Ozzy Osbourne's solo band). They too were playing against a backdrop of shortages, strikes, and evolving attitudes around race and sex. For the Brits, though, the ancestral memories of class-based inequality ran deeper, and the liberation promised by their sector of rock 'n' roll was more desperately sought. Whereas an Aerosmith or an Alice Cooper or a ZZ Top at least retained the confidence that their country, for all its problems, was still the richest and freest in the world, the boogie merchants out of Sheffield or Glasgow or Dublin knew their society's best days were behind it and played accordingly.

Among these first-generation heavy metal outfits were Budgie, from the coal-shipping Welsh city of Cardiff, whose pummeling "Breadfan" was a worthy rival to Sabbath's "Paranoid" in the killer riff sweepstakes and a cult favorite of many later British and American acts. Sharing Sabbath's Vertigo label from 1972, the long-lived Status Quo enjoyed a loyal British following through their consistently upbeat, uptempo bluesy guitar rock like "Down Down," "Roll Over Lay Down," and "Wild Side of Life." Another act initially signed to Vertigo was Uriah Heep, named after a character in Dickens's *David Copperfield*. With a fluctuating membership over several years, Heep scored with progressive proto-metal in "The Wizard" and "Easy Livin'" and albums titled *Demons and Wizards*, *The Magician's Birthday*, *Wonderworld*, and *Return to Fantasy*, all abetted by regular touring in the United Kingdom, Europe, and North America. Uriah Heep were one of many sub-Zeppelin, sub-Sabbath British groups—drummer Lee Kerslake and bassist Bob Daisley also had tenures as Ozzy's rhythm section—bringing cosmically heavy rock 'n' roll to the provinces when bigger names were filling the LA Forum or Madison Square Garden. And Foghat, descended from the pioneering blues act Savoy Brown, reached a wide audience on both sides of the Atlantic with enduring hits in "Slow Ride," "Fool for the City," and the great touring anthem "Eight Days on the Road." Singer-guitarist Dave Peverett's piercing vocal projection compared well with that of arena-rock gods like Steve Marriott and Robert Plant, while the powerhouse instrumental chops of lead guitarist Rod Price, drummer Roger Earl, and bassist Craig MacGregor were heard to devastating effect on their definitive cover of Muddy Waters's "I Just Want to Make Love to You." Yes, it was all derivative, mindless, hair-tossing, whoa-yeah-baby overdriven riffery, but it was also state-of-the-art rock music in the crumbling Britain of 1975.

A different strain of raunch, coming out of a different aspect of working-class culture, was infecting the United Kingdom around the same time. Glam rock figures, with David Bowie, Marc Bolan of T. Rex, and Roxy Music at the forefront, had turned away from the artfully disheveled sartorial and musical philosophies of Creedence Clearwater Revival or the Band to present themselves as glittery, ultramodern urban superstars—even if their record and ticket sales didn't truly justify the conceit. Genuine or contrived sexual kinkiness was also part of their act. Yet in Britain, anyway, such playing at dress-up was an expression less of aristocratic debauchery that of the music hall pantomimes that had long been a staple of commoners' fun. Slade, a straightforward gigging quartet out of Wolverhampton, around Birmingham, enjoyed a short but intense period of leading the glam pack after they came under the management of Newcastle-born Chas Chandler, formerly of the Animals and the man who'd assembled the Jimi Hendrix Experience. Chandler took Slade's loud, aggressive stage act and hook-laden songs and emphasized their outrageous dress and other postures to earn a magic couple of years of hit records and sold-out shows: the massively muttonchopped singer-guitarist Noddy Holder wore a mirror-covered top hat to reflect under spotlights, while guitarist Dave Hill wore shiny metallic costumes, high-heeled boots, and splotches of cosmetic sparkle on his face. "For a period, there were no groups around that knew the same wage-packet type of background as the football fans," Chandler explained of his clients' sudden popularity; "it was very much a students' thing. Now it is back to the people."[14] Hill also wore "Super Yob" T-shirts and played a customized "Super Yob" guitar (*yob*: English slang for hooligan or lout). Slade's best-known works were titled in echo of their native Black Country's linguistic idiom, as in "Cuz I Luv You," "Tak Me Bak 'Ome," "Mama Weer All Crazee Now," and "Cum On Feel the Noize." It was ersatz glamour for an audience that had never known much of the real thing, from artists who hadn't either. "I think people are getting the same sort of excitement from our act as they do from soccer," Holder commented in 1973, while Hill elaborated, "I couldn't be camp if I tried, because my background is working class. . . . People, especially in the North, work hard all day and when they go out at night they want to be entertained."[15]

Also tied the British glam wave was Mott the Hoople. Provided by songwriter David Bowie with a generational manifesto of rock 'n' roll devotion in 1972's "All the Young Dudes," the Ian Hunter–led group had a short stint up the British and American charts: they had the glam look and epicene suggestiveness of their mentor but played solid crowd-pleasing shows uncluttered by progressive or jazzy fripperies. "Jazz in Britain was middle and upper-class-type music," Hunter declared. "It wasn't balls music."[16] He also claimed of the band, "Mott are the original working-class heroes because of the simple fact that people can identify with us. They look upon Mott as being real."[17] Mott the Hoople guitarist Mick Ralphs later became a member of the decidedly un-glam Bad Company, signed to Led Zeppelin's Swan Song vanity label in 1974. With ex-Free singer Paul Rodgers at the microphone, Bad Company purveyed a blunter brand of hard rock than Hoople's under the self-conscious ironies of Hunter, and the foursome capitalized on their Zeppelin connection to some success in America. Their most memorable tunes included "Run with the Pack," "Shooting Star," and the self-celebrating "Bad Company." Lester Bangs labeled Bad Company a "notable addition to the British Working Class . . . whose stock-in-trade are the most predictable of heavy riffs and rodomontades to the effect that they are 'bad men.'"[18]

It was David Bowie himself, at least in the most drugged and delusional phase of the mid-1970s, who made the most extreme gestures beyond class-based populism to the dark, discredited politics of fascism. His Thin White Duke persona evoked the cabaret decadence of Weimar Berlin, and in numerous interviews (the Diamond Dog was always a talkative publicity hound) he admitted a fascination with the propaganda skills of the Nazis and held forth with half-formed opinions on Britain's need for "an extreme right front [to] come up and sweep everything off its feet and tidy everything up" (1973),[19] also announcing "I believe Britain could benefit from a fascist leader" (1976).[20] In a country beset by shutdowns and terrorist bombings, where the future of democratic government concerned serious social scientists as much as coked-up rock stars, Bowie's inflammatory flirtations with the far right only stirred more unease.

Outside of glam rock's penchant for ostentation, and away from the cosmopolitan media whirl of London, British rockers took a humbler perspective. From Scotland came the craggy blues of Nazareth, another ensemble that fed the unpublicized public appetite for no-bullshit thud when countrymen Rod Stewart and the Bay City Rollers were claiming all the press. Nazareth were distinguished by singer Dan McCafferty's sandpaper rasp, highlighting a strong run of original hits between 1973 and 1977, such as "Razamanaz," "Broken Down Angel," "Hair of the Dog," "Turn On Your Receiver," and the very pretty "Sunshine," as well as an imaginative selection of cover tunes on albums and singles, among them blistered takes on Joni Mitchell's "This Flight Tonight," Roy Orbison's "Love Hurts," Woody Guthrie's "Vigilante Man," and a heavier-than-heavy destruction of Bob Dylan's impoverished family tragedy, "The Ballad of Hollis Brown." Ironically Nazareth (named after a reference to the Pennsylvania burg in the Band's "The Weight") were more popular in Europe and North America than their native country, but for decades they toured tirelessly around Germany, Poland, Canada, and the United States to a faithful following. They were the Scottish arena-rock equivalent of New Englanders Aerosmith or the Canadian Bachman-Turner Overdrive, serving up grade-A rock 'n' roll to the ordinary fans residing in the rust belts and backwaters of many nations. Years after their string of chart successes were behind them, Nazareth continued to attract crowds at small venues across the globe. "Going out and doing your work is how we came up," McCafferty told a Canadian reporter in 2007. "Touring is a natural thing. This is going to sound a bit philosophical, but folks are folks. At the end of the week [a guy] wants to have a few beers and have a good laugh because he's worked all week. There's a lot of people out there looking for a live band. So it's just a good night out."[21]

And more peripheral than Scotland, the Emerald Isle produced one of the best and baddest rock groups of the era in Thin Lizzy. With a core membership of drummer Brian Downey and the charismatic half-Celt, half-Caribbean poet Phil Lynott on bass and vocals, the Dublin-formed Lizzy evolved from the uniquely Irish folk rock of their first hit, a rough electric version of the traditional highwayman ballad "Whiskey in the Jar" in 1972, to the early metal of their later albums *Live And Dangerous*, *Bad Reputation*, and *Black Rose: A Rock Legend* a few years later. Ireland, of course, had major social problems of its own then, with the murderous bombings and British military interventions of "the Troubles" in Belfast and Londonderry; in time the Lizzy lineup would reconcile Catholics and Protestants on the same stage. A rotating flock of guitarists performed with the band, including Irishmen Brian Bell and Gary Moore, the English John Sykes and Snowy White, and the classic pairing of Scotsman Brian Robertson and American Scott Gorham, whose instruments were tightly woven together on several key Lizzy records. Thin Lizzy stood apart from many of their rock contemporaries, not only in their Irish origins and the biracial visibility of Lynott in the spotlight but also in the singer's deeply felt lyrics of both wistful longing ("Cowboy Song," "Still in Love with You," "Don't Believe a Word") and noirish city life ("Cold Sweat," "The Toughest Street in Town," "Waiting for an Alibi," "Johnny the Fox Meets Jimmy the Weed," the merciless "Johnny"). Raised by his maternal grandmother in a rough part of Dublin, Lynott had known real prejudice and real poverty. There was no empty bluster to Thin Lizzy, no throwaway evocations of sex or sci-fi or Satan. Their heaviest material, like "Genocide," "Are You Ready," and "Baby Please Don't Go" (an original, not a cover of the Big Joe Williams blues), approached plutonium-level intensity.

It was ideal music for a largely male fandom who were then getting from rock 'n' roll what their fathers might have once got from competitive sports—Lynott called Thin Lizzy's audience "supporters," as in soccer partisans—and the band's ceaseless concert schedules in Britain, Europe, North America, and Australia were hardly less of a physical workout, especially with the steady amounts of drink and drugs flowing through the musicians (Lynott eventually died from complications related to a heroin habit in 1986). Thin Lizzy opened for Slade in the UK and for Bachman-Turner Overdrive and Aerosmith in the States, reaching a ready-made market of restless young guys looking to let off some steam, and their two best-known works confirmed the sense of masculine solidarity. "Jailbreak," the title track from their 1976 album, rides on a sibilant groove laid down by the deceptively subtle Downey, where Lynott warns the listener that he and the boys mean business and some won't survive tonight's trouble, while the same disc's "The Boys Are Back in Town" is an exuberant celebration of male bonding that remains an anthem of testosterone-fueled good times to this day. The bar and grill where the boys gather was inspired in part by a real after-hours club in Manchester where Lynott and the rest of Lizzy caroused with local underworld figures, off-duty police, show business people, and players from the Manchester United football team, in a warm spring night's utopia of crazy cats, flowing drink, and favorite songs blasting from a corner jukebox.

Who was the audience for all this? As in other parts of the world, it was difficult to know with certainty what social background or income bracket defined the people tuning their radios to, purchasing records by, or catching performances of any of these acts. Even so, the data on the British economy over the years the artists were at their most popular is plain: from the middle of the 1970s to 1984, unemployment gradually rose to a peak of 12 percent, while inflation hit a disastrous 24 percent in 1975 and stayed in double digits for several years. Thin Lizzy, Status Quo, Nazareth, Foghat, and Black Sabbath probably drew their share of educated, middle-class punters as much as they appealed to dropouts and day laborers, but all would have felt the crises of joblessness and budget tightening around them. In the cacophony of the period's British pop, moreover, a Budgie or a Uriah Heep would have sounded much different—and would have meant something different—than an ABBA or an Osmond family, or a Fairport Convention or a Steeleye Span, or an Electric Light Orchestra or a King Crimson. For teenagers and young adults (themselves two quite distinct categories), professed taste in music shaped and signified personal identities already being formed by home neighborhood, family roots, and household earnings. Some music was juvenile, danceable confection; some was cerebral, cryptic complexity; some was provocation; some was pandering. For a specific cohort of recessional Britain's listening populace, their choice of martial, manly rock 'n' roll would have fortified a sense of self increasingly battered by automation, immigration, urban decay, and the dole.

Well apart from any commercial acts competing for air time or sold seats was pub rock. A phenomenon confined to Britain, and particularly to London, pub rock was an ephemeral but distinct movement of small-scale, small-ambition performers content to entertain live in local spaces rather than chase the golden cup of a record contract and big gigs: when the mainstream music industry was constantly scouting a next Beatles, or a next T. Rex, to fill Wembley Stadium or the Hammersmith Odeon, bands like Brinsley Schwarz, Dr. Feelgood, Eddie and the Hot Rods, and Ducks Deluxe were subsisting on weekend spots at the Hope and Anchor in Islington or the Tally Ho in Kentish Town. The music was a conspicuous nod backward to short, 1950s-style rock 'n' roll numbers rather than the overproduced, overthought, and overlong concept albums preoccupying the major labels and the trade press. And there was a practical economic component at play, as well—artists signed to record companies were expected to play in theaters to recoup whatever investment had been made in them and to charge a corresponding amount for tickets, which made them too expensive for bookings in mere bars. Pub rockers filled the gap. Their essence was less in the class circumstances of the spectators, who were often just young drinkers who liked a competent in-house show to soundtrack their Saturday nights, than in the musicians themselves, openly unembarrassed by their spots at the very bottom rung of a very tall show business ladder. Nick Lowe of Brinsley Schwarz, an act that had a few years earlier attempted a conventional breakthrough with a heavily hyped New York debut that bombed big time, eventually came to appreciate missing out on the usual markers of stardom: "Since then I have had occasion to fall to my knees to give thank for that experience," he said (Lowe later won more respect than celebrity as a songwriter and producer). "It gave me an early taste of the lure of fame and how it can come and kick you in the ass."[22]

The most important thing about pub rock was that it begat punk. The punk ethos also scorned grand notions of rock 'n' roll glamour and rock 'n' roll royalty, only with more open contempt than pub rock ever expressed. Traceable, at least in some histories, to "Anarchy in the UK," EMI's first single from the Sex Pistols in November 1976, the punk movement was initially seen as a class revolt as much as a cultural one. The same walkouts, unemployment figures, price increases, and entrenched social stratums that confronted the musicians in Slade or Foghat were also looming over the generation that formed the Pistols and their followers; it was a cohort that did not even have the encouraging memory of better times just five or ten years before. The ubiquitous "No

Future" punk slogan was a realistic summary of the personal prospects faced by many in its hearing. Yet punk's class consciousness was often drowned out by its broader attacks on supercilious journalists, hostile onlookers, and media decorum generally. "My father was a crane driver, but I don't see that any of my background has any effect on me whatsoever,"[23] spat the Pistols' Johnny Rotten.

Certainly numerous punk bands did put out clear political messages. Sham 69 and the Cockney Rejects were bluntly working class in their songs and performances, while Crass offered a kind of Dadaist anarchism. The most influential punk politics were those espoused by the Clash, whose albums *Give 'Em Enough Rope* (1978), *London Calling* (1979), and *Sandanista!* (1980) introduced urgent if not always coherent socialist rhetoric to a wide audience in Britain and, later, North America. To the first and subsequent wave of young people who grew up with punk, Clash songs like "Career Opportunities," "Clampdown," "English Civil War," "Spanish Bombs," "The Call Up," "London Calling," and their pointed cover of the 1966 Bobby Fuller Four hit "I Fought the Law" are named as the starting points for a social awareness and activism few other rock 'n' roll bands could have ever inspired. The Clash were smart and engaged where so many others were stoned and oblivious. "We're not just another wank rock group like Boston or Aerosmith,"[24] key songwriter and vocalist Joe Strummer told *Rolling Stone* in 1979.

It was perhaps indicative of punk's inner contradictions, though, that Strummer, né John Mellor, was not a product of an East End slum but actually the son of a British diplomat and had formerly adopted the pseudonym Woody, as in Guthrie; Strummer had been deeply affected by the suicide of his teenage brother, who himself had become immersed in the far-right movement of late 1960s Britain. Under Strummer's leadership the Clash were one of the few punk bands to explore reggae and other music outside the minimalist parameters of the genre, and the group's first single, "White Riot," took on the violent anti-immigrant outlook stirring urban centers, already hit by unemployment and strikes, across the nation. The Clash were prominent in the United Kingdom's Rock against Racism campaign, and Strummer, emulating Guthrie, affixed a provocative decal to his guitar: "IGNORE ALIEN ORDERS." "My politics are definitely left of center," he told a reporter. "I believe in socialism because it seems more humanitarian, rather than every man for himself."[25]

Yet what the public at large more often heard in punk rock was not the political commitment of Strummer or of punk-descended artists like Billy Bragg, but rather the music's bohemianism and shock effects—the green mohawk haircuts, the safety-pinned clothes and body piercings, the exaggerated vocal accents of yobbish London or Manchester. Punk, to many listeners, was an exercise in style designed to offend the pop music establishment rather than overthrow its equivalents in government or business. There was also suspicion, in Britain and elsewhere, about whether the punk base was a true uprising of the disenfranchised and underemployed or only the slumming of the educated and the relatively privileged. Mott the Hoople, Uriah Heep, and Bad Company had their middle-class collegian fans too, of course, but those ensembles had never claimed a class allegiance (or had reviewers claim it for them) as stridently as the punks. There again was the paradox of proletarian authenticity: if you made a point of saying you had it, you quite likely didn't.

Indeed, other acts whose first appearances coincided with the punk explosion had more credible, and more long-lasting, downmarket appeal. One such British entry was a trio led by the former bassist of Hawkwind, perennially dysfunctional and perennially mind-altered purveyors of heavy psychedelia. Gradually assembling and jettisoning members while hustling for record deals and club dates around London, the eventual threesome developed a formidable sonic and visual brand that was distinct from the adolescent insolence of punk or the ironic detachments of New Wave. Listeners who braved the first albums in 1977 and 1979 couldn't believe what they were hearing; audiences who came to the gigs didn't think they would ever hear again. The singing bass player had warned them not to expect the fractious discord of a concert by Siouxsie and the Banshees, the Damned, the Buzzcocks, or the Sex Pistols or the Clash. "We are *Motörhead*," Lemmy would announce, in no uncertain terms. "We play *rock 'n' roll*."

While early reviewers and marketers sometimes lumped Motörhead in with punk, the work of the classic configuration of 1976 to 1982 had its real roots in the hard blues of previous eras, albeit sped up to barely controllable tempi and amplified, as an early tour program advertised, "Beyond the Threshold of Pain." Leader Ian "Lemmy" Kilmister, son of a vicar who'd abandoned his young family, was some ten years older than most of the upstart players around him and had seen the Beatles play in the Cavern Club and briefly roadied for Jimi Hendrix. He was no delinquent with spiked hair and a ripped T-shirt, and neither were his sidemen. "It was just a lot of kids," drummer Phil "Philthy Animal" Taylor said of punk rock players and fans. "I think punks liked Motörhead more than we liked their music."[26] "I was never that taken with punk music," agreed guitarist "Fast Eddie" Clarke. "I liked the attitude and everything, but . . . the singers were singing out of tune, guitars weren't in tune."[27] There was certainly an overlap between Motörhead's enthusiasts and those of punk bands, but Motörhead's better musicianship and more consciously professional work ethic kept them operational long after punks had gone home. By 1979 their stage set featured a giant prop warplane hovering over the band and its near-lethal sound system. "Having the bomber and stuff like that, and generally so fucking loud you couldn't hear yourself think," Clarke recalled fondly. "It was fucking great in those days getting your ears blasted out, you know?"[28]

The songs themselves, too, had more maturity than mere rebellion. Playing with an accomplished abandon that prefigured thrash metal, they reigned for several years at the extreme limit of rock volume, speed, and distortion—Motörhead barely rose above cult status in North America, but they had an intimidating reputation that kept them touring the world through many cycles of musical fashion. Lemmy played his bass like a four-string guitar and vocalized up into his microphone, his neck bent back in apparent apoplexy, which made for an indelible picture in the midst of an almost intolerable wall of noise.

For his part, Lemmy liked punk, and in time Motörhead would collaborate with American punkers the Plasmatics to do a version of Tammy Wynette's "Stand by Your Man" and cover "Anarchy in the UK," but they also did stronger takes on John Mayall's "I'm Your Witch Doctor," ZZ Top's "Beer Drinkers and Hell Raisers," the Motown obscurity "Leaving Here," the R & B chestnut "Train Kept a-Rollin'," and the frat-house standard "Louie Louie." And it was in its originals where Motörhead most made its mark: the infamous "Acc of Spades," all nihilism and fate, at 130 decibels; "(We Are) The Road Crew," a careening tribute to the working class within rock 'n' roll itself; "Metropolis," pure malice; "Love Me Like a Reptile," pure depravity. No punks were ever this brutal, or this adult. After Taylor and Clarke left the band and a varying cast of players (including ex–Thin Lizzy guitarist Brian Robertson) came and went, frontman Lemmy essentially became Motörhead and built a towering, mole-dotted persona as rock's ultimate Bad Man, impossibly ugly, utterly dissolute, yet nevertheless oddly righteous. A dedicated consumer of acid, alcohol, and amphetamines ("motorhead" was slang for a speed freak), Lemmy had known numerous heroin casualties, including a girlfriend, and presciently cautioned young fans to "Stay Clean," bragging he would only be "Killed by Death" while "Dancing on Your Grave." Elsewhere his band counseled "(Don't Let 'Em) Grind Ya Down," "Eat the Rich," and told off the wealthy and the dominant, "Just 'Cos You Got the Power."

But some of Motörhead's character had a harsher edge. Like Steppenwolf and Lynyrd Skynyrd in the United States, they were adopted as favorites of motorcycle outlaws in England. "None of us ever claimed that we were bikers," Taylor clarified. "But we just kind of looked like bikers, because in those days, if you wore a leather jacket you were a biker or you were affiliated with bikers."[29]

What's more, the gothic typeface and umlaut of their name, their tusked and helmeted "War Pig" logo, the Luftwaffe Heinkel aircraft on the cover of the *Bomber* album, the members' black attire, and Lemmy's (American-made) Rickenbacker basses and Iron Cross necklace—all suggested a Teutonic severity that carried uncomfortable implications. Here was a group whose leader sang about standing up to power while himself backed by an overpowering force of sound, while fans (young, mostly male, and almost entirely white) celebrated the music's liberating qualities by banging their heads and raising their fists in massed ranks. What did those recall? It scarcely helped matters that Lemmy became a collector of Nazi memorabilia. "I liked the designs," he said. "I think the designs are very attractive. I think [the Nazis] got a hold of a lot of people just through skilful marketing."[30] No one ever accused anyone in Motörhead of truly holding Nazi-like beliefs or of stoking them in their audience, but their onslaughts seemed to bring out a streak of British culture whose logical ends were darker than anything a mere rock 'n' roll act could project.

That punkers like the Clash were obliged to participate in Rock against Racism benefits, for example, showed how the politics of restless British youth of the 1970s and 1980s didn't all incline in one direction. As evidenced by the short life of Joe Strummer's brother, some of the disaffected were drawn to the alternative of the extreme right. Skinheads had been around England since the 1960s, deliberately eschewing the long hair and neo-Renaissance costume of the hippies for shaven scalps, suspenders, and work boots; they also rejected the hippies' peaceable affectations for postures of belligerence and racial chauvinism. The skinhead tribes were vocal in their identification with the white working class, and skins were occasionally charged with assaults or murders of South Asians or Blacks unfortunate enough to have crossed their path alone or unprotected.

In 1973 a landmark academic survey by the University of Leicester confirmed that British teenagers' predilections for pop music often broke down along socioeconomic lines, with "progressive" figures like John Lennon and Mick Jagger favored by middle-class kids but disdained as insufficiently masculine by their poorer classmates. "Many working class groups resent the apparent intellectualization of pop and have reacted against it," the survey's authors found. "The 'skinheads' who emerged in London in 1969 represented a reassertion of the basic values and interests of the male working class peer group—cleanliness, toughness, and fighting ability."[31] Thus some skinheads had found community in the rhythmic drive of reggae (despite its Black Caribbean origins), but after punk rock demonstrated how any gang of semi-competents could start a band, a few from this fringe began to create their own plainly racist rock songs. This sub-subcategory, dubbed *Oi!* for the street dialect of its followers, was usually too toxic for record contracts or radio airplay, but a fistful of groups gave shows and made singles for a volatile audience of skinheads and assorted fascist wannabes. Oi! was "the only music that talks about what's really going on in Britain,"[32] declared Carl Fisher of Blitz, while Ian Stuart of the Oi! band Skrewdriver (best-known track: "White Power") claimed in a 1982 interview: "Our support is extremely loyal. We have a regular crowd of 500 people who are loyal white nationalists."[33]

Simmering racial resentment was not confined to small-timers like Blitz and Skrewdriver. Aside from David Bowie's ill-advised endorsements of fascism, other British stars were known to have expressed bigoted views from much higher platforms. On an early US tour in 1979, it was reported that New Waver Elvis Costello had spoken of "jive-assed niggers"[34] in an inebriated barroom conversation with musicians Stephen Stills and Bonnie Bramlett, and Rock against Racism itself had been launched in reaction to guitar god Eric Clapton's similarly drunken rant from a Birmingham stage in 1976: "I think we should vote for Enoch Powell," Slowhand told his audience. "I think we should send them all back. Stop Britain from becoming a black colony. . . . Get the wogs out. Get the coons out. Keep Britain white."[35] ("Since then I have learned to keep my opinions to myself," Clapton later wrote in his autobiography, "even though that was never meant to be a racial statement.")[36] Public outrages of this sort were rare in Britain, but the nativist views they reflected were commonly shared in private.

The election of Conservative party leader Margaret Thatcher as prime minister in May 1979, certainly, was far more significant than the latest pop star scandal. Thatcher came to office pledging to undo the previous decades' buildup of inflation and national debt; admirers looked to her to restore Britain's international standing and to tame its domestic disruptors in the unions and the sprawling welfare state. But hopes for a return to Britannic glory came up against the modern realities of economics, politics, and culture, and Thatcher's tenure over the next decade was to see a radical and often painful transformation of life across the United Kingdom. National unemployment peaked under her government, and, notwithstanding her professed dedication to traditional families, divorce and illegitimacy rose. In 1981 riots, often with whites and nonwhites pitted against each other, tore through Liverpool, the London district of Brixton, and other cities, followed by more riots in Birmingham in 1985. The City of London became an international financial capital, while the mining and factory towns of the Midlands and the north were gutted from within. Various offshoots of pop music responded to this directly and indirectly—it was the era of the Culture Club, Wham!, the

Thompson Twins, and Frankie Goes to Hollywood—but one vital strand was labeled the New Wave of British Heavy Metal.

With the old warhorses Led Zeppelin, Black Sabbath, and Deep Purple disbanded or disintegrated, younger acts raised on "Whole Lotta Love," "Paranoid," or "Smoke on the Water" took the orchestration and lyrical maxims of those groups' music to the next level. The new bands had also adopted some of the punk spirit, playing faster, louder, and sometimes more crudely than their exemplars, out of both anger and amateurishness. They were not coming down from the rainbow unity of the late 1960s, as were the earlier artists, but stuck inside the bitterly polarized society that the policies of Margaret Thatcher had wrought. Several NWOBHM outfits came from the depressed towns of Britain's own rust belt, like Saxon, from Barnsley, where George Orwell had reported some of *The Road to Wigan Pier*, and Raven, from Newcastle, whose once-busy shipyards were shutting down by the 1970s. "When we first got together," remembered Raven bassist and singer John Gallagher, "there was a circuit of working men's clubs. You'd sign up, get cheap beer. . . . We learned our trade from being three feet in front of somebody who was looking at you going, 'Impress me.'"[37] Also from Newcastle were Venom, pioneers of the emergent style of death metal, who made albums titled *Welcome to Hell* (1981), *At War with Satan* (1984), and *Possessed* (1985). "Death metal is basically saying things that Sabbath didn't have the balls to say," declared leader Conrad Lant, alias Cronos. "We Are the Evil Dead to their Hammer Horror."[38] And the rusting steel center of Sheffield in Yorkshire produced Def Leppard, who made a huge American hit with their 1983 album *Pyromania*, on the heels of their grittier records *On through the Night* (1980) and *High 'n' Dry* (1981).

The most successful band to be sorted into the NWOBHM were Iron Maiden, whose vocalist Bruce Dickinson later rejected the term. "The NWOBHM was nothing of the sort," he wrote in a 2017 memoir. "It was an 'old wave' that had been ignored by the mainstream media in favor of punk, which, with its Vivienne Westwood fashion links and faux-class-war rhetoric, was more palatable to journalists who had aspirations beyond mere music."[39] Formed in London's East End in the 1970s, Maiden became an international attraction in the next decades, growing vast fan bases in Europe and the Americas and giving epic stadium gigs around the world. Like Motörhead, Iron Maiden comprised relatively accomplished players who had no time for the incompetence-as-integrity dogmas of punk rock. "We hated the punk movement," bassist Steve Harris confirmed. "When punk was happening, it was really difficult to get gigs unless you had Day-glo hair and played out of tune. . . . There were always fans there; we proved that when we started playing gigs and would get packed houses everywhere. It's just that the press didn't really write about these rock bands, us included."[40]

Aside from Dickinson's soaring registers (his voice was compared to an airraid siren), Maiden was noteworthy for its peculiarly Anglo brand of rock. Since Led Zeppelin's Viking saga "Immigrant Song" in 1970, British and Continental metal groups had been straying further and further away from the African American blues that was the music's fundamentals, the Teutonic juggernaut of Motörhead being a prime example. Band names like Saxon, Celtic Frost, Candlemass, Bathory, Witchfinder General, and Tygers of Pan Tang announced their long distance from the Mississippi Delta or Chicago's South Side before they ever played a note. Maiden was no different. Like many hard rock six-stringers of their day, guitarists Adrian Smith and Dave Murray were trying quasi-classical scales rather than the pentatonic lines of Robert Johnson or Jimi Hendrix, lending a Romantic, almost Wagnerian feel to numbers like "The Evil That Men Do," "Two Minutes to Midnight," and the Native American bloodbath "Run to the Hills."

The lyrics, mostly by Harris but howled by Dickinson, a coal miner's grandson and a history buff who'd had a short stint in the British Army, also put Iron Maiden firmly at home in the Old World. Favorite tracks included a thirteen-minute adaptation of Samuel Taylor Coleridge's "The Rime of the Ancient Mariner," while "Aces High" set the Battle of Britain to Nicko McBrain's breakneck drumming and Smith and Murray's furious solos, and "The Trooper" was inspired by Tennyson's "The Charge of the Light Brigade," about the Crimean War. In concert, "Aces High" was preceded by a playback of Winston Churchill's "We shall fight them on the beaches" speech of 1940. Iron Maiden album covers and performances were distinguished by their recurring mascot Eddie, a hideous zombielike creature envisioned by illustrator Derek Riggs; among many scenes, Eddie turned up waving the Union Jack across a battlefield and downing Messerschmitts from the cockpit of a Spitfire, but he was never found waiting his turn in the dole queue or lying around in a council flat. Eddie and Iron Maiden offered a vengeful fantasy of national heroism that worked because they were so removed from the actual conditions of multicultural, Thatcherite Britain in which most Maiden listeners resided.

Predating Maiden by a few years but scaling similar heights of success during the 1980s were Judas Priest. Priest too was part of a rising cohort of post-counterculture metal musicians and fans. Though they had opened for Led Zeppelin at the ill-starred Oakland shows in 1977 (Zeppelin's security team was charged with assaulting a backstage employee), they had slowly jettisoned the hippie or acoustic affectations of the older era and came to embody the music's fully electroplated, tool-and-die leitmotif: Judas Priest put the metal in heavy metal. As with Iron Maiden, the band's stage attire included plenty of leather and spandex, along with studded bracelets and other couture, and singer Rob Halford occasionally rode a Harley-Davidson motorcycle onto the stage. The Priest look codified the near-S&M fashions worn by their British, American, and European rivals and imitators during the decade, like Dokken, Accept, Krokus, the Scorpions, Manowar, and numerous others; Halford brandished a whip in some appearances. Messages of peace and love belonged to a distant epoch.

Like Iron Maiden, Judas Priest played harmonically complex and rhythmically accelerated two-guitar hard rock, busy with thickly distorted barre or power chords, where the propulsive riffs of Black Sabbath or Deep Purple seemed to have been hotted up into overdrive. Guitarists Glenn Tipton and K. K. Downing prowled the boards, and the increasingly common video promos, with menacing grimaces while they chugged away on their angular guitars and violently wrenched their instruments' intimidating metal tremolo and bridge apparatuses back and forth. Priest played little that could be recognized as the blues, and seldom did they venture into the syncopated funk cadences of Zeppelin or Aerosmith. Halford's vocal range was the most audible Priest signature, a uniquely sustained, operatic pitch—the prototype of Bruce Dickinson's own wail—which again harked back to a classical tradition. After slogging through several lineup, label, and management changes, they hit their commercial stride after signing with Columbia Records and found a following with 1979's live album *Unleashed in the East*, followed by *British Steel* (1980), *Point of Entry* (1981), *Screaming for Vengeance* (1982), and *Defenders of the Faith* (1984), the titles alone stating the comradely, combative mood of their track listings. Priest's most popular songs included "You Got Another Thing Comin," "Turbo Lover," "Victim of Changes," "Hell Bent for Leather," "Living after Midnight," "Breaking the Law," and covers of Fleetwood Mac's "The Green Manalishi (with the Two Prong Crown)" plus a wildly improbable "Diamonds and Rust," first sung by Joan Baez. Everything was dark, fast, hard, and bristling with implied ferocity.

It may have had to do with the band's Midlands roots in West Bromwich. In 1977 Halford alluded to the Birmingham car factory from which their first followers were drawn: "If you are working at British Leyland for eight hours a day putting nuts on machinery you need *some* relief."[41] At the height of Judas Priest's American popularity, the singer told *Creem* magazine, "Our background's working class and normal. I think that's why there are so many good bands from Birmingham, why heavy metal comes from the Midlands. If you live in a council house on a really bleak estate—where I'm from—and you look out of the window every morning, you think 'God, there must be something better than this!' "[42] Generally scorned by the rock critical class, Iron Maiden, Priest, and their ilk cultivated a close allegiance with their fans, consistently promising and usually delivering spectacular shows over grueling tour schedules across the secondary and tertiary markets of North America and Europe. "You get narrow-minded critics reviewing the shows," Halford said, "and all they think about heavy metal is that it is just total ear-splitting, blood-curdling noise without any definition or point. This is a very, very professional style of music. It means a great deal to many millions of people. We treat heavy metal with respect."[43] "Judas Priest wrote for audiences—for live audiences," Glenn Tipton maintained. "People tend to forget that. . . . There is nothing like the feeling of stopping in the tune and hearing everyone in the audience sing the chorus 'Living After Midnight.' I used to shiver with emotion."[44] Like Motörhead and Iron Maiden, the Priest's most devoted adherents were largely male, who either missed the homoerotic elements in the quintet's image or perceived them as models of masculine cool, and who had no inkling that Rob Halford himself was a closeted gay man.

At some level never quite articulated, as well, Judas Priest may have stood for the legions of disgruntled youth growing up under Margaret Thatcher and her American partner in laissez-faire conservatism, Ronald Reagan. Over the Western world, the thirty-year economic boom following the Second World War was decisively buried under an avalanche of high interest rates, government cuts, and deindustrialization. "The nation was coming off the back of a number of very turbulent years under Margaret Thatcher," Halford noted of Priest's timing. "The recession and the strikes and the street riots were very difficult for a lot of people, and we felt a real kinship with them. 'Breaking the Law' was almost a political protest song. . . . 'Grinder' [from the same *British Steel* album] was about rejecting the establishment. I saw the system as the grinder, and it was grinding people up."[45] "Breaking the Law" turned into a manifesto for millions of white American suburbanites and British working-class kids, growing up completely wasted, out of work and down, and entertaining a conceit that they had had every promise of a golden future broken and that nobody cared if they lived or died.

At the time, some adult commentators weren't buying it. By the 1980s heavy metal had become a full-fledged US pop-cult phenomenon, its makers and spectators subject to anthropological study in a variety of media. Some of the studies were unfazed by the mystique of dry ice and Marshall amps. A short 1986 documentary, *Heavy Metal Parking Lot*, earned a word-of-mouth reputation for its cinema-verité interviews with jerseyed and mulleted attendees outside a Judas Priest show at the Capital Center in the bedroom community of Landover Maryland—a tribal gathering of semi-drunken, cheerfully oblivious dudes and chicks looking forward to the brief escape of a rock concert before resuming their banal young existences, the real-life antiheroes of "Breaking the Law" revealed as mostly futureless high school yahoos. A 1988 film, *Decline of Western Civilization Part II: The Metal Years*, went backstage for candid interviews with Ozzy Osbourne, Lemmy of Motörhead, Steve Tyler and Joe Perry of Aerosmith, and Alice Cooper, among others, depicting them more as veteran showmen plying a temporarily popular bit for all it was worth, rather than spokesmen for any meaningful philosophy. "Nobody's original out there," admits Ozzy in the picture. "We're all thieves."

For all heavy metal's lucrative prominence on the tour circuit and in the record stores, a social backlash of "family values" had developed in parallel with the genre, and several parental and religious lobbies in the United States raised objections to what they heard as metal's promotion of violence, drugs, promiscuity, or devil-worship. Even less panicked observers detected something cynical in the bands' (or the music business's) claims to be merely reflecting their audiences' frustrations in a troubled society, when they may have been just as inclined to actively encourage them. "According to the popular stereotype, which is corroborated by years of expensive research by radio and record company consultants, heavy metal fans are usually white working-class males between the ages of 12 and 22," wrote critic Liam Lacey of the Toronto *Globe and Mail* in 1984, proposing that the music granted listeners "the brief vicarious experience of controlling vast amounts of power before they settle down to real life."[46] "Their bikers' boots and jackets, demonic hair and vicious-looking jewelry are a fashion statement that resoundingly rejects middle-class security," the advertising journal *Adweek* wrote assessing the metal audience in 1989. "Dedicated to living on the edge—actually, stylistically or musically—heavy-metal fans are an energetic and growing community. It's that kind of grassroots dedication that is making its fans attractive to marketers, especially since metal's core audience—primarily 12–25-year-old white males—are generally a tough segment to reach."[47] Given a huge demographic of adolescent consumers, it might have been a tempting strategy for Iron Maiden, Judas Priest, or their corporate sponsors to flatter their listeners as angry and alienated, the better to sell their musical celebrations of dominance and belonging.

For Judas Priest, this imperative was literally put on trial in 1990, when the band was named in a Nevada lawsuit claiming two young men had committed or attempted suicide while under the influence of Priest's "Better by You, Better Than Me," and other songs from their 1978 album *Stained Class*. In 1985, eighteen-year-old Ray Belknap died from a self-inflicted shotgun blast, while his twenty-year-old friend Jay Vance was grievously disfigured after he used the same weapon on himself; he died of a drug overdose in 1988. Much of the plaintiffs' evidence concerned alleged "back-masking" on the record, whereby subliminal urgings to "do it" reached the victims' subconscious minds and thus provoked their suicidal actions. Despite testimony from supposed experts, the back-masking theory was widely discounted, both inside and outside the courtroom; any intelligible language heard on a reversed record could only be perceived through suggestion or a preconceived willingness to make it out. The members of Judas Priest appeared at the trial and solemnly avowed they had never implanted any secret speech into their music, while others pointed out that even if the subliminal technique actually worked, it was unlikely the offending artists would try to kill off their own customers with it. In the end the lawsuit was dismissed, but Rob Halford later admitted, "The trial shook us up, because it came from a country that we love dearly."[48]

The case against Judas Priest, in truth, revealed another kind of culpability in the relationship between heavy metal performers, their public, and the environment that brought them together. Young guys like Ray Belknap and Jay Vance had not turned to Priest for themes of optimism or faith: "Breaking the Law," and other cuts like "Beyond the Realms of Death" and "Electric Eye" offered a gloom that was somehow cathartic, both validating the embittered emotions of teenage listeners and serving as an outlet for them. Why so many people in the spring of their lives might feel the need for such pissed-off, pessimistic music was not hard to guess. Vance had been beaten by his father, a heavy drinker who had been laid off from a local auto plant, while Belknap had been raised in a broken home with a newly Christian mother and a series of male partners, themselves sometimes abusive. Situations like theirs had proliferated in Britain, the United States, and many other countries during this era, as a once-confident middle class shrank and the security of even modestly paying jobs diminished. To this cohort, the noble causes of U2 or the Alarm, the foppish couture of Duran Duran or the Style Council, and the elegant angst of Tears for Fears and Simple Minds—all popular with other ages or other strata—meant little. Sociologist Donna Gaines's 1991 book *Teenage Wasteland* diagnosed heavy metal fandom as a worldwide condition: "Yet now, the international electronic eye of TV broadcasts disaffected post-glasnost Soviet youth into our living rooms—cynical, alienated, dressed in Iron Maiden and Ozzy T-shirts, hanging out, partying in vacant lots, alcoholic," she wrote. "They too fear they have 'no future.' Restless, wasted youth now appear as an international malaise among the industrialized nations."[49]

It had all made a fertile landscape for acts like Judas Priest, whose musicians had already experienced a foretaste of the new economic reality while growing up in the rusting English Midlands that had generated their group, plus Black Sabbath, Slade, Mott the Hoople, Thin Lizzy, Bad Company, and a universal audio lexicon premised on decline and despair. "I do feel haunted when I hear about their lives," Priest guitarist K. K. Downing said of the two lost souls at the Nevada back masking trial, "'cause they were the same as mine. . . . I do feel angry, though, when they play all that backward surf music and talk about the *harm* our music did these kids, 'cause I think it was the best thing they had."[50]

7

For Those About to Rock

A society of utility, for all the indisputable ways that it exploited men's
health and labor, and in an industrial context broke the backs and
spirits of factory workers and destroyed the lungs of miners, had one
saving grace: it defined manhood by character, by the inner qualities
of stoicism, integrity, reliability, the ability to shoulder burdens. . . . In
a culture of ornament, by contrast, manhood is defined by appearance, by youth and attractiveness, by money and aggression, by posture and swagger and "props," by the curled lip and petulant sulk and
flexed biceps.

Susan Faludi, *Stiffed*

In 1963, when the large Young family left their native Scotland to settle on the
other side of the world in Australia, their youngest child was at first baffled by
the new environment. He saw teenagers mimicking Californian culture and
listening to the Beach Boys' "Surfin' USA." It seemed an impossibly long distance from the soot of Glasgow to the constant antipodean sunlight of western
Sydney, even out in the working-class suburb of Burwood. "Mum," eight-
year-old Angus reported back home, "I think they put us on another planet."[1]

For Britons recovering from the bombing and rationing of World War II,
the faraway former colonies of Australia, New Zealand, and Canada may as
well have been somewhere else in the universe. Huge in area, inhabited by
exotic species of flora and fauna, and sparsely settled by Europeans who had
already pushed native inhabitants roughly aside, the countries offered tanta-
lizing prospects to English, Irish, and Scots immigrants anxious to leave the
painful histories and limited opportunities of their home islands. During
the 1950s and early 1960s, Australia had especially encouraged British and,
subsequently, European newcomers, even as quasi-official "White Australia"
policies put sharp restrictions on Asian arrivals. Despite the cosmic upheaval
represented by their relocation, Angus and the rest of his family—including
brother Malcolm, two years his senior—continued to dabble in the pastime
that had sustained them in their journey from up north to Down Under, over

Takin' Care of Business. George Case, Oxford University Press (2021). © George Case.
DOI: 10.1093/oso/9780197548813.003.0008

patriarch William Young's skepticism. The elder Young had been employed in the practical trade of painting in Glasgow's shipyards, after a stint as an airplane mechanic during the war. "My father wanted to get us all off the music kick—he thought we should be working," Angus recalled. "That was his thing. That's why he moved to Australia."[2]

In Australia, the next member of the Young clan to ignore William's edict was brother George, who quickly formed a group with some fellow emigrants while still residing at the barrack-like quarters where they'd been sent upon deplaning from Scotland, among them Dutchman Johannes Vandenberg, alias Harry Vanda. This band, the Easybeats, connected with Sydney-based Alberts Productions to achieve some recording and performing success in mid-1960s Australia, which was then starved for homegrown rock 'n' roll talent. With this momentum behind them, the Easybeats then went to London, where they had their greatest achievement in the worldwide hit "Friday on My Mind," released in late 1966. Though the song was built on Vanda's distinctly pulsing guitar line, which pushed it toward the edge of psychedelia, its lyrics, exuberantly sung by Stevie Wright, remained at the street-level concern of ordinary blokes laboring through each day of the work week at the behest of the rich man, awaiting the weekend hours when they could spend their bread and lose their head. The sound was shimmering power pop, but the implication was class struggle.

Alas, the international popularity of "Friday on My Mind" was not matched by the Easybeats' other material, and like so many other acts following a single score, the quintet gradually collapsed in a series of bad deals, personal problems, and misguided creative efforts. The partnership of George Young and Harry Vanda continued, however, and, allied with Alberts Productions, they remained active in the Australian music industry as songwriters and producers. With the Easybeats experience behind them, the pair had acquired a healthy respect for the business aspect of show business: inspired music, they'd learned, was no more vital to pop profitability than secure contracts, committed labels, clear career plans, and, as much as anything, a steady work ethic and predictable product. Always on the lookout for new potential, by the mid-1970s Vanda and Young made their greatest discovery within George's own family, to whom they would apply their Easybeats lessons to unparalleled achievement. Vocalist Stevie Wright would look back, "The Easybeats were a rock band as much as we were a pop band. I'm really proud AC/DC continued the job we set out to do."[3]

Angus and Malcolm Young had been playing guitars together since boyhood, and by late 1973 they were performing in a prototype of the ensemble they would lead for another four decades. The band had been named by their level-headed sister Margaret Young (the family's only girl), whose sewing machine could run on both alternating and direct current electricity; it was also Margaret who suggested Angus continue to wear his uniform from Ashfield Boys' High onstage, since he would rush home from the hated institution and plug in to his amplifier without bothering to change anyway (nonetheless, at some of their first public recitals, Angus would wear Zorro or gorilla costumes). "Other kids would come to school with the latest Top 40 thing, but I was always buying imports like Muddy Waters," Angus said of his primordial influences. "When I heard [Little Richard's] 'Great Gosh Almighty' I thought it was the second coming. As soon as I had the money I bought 'You Keep A-Knockin.'"[4] Malcolm too had his mentors, including the Rolling Stones, Them, and the blues-rock bands of the late 1960s. "You know, we used to like Canned Heat from way back, and we would just jam on stuff, around their ideas at the time, and we'd put a bit of boogie into our own material,"[5] he said subsequently. The siblings were perfecting an interplay that showcased both of their respective abilities—Angus the excited soloist and Malcolm the impassive rhythm player steadfast at his back. Every naughty schoolboy needs a tough older brother glowering behind him.

In AC/DC, Angus and Malcolm initially played with several vocalists, bassists, and drummers, but they eventually settled on Phil Rudd on drums and (more precariously) Mark Evans on bass, while new manager Michael Browning and older brother George Young continued to counsel professionalism and big ambitions. They were getting pub and theater gigs in Sydney, Melbourne, and other cities and towns in Victoria, New South Wales, and South Australia, and were looking to cut some studio tracks, which George and his partner Harry Vanda would produce under the aegis of Alberts Productions. Always at the center of the enterprise, Angus and Malcolm were very tight, Evans remembered. "The Youngs are real Scottish working class, really good strong family, you know, staunch. Very hard, though. . . . One thing I will give them, they had an absolute solidity of purpose."[6] "It's not too fancy in Australia," said Phil Rudd. "We play it sort of straight. AC/DC were particularly looking to play it straighter than anyone else, you know?"[7] "This is a nine-to-five sort of gig," Malcolm was to sum up, thinking of his short teenage job in an Australian undergarment manufacturing plant. "It comes from working the factories, that world. You don't forget it."[8] Had these been all AC/DC's strengths—two determined guitarist brothers committed to basic rock 'n' roll, with a third advising behind the scenes, leading a reliable rhythm section—they might have remained an active, modest regional attraction in their native country. But in September 1974, they had taken on a new singer who would redefine the group and change their fortunes forever.

Ronald Belford "Bon" Scott was another Scottish transplant in Australia, who'd arrived on the island continent from the town of Kirriemuir in 1952. Scott was six. A few years later the family settled in Fremantle, outside of Perth, on the country's distant west coast, where his father was employed as a window framer. Ron was the eldest of three boys, and by his early teens he was already in trouble for skipping school, running with a gang, fighting, and, as a police report had it, having "unlawful carnal knowledge" with underage girls. At sixteen he did two years' time in a tough juvenile institution. He got several tattoos. Released at the end of 1963, Scott, like thousands of others of his generation in the wake of the Beatles and local heroes like the Easybeats, began to chase a dream of musical stardom. It was better than jail.

For a while, he had promising but ultimately abortive stints singing in two Australian acts: the Valentines were a short-lived teenybopper group in which Scott was sold, unbelievably in light of his later persona, as a doe-eyed heart-throb, while Fraternity was made up of Band-style folk rockers who'd tried and failed to make an impression on the British scene and then returned to Adelaide in defeat. He was recovering from a near-fatal motorbike accident he'd had after a drunken fight with one of a string of female partners when he connected with a friend from the Valentines, who told him about a hopeful new band from Sydney who wanted a new singer. Older than Angus and Malcolm Young by several years—he was already twenty-eight—Bon Scott joined AC/DC with the unsentimental perspective of a man who'd made two shots at rock 'n' roll glory and missed each time. This was likely his last chance. He'd found out the hard way that it was a long way to the top.

Between 1975 and 1979, with Bon Scott singing and writing most of the lyrics, AC/DC created a catalog of music that has endured as some of the most memorable and powerful in the genre. Today Scott's songs regularly blare out from classic rock radio, at sporting events, on movie soundtracks, and in newer acts' covers, while the AC/DC brand—the group, the records, the logo, the idea—is recognized around the world. Now among the biggest-selling recording artists of the recording artist era, the Thunder from Down Under have come to stand for an international subculture of eternal young adult maleness that encompasses all ages and genders: if Bach is the sound of God whistling while He works, AC/DC is the sound of God ordering another round in a strip bar on Friday night.

Several factors went into making this reputation. There was Angus, first of all, dressed in shorts, knee socks, and a school blazer: a cute theatrical gimmick instantly blown apart upon hearing the guitarist's fluency with trilled blues bends on his indispensable Gibson SGs. Any punters' assumptions that some amateur kid was being used as the band's mascot were abandoned the moment the younger Young took center stage. He was unstoppable, playing on his back, playing one-handed, skipping, duck-walking, being carried on Bon Scott's shoulders, and throwing his small frame around the boards in concert-length frenzies. It was all meant to win over tough crowds, a skill AC/DC had learned on the provincial circuits passing through Geelong, Moorabin, Cooma, and Rangaratta. Sometimes extreme measures were called for. "I saw Angus tip a jug of beer over a guy's head one day who just sat there looking at us," Phil Rudd recounted. "Just couldn't get a rise out of this guy. That was at the Station Hotel in Melbourne, which is sort of a cool gig, you know, sort of too cool to be clapping and be all enthusiastic."[9] "I remember there was many a time in Australia, playing in these outback places, where we'd have to put up bail money,"[10] Angus corroborated. "When you're onstage you know people have paid to see the high-diving act, so our attitude has always been that these folks are going to see the high-diving act.... [11]When I started doing this, I thought, 'You gotta give it 200 percent.' Because it was your survival. It was the job, what was going to put food on the table."[12] When it came to guaranteeing quality rock 'n' roll entertainment, the bad boys in AC/DC were old pros.

They had a unique sound. Unlike many hard rock groups of the mid-1970s, AC/DC did not play tricky riffs, ambitious power ballads, or thick slabs of distortion. Many of their boogies were built around the same basic open guitar chords of A, B, C, D, E, and G that beginners learn; they took simple intervals, licks, or single-string bends that would have taken up two bars in pieces by Bad Company or Alice Cooper and repeated them across entire songs. In this way they resembled Creedence Clearwater Revival, perfecting the structural bases of rock's originators instead of innovating away from them. Like CCR with John and Tom Fogerty, too, AC/DC had an irreplaceably fraternal empathy between rhythm and lead guitar players. They had no keyboards, acoustic guitars, or vocal harmonies in their arrangements; only when Malcolm Young and Mark Evans (later dropped and replaced with Cliff Williams) marched up to their microphones to join in the choruses was Scott accompanied by a backup gang. Angus Young did not employ a battery of outboard electronic effects to play through, as did other lead guitarists in the era—his amplification was somewhat overdriven but, more importantly, very loud. Malcolm was the real source of AC/DC's audio weight, hammering out full-strum sequences on his battered Gretsch Jet Firebird (a uniquely unhip instrument among the usual Gibsons and Fenders) to lay down the brawny heft supporting his brother's impeccably executed pentatonic runs. "Malcolm's guitar is always set up with his railway-track strings, that old-style setup where if you hit 'em you break your fuckin' fingers," Angus said describing the heavy gauges on the Gretsch. "But I have to say if you're doing a solo in front of a great rhythm player like Malcolm, you know even better the direction to go in, you know?"[13] Underneath everything was Phil Rudd's muscular drumming. His playing, and the Youngs', was minimalist by choice rather than necessity—skilled musicians working at the core of their talents rather than at the limit of their techniques.

But Bon Scott created the AC/DC ethos. Malcolm Young characterized him as the band's father figure: "He was only a few years older than us, but he had that thing—he could sort something out with two words."[14] "Bon was really quite a guy," Rudd remembered. "He had a lot of poetry in him; he saw the world his way and wrote about it, in his inimitable way. Sometimes a bit . . . not in the way you'd like to explain it to your mom, but still with a sly kind of cheeky smile."[15] Though plenty of rock lyricists from Bob Dylan and the Band's Robbie Robertson on down had affected world-weariness, Scott was worldly. There's a difference. Other writers were more literate or more sophisticated in their imagery, but none were as credibly sleazy as Scott. He also put a strong undercurrent of humor into his verses—someone once described them as a cross between Chuck Berry's and Benny Hill's—whereby the double entendres made his jadedness sound all the more genuine. It was those couldn't-care-less insinuations of his stories, the smirk of someone who'd already seen the seamiest side of life and didn't worry about offending anyone who hadn't, that defined him. The most common compliment given to Scott's AC/DC songs is that he had lived them: the leering pickup patter of "Live Wire," "High Voltage," and "Bad Boy Boogie," put to no avail in "Shot Down in Flames"; the travails of working rock bands in "Highway to Hell," "Long Way to the Top," "Show Business," and "Ain't No Fun (Waiting Around to Be a Millionaire)"; the endless carnal one-night stands and their resultant complications, reported in "You Ain't Got a Hold on Me," "Touch Too Much," "Gimme a Bullet," and the independently verified chronicle of "Whole Lotta Rosie," about a large Tasmanian lady whose dimensions were estimated at 42-39-56. "I woke up one morning and looked over at Bon's bed and I thought, Jeez, he's done it," said roadie Pat Pickett. "I could see underneath [Rosie], this tiny little arm with tattoos on it was sticking out."[16]

In an unpublished profile, Scott revealed that of his favorite records, he "didn't mind" ZZ Top's *Tres Hombres*, and his rhymes certainly extended the Texas trio's verbalization of indiscriminate, perpetual masculine horniness (musically, as well, AC/DC's "Ride On" sounds a lot like ZZ Top's "Jesus Just Left Chicago"). Many of his songs flirted with sexual ambiguity, a quality accentuated by the very name AC/DC; of the singer's teenage reformatory term, a Bon Scott biographer hinted that "sexual favors were taken, not given."[17] Both "TNT" and "Dirty Deeds Done Dirt Cheap" mention back doors, while "The Jack" addressed venereal disease (disguised in card-playing metaphors), and "Big Balls" (about dance parties) and "She's Got Balls" (about a strong woman) offered more lewd wordplay. "Little Lover," "Squealer," "Love at First Feel," and Scott's recitals of "Can I Sit Next to You Girl" and "Soul Stripper" could have been indicted on morals charges. Females were often described in the third person, as from one boasting bro to another: *She's got balls; she* was a squealer; *she* was a soul stripper; *she's* got the jack; *she* told me to go to hell; when it comes to lovin', *she* steals the show. Without a great vocal range to employ, Scott's performances were embellished with mock-posh flourishes in "Big Balls" and ad-lib squeals of feigned delight or outrage in "Whole Lotta Rosie" or "Dirty Deeds Done Dirt Cheap." He often appeared in concert bare-chested but for a denim vest or stripped to the waist, singing his most risqué lyrics with theatrically arched eyebrows and rolled eyes. In the solo interlude of "Go Down" it sounds for all the world as if Scott is actually getting a blow job.

But other pieces took on more serious themes: the dangers of hard drugs, in "Overdose" and "Gone Shootin'" (Scott had encountered heroin through a girlfriend who was a user), and the dishonesty and unfairness inherent in an insurmountable socioeconomic order, in "Jailbreak," "Dog Eat Dog," "Down Payment Blues," "Sin City," and "Rock 'n' Roll Singer," the last of which featured Scott's spoken diatribe against nine-to-five living, collars and ties, moral standards, golden handshakes, silly rules, and every other lesson imparted by the educational system. In this fashion AC/DC also resembled CCR, insofar as their populism hit harder than that of other artists more ensconced on the soapbox. Scott was occasionally spotted wearing a Lynyrd Skynyrd stars-and-bars belt buckle and had spoken of his fondness for straight-talking Southern rock. As the group began to make commercial headway outside of Australia, in a 1977 interview with the British paper *New Musical Express*, Scott opined, "The music press is totally out of touch with what the kids actually want to listen to. These kids might be working in a shitty factory all week, or they might be on the dole—come the weekend, they just want to go out and have a good time, get drunk and go wild. We give them the opportunity to do that."[18]

To paraphrase Grand Funk Railroad, AC/DC was an Australian band: thoroughly road-tested in their homeland, they were tirelessly taking to the stages of Europe and North America by the late 1970s, to the detriment of bigger names they were booked with. In many instances fans who only knew Australia for kangaroos and "Waltzing Matilda" were coming to see headline acts and found AC/DC to be the more impressive rock group. Older bands at the top of the bill, like Black Sabbath in Germany and Ted Nugent, Alice

Cooper, or Aerosmith in the States, had their complacent, worn- or drugged-out asses handed to them by Bon Scott and the Young brothers. "There's been an audience waiting for an honest rock 'n' roll band to come along and lay it on 'em," Scott told the US magazine *Circus*. "There's a lot of people coming out of the woodwork to see our kind of rock. And they're not the same people who would go to see James Taylor or a punk band."[19]

At this point, though, punk rock was the preference of many pop music critics and journalists, and it was here where the divide between the tastemakers and the average listeners within the rock community became irreparable. In December 1976 *Rolling Stone* magazine, whose publisher, Jann Wenner, had hated hard rock since Grand Funk and Led Zeppelin, assigned Billy Altman to review *High Voltage*, AC/DC's first US-released album (they had signed with Atlantic Records' Atco label the previous year). In a short writeup later held as an example of egregious rock snobbery, Altman declared, "AC/DC has nothing to say musically (two guitars, bass and drums all goose-stepping together in mindless three-chord formations). . . . Stupidity bothers me. Calculated stupidity offends me."[20] At first the roughness of AC/DC's presentation led them to be categorized as punk rockers by some industry people on either side of the Atlantic, but the band would have none of it. "None of us were into [punk]," avowed Phil Rudd. "AC/DC wasn't a punk band. We were a rock band. . . . We were that sort of band, a no-bullshit band."[21] "At that time, we were giving punk music a good name," agreed Angus Young. "We weren't a punk band, but they'd put us on the same bill as punk bands."[22]

As in Great Britain, America's punk and new wave pioneers were sometimes extolled for a political progressivism that they didn't always live up to. Some groups definitely staked out a leftish or at least insurgent identity, like Black Flag and the Circle Jerks from Los Angeles, or Devo from the industry town of Akron, Ohio, or San Francisco's Dead Kennedys, whose 1980 record *Fresh Fruit for Rotting Vegetables* featured parodic commentaries titled "California Über Alles," "Kill the Poor," and "Stealing People's Mail." Other US acts, however, were more notable for their appropriations of jarring, knowingly kitschy musical and sartorial styles than for their civic agendas: Blondie, the B-52s, Patti Smith, the Talking Heads, the Cars. They were provocative, maybe, but they weren't representatives of any broader underlying public constituency. In 1977 New York's Talking Heads toured Europe with their neighbors from the borough of Queens, the Ramones. Talking Heads manager Gary Kurfirst found the leather-clad Ramones, one of the most popular and influential punk acts of their own and later times, to be incompatible travel mates with his clients. "The Talking Heads adored [Europe]," he recalled. "It was really yuppie chic at work. The Ramones were like Archie Bunker at the Vatican. . . . They hated the food and just looked for hamburgers everywhere."[23] The Ramones excelled at fast and very primitive rock 'n' roll (Motörhead paid them homage in their song "R.A.M.O.N.E.S."), but there was little in their music that really stood for anything. The "anarchy" or "authenticity" ascribed to punk and new wave was usually more in the minds of its journalistic apologists than in the conscious principles of its players.

From the second half of the 1970s and throughout the 1980s, in fact, while punk evolved into alternative and numerous punkish acts in North America and Europe developed small followings, they were regularly well outsold in records and concert tickets by hard rock groups detested by everyone except audiences—"Heavy metal rules, all that punk shit sucks," slurred a typical subject of the Judas Priest-related documentary *Heavy Metal Parking Lot*. Two of the biggest albums of 1979 were the certified dinosaur music of Pink Floyd's *The Wall* and Led Zeppelin's *In through the Out Door*, while a third was the first million-seller for an avowedly non-punk quintet from Australia, AC/DC's *Highway to Hell*.

Why was this? One standard explanation has been that the Replacements, Hüsker Dü, and R.E.M. were just too challenging, too original for the brainwashed rabble of middle America, who only wanted their MTV, their Top 40 radio, and their suburban strip malls. Yet some of the relative public aversion to punk, new wave, and alternative during these years was likely due to a sense of critical condescension, and to the fairly obvious technical limitations of the music itself. In her study *Teenage Wasteland*, Donna Gaines recognized the holdouts: "It was these primarily male white suburban teenagers that kept the faith. . . . Here they were, through the late 1970s and early 1980s, getting bashed for uninformed commercial tastes, yet resisting the trendy 'new wave' imports, adhering instead to local traditions of class and community."[24] "Our audiences liked long hair; punks had short hair," the FM radio consultant Lee Abrams elaborated. "Our audience loved great guitar players; most punk musicians seemed like they had gotten a guitar a few months before."[25] The willfully amateurish, deliberately abrasive posture of punk and its derivatives was taken as an insult by people who could never have afforded such impertinence at their own jobs; the members of AC/DC, in contrast, were proficient craftsmen who approached performing and recording as professionals, to whom satisfying fans, rather than throwing their supposed alienation back at them, was a given objective. Angus Young's virtuosity on guitar was a straightforward attribute that an ordinary seventeen-year-old punter could easily appreciate, whereas the do-it-yourself garage aesthetic of, say, Sonic Youth's Thurston Moore was too much of an in-joke at the expense of virtuosity itself.

Even as their sales or visibility rose, the hard rock of AC/DC and the punk rock of the Ramones were hardly the only choices in pop music available. Throughout the 1970s a considerable chunk of the entertainment market cashed in on a nostalgia fad, of which the rock 'n' roll of the 1950s and early 1960s was a major component. As early as 1969 a recurring "Rock 'n' Roll Revival Show" had been staged in New York City and other venues in the United States, as impresario Richard Nader assembled a lineup of stars from the medium's original era: Bill Haley, Chuck Berry, the Platters, the Coasters, Jerry Lee Lewis, Bo Diddley, Little Richard, Chubby Checker, Fats Domino, and others, all then only in middle age and, in some cases, grateful for the paying gig. A regular package tour of the Rock 'n' Roll Revival performed for several years thereafter (the 1971 edition at Madison Square Garden, where ex-teen idol Rick Nelson was booed when he performed newer material, was the subject of Nelson's hit "Garden Party"). Sha Na Na, a younger set of Columbia University students who gave theatrical performances of 1950s doo-wop and rock 'n' roll, interspersed with comedy sketches of 1950s greaser and hot rodder archetypes, built a steady career after an incongruous appearance at Woodstock in 1969 and in the later Revival tours. They even got their own syndicated television show in 1978. The show's producer, Pierre Cossette, told *Billboard*, "The concept was to capitalize on the '50s nostalgia craze."[26]

The craze was real, and revealing. Twenty years after the decade had passed, a wave of 1950s-themed movies, plays, television and records rolled through America's entertainment landscape: the 1971 Broadway musical *Grease*, adapted into a successful film in 1978; George Lucas's 1973 top-grossing coming-of-age picture *American Graffiti*, which generated its own hit soundtrack album (the cinematic device of scoring with wall-to-wall pop singles would be widely copied); the TV series *Happy Days*, which debuted in 1974, running for several seasons thereafter and spawning another 1950s-set show, *Laverne & Shirley*; and a range of other cinematic efforts, like 1974's *The Lords of Flatbush* and 1978's *The Buddy Holly Story*, as well as a rack of "jukebox hits" or "sock hop memories" compilation albums. Most of these were sanitized representations that focused more on the frivolous fads of the period—hula hoops, drive-ins, et cetera—and avoided more complex topics like McCarthyism and the emerging civil rights movement. But for people in their thirties and forties in 1975, such offerings were reassuring reminders of a more "innocent" time, when America's global power and domestic stability were not in doubt. Even (or especially) kids not alive during the actual 1950s absorbed these portraits of a more wholesome society that contrasted with the supposed moral and economic rot of their own environment. What was crucial in 1950s nostalgia was that the once-threatening products of early rock 'n' roll could now be heard not just as catchy commercial records by talented artists—which they certainly were—but as comforting signifiers of an age described in *American Graffiti's* screenplay as "back when things were simpler and the music was better."[27] This perception was heightened with the 1977 death of Elvis Presley and the resultant resurgence of the King's classics on the radio and in television ads. After years of upsetting the adult or offending the responsible, a certain kind of rock songs were now warmly accepted by responsible adults themselves.

At this point, too, a whole other genre of youth-oriented music was competing with contemporary rock. Already splintering their output between the likes of AC/DC, the Ramones, and Sha Na Na, producers, promoters, broadcasters, and retailers had now discovered the next Next Big Thing: disco. Released in late 1977, the soundtrack album for the disco drama *Saturday Night Fever*, featuring the Bee Gees' "Stayin' Alive" and "Jive Talkin'," became a no. 1 record internationally and in time would be ranked as the highest-selling film soundtrack ever. A crowded floor of other popular dance singles in that and later years included the Trammps' "Disco Inferno," Donna Summer's "Last Dance," "Hot Stuff," and "Love to Love You Baby" (strangely enough a private favorite of Bon Scott), Alicia Bridges' "I Love the Nightlife (Disco 'Round)," Chic's "My Forbidden Lover" and "Good Times," and the Village People's "YMCA" and "Macho Man." More movies (*Roller Boogie, Skatetown USA, Thank God It's Friday, Xanadu*), TV programs (*Dance Fever, Solid Gold, Makin' It*), and anthology records (*Disco Nights, Disco Super Hits, Disco Dynamite, Disco Fever 1979*) hustled aboard the bandwagon. Even those normally oblivious to pop fashions were aware of disco—the insistent grooves, the smooth vocals, the slick productions, and the pervasive images of sharply dressed young men and women (notably *Saturday Night Fever's* white-suited star, John Travolta) showing off their best moves under the mirror balls of Xenon, Studio 54, or Danceteria.

Disco's entry into the listening and dancing preferences of mainstream America may have indicated an accompanying acceptance of the key groups who had fostered the music and the lifestyle: Black, Hispanic, and, not least of all, gay. For a brief moment, the sexual permissiveness, pharmaceutical indulgence, and racial diversity that were prominent in disco culture looked to have been a triumph of post-1960s values in a wider society. But then came the backlash. Punk rock had never really sparked such a reaction; most of its detractors simply didn't buy the records. Disco, however, provoked an unusually hostile response that was vociferous enough, and organized enough, to impact the music's place in the industry itself. Only a year or two after *Saturday Night Fever's* ascendancy, a counteroffensive of "Disco Sucks" iron-on decals, lapel pins, and other products had begun. "Disco Sucks," a comedy song by an American act called Chuck Wagon and the Wheels, became the movement's battle cry, even as it parodied the country format in which it was delivered. Rocker Frank Zappa's satirical number "Disco Boy," from his 1976 album *Zoot Allures*, was revived, and a Canadian novelty disc, "Disco's in the Garbage," received heavy rotation on rock radio stations in 1979. On July 12, 1979, a "Disco Demolition Night" at a Chicago White Sox–Detroit Tigers baseball doubleheader in Chicago's Comiskey Park turned into a small riot, when local rock DJ Steve Dahl gave listeners discounted admission if they brought a disco record to be blown up in a controlled explosion. The promotional stunt got out of hand, as many of the attendees arrived drunk or stoned, storming the field and leaving the grounds unplayable. As quickly as it seemed to have caught on with everyone, disco turned very uncool everywhere.

Since the Comiskey Park revolt and similar episodes, many social historians have read into them a coded demonstration of straight white antipathy toward the non-straight, nonwhite Others who were associated with disco music. "White males, eighteen to thirty-four, are the most likely to see disco as the product of homosexuals, blacks and Latins, and therefore they're most likely to respond to appeals to wipe out such threats to their security,"[28] Dave Marsh of *Rolling Stone* argued in late 1979. But in an odd way, the presumed bigotry of the disco haters may have masked a more basic resentment, that of scruffy T-shirt- and denim-wearing dudes toward dressed-up and bejeweled dandies. Disco became an insult, denoting the personal vanity and preoccupation with grooming ascribed to Travolta-like males; the same unkemptness a traditionalist like Merle Haggard once condemned in the hippies had itself become a traditional virtue. The barbarians were starting to work the gate.

What's more, disco seemed to valorize the very standards of conformity— designer outfits, neatly trimmed hair, fitting in at exclusive clubs—that rock 'n' roll had stood against for so long. Steve Dahl, the instigator of the Comiskey Park fracas, griped about the expectations imposed by *Saturday Night Fever* and its fashions: "You have to look good, you know, tuck your shirt in, perfect this, perfect that."[29] Disco Demolition Night's participants were largely from Chicago's blue-collar southwest side, where slick clothes and accessories were unseemly extravagances. "When I jumped on the outfield, there was this moment of liberation where I thought, I don't have to be like everyone else," recalled Comiskey partier Tony Fitzpatrick. "By the time there were a few hundred people running around out there, they all had the same fucking goofy grin on their faces. It was like it's OK for a long-haired kid who likes rock 'n' roll to be free and stupid."[30] Even though many of the individuals dancing at discos and purchasing disco records were no wealthier than the guys yelling

"Disco sucks" and ceremonially smashing disco merchandise (indeed, they may have been on average poorer), the campaign against disco amounted to pretend poverty versus affected affluence.

Discophobes also subscribed to a belief that rock was the legitimate creation of named musicians, as opposed to the generic background rhythms assembled by disco's producers and studio instrumentalists. The view was simplistic—unlike punk, disco's players usually boasted some pretty respectable chops—but it derived from powerful myths about artistic individualism and autonomy that were central to rock 'n' roll. Rock 'n' roll had confessional lyrics, distinct personalities, and heroic solos, but a lot of disco seemed to have been engineered into anonymity. Accusations that disco's antagonists were really just malicious rednecks, and that punk's antagonists were really just cowed philistines, prefigured the glib patronizing that impaired the persuasiveness of liberal rhetoric for many years and culminated in a basket of deplorables. Finally, there may have been an inferred distrust of the mass hype machine in the anti-disco position: an early instance of a grassroots movement rejecting what it heard as propaganda for a phony or elitist platform. "When we came to the States in '77," Malcolm Young said of AC/DC's initial US visit, "they told us the timing was wrong for our style of music. It was the time of soul, disco, John Travolta, that type of stuff."[31] "I hadn't even heard a lot of the music here at the time—I thought it would be more rock," added brother Angus. "But when we got here it was a disco-type thing. What was real strange was that although the media was pushing this really soft music, you'd get amazing numbers of people turning out to hear the harder stuff."[32]

As the disco fad died out, "the harder stuff" really remained the steadiest attraction to young listeners, even well into the 1980s. The male and female consumers of heavy metal and hard rock held strong but largely unspoken (or unconscious) criteria for which music and musicians they identified with. Straight young men saw their physical instincts legitimized in the lechery of Ted Nugent or the ribald rhymes of Bon Scott, but the confessed or hinted orientations of Elton John, Freddie Mercury, or David Bowie were harshly rejected. Acts with record-selling single albums such as Peter Frampton (*Frampton Comes Alive*), Fleetwood Mac (*Rumors*), or Boston (*Boston*) were perhaps too regal in their success for ordinary small-town youth to see as reflections of themselves, whereas steady strivers Montrose, Rick Derringer, or Triumph were paying their dues on the arena circuit. Young women, for their part, may have admired the tough rock-chick models of Heart, Pat Benatar, or Joan Jett (Jett eventually covered AC/DC's "Dirty Deeds Done Dirt Cheap"), but they scorned the soft focus of Olivia Newton-John or the avant-gardism of Patti Smith. As personal and political philosophies began to develop in millions of record buyers' unformed minds, it was never enough just to like some artists; others, always, had to be hated. The rancorous partisanship that later came to town halls and polling stations was previewed in record stores and radio dials. Whether driven by peer pressure, group prejudice, or a nascent class loyalty, the parameters of teenage taste were fickle but unforgiving.

Ironically, some of the same invisibility that audiences distrusted in disco was accepted in rock 'n' roll bands; perhaps the distinction lay in the fact that even little-known rock groups consisted of fixed lineups, whereas other categories of pop were more likely to be made by ad hoc teams of session staff. But some critics weren't convinced. In a 1982 *Rolling Stone* article, Steve Pond placed the popular rock acts Styx, Rush, Journey, Foreigner, and REO Speedwagon in a class of "faceless bands," quoting an unnamed record executive who explained, "Radio stations all have their little target audiences, and they zero in on them. . . . Anything that polarizes your audience, like New Wave, is too much of a risk to put on the air. To radio, faces don't matter. . . . Not only does radio's institutionalized format guard against anything different, but it guards against anything with much personality."[33] This theory in turn prompted a rebuttal in a later issue of *Billboard*, where contributor Michael R. Lee wrote, "Somehow, the fact that these bands attained great popularity and yet couldn't be identified at a typical supermarket rankled quite a few critics and people within the industry. . . . The implication of faceless band disease has been assessed thusly: there is something wrong with a country that enjoys music by unseen faces. Since it is tougher to blame the country, they blame the bands. Maybe it is the country."[34] And radio programming expert Lee Abrams told of a conversation he'd had with *Rolling Stone* writers and editors around this same time: "They kept talking about how great these obscure punk bands like Gang of Four were and how much commercial rock bands like Styx sucked. At one point I said to them, 'You know, if you would just go and spend a week in St. Louis, you would look at this all very differently.' "[35]

Critics of faceless bands and the country that enjoyed them were right about one thing, at any rate: rock's major conduit of radio had been fragmented into numerous target markets that increasingly segregated listeners by age, region, income, and particularly race. Where once the Supremes, Aretha Franklin, and Marvin Gaye had been carried by the same airwaves that transmitted the Rolling Stones, Simon and Garfunkel, or the Lovin' Spoonful, since the late 1970s Black and white artists were less and less likely to be heard on the same broadcast programming. The compartmentalization continued into the video era, as Michael Jackson, Whitney Houston, Tina Turner, and Prince made blockbuster records but were nevertheless considered crossovers from their home—that is, Black or "urban"—audience.

In 1985 a group of African American musicians and writers formed the Black Rock Coalition to draw attention to the growing marginalization of Black rock 'n' roll performers by radio and record labels. "People [were] telling me my music wasn't black enough," BRC founder and Living Colour guitarist Vernon Reid said of his frustrations in getting signed. "That was weird. Because I *am* a black person, aren't I? Where I'm coming from is black."[36] That is, a Black musician whose music wasn't audibly soul, R&B, or rap would have a hard time being accepted as anything else. *Billboard* quoted Reid asserting, "The members of the BRC are neither novelty acts nor carbon copies of the white acts who work America's apartheid-oriented rock circuit. We will not be denied our due by demographics that claim our appeal is limited, nor will we tailor our music to fit the narrow straitjackets the industry has custom designed for black artists."[37] Reid's apartheid quip played on the standard designation of AOR, for "album-oriented radio," which allotted such generous airtime to Journey, Styx, and REO Speedwagon. In 1987 the NAACP reported of the music business, "No other industry in America so openly classifies its operations on a racial basis."[38] The issue was not that whites instinctively disliked Black acts, or vice versa—as some had speculated of the anti-disco movement—but that the trade's Black and white gatekeepers functioned as if they ought to. It did not bode well for the society they shared.

Some of the faceless bands, which might also have numbered Toto, Night Ranger, Asia, and the Jefferson Airplane offshoot of Starship, were often perpetrators of the safe and slick music they were charged with purveying— big, empty stadium rock songs about love or rocking on, expertly played and sung but emotionally predictable. By then, perhaps, during the back-to-back recessions of Jimmy Carter's US presidency and Ronald Reagan's first term, safety and predictability were things many consumers honestly needed, whether from want ads, mortgage rates, grocery bills, gas prices, or rock 'n' roll. Yet within the set lists of the faceless bands were some occasionally inspiring tunes that may have touched, albeit lightly, a few social nerves: Styx's down-and-dirty "Midnight Ride" (1975) and "Blue-Collar Man" (1978), as well as Journey's cavernous "Wheel in the Sky" (1978) and their eternal "Don't Stop Believin'" (1981), starring a small town girl and a city boy from south Detroit, with vocalist Steve Perry declaring he was workin' hard to get his fill. "We're not a Rod Stewart-type group," Styx guitarist James Young told Steve Pond in the *Rolling Stone* piece, "and we're not in a position like Talking Heads, where whoever in New York is in charge of setting trends in the rock press likes us. We're all down to earth. . . . We're not trying to inject glamour into it."[39] Composed by keyboardist Jonathan Cain, "Don't Stop Believin'" came out of Cain's impression of Journey's audiences, which he'd noticed while still a member of the group's opening act, the Babys. "Watching the shows as a fan while I was on tour with Journey," he wrote in 2018, "I noticed that the core Journey fans were blue-collar folks who were eager to rock and had spent hard-earned money to see them in concert. . . . *Let's sing to those dreamers,* I thought."[40]

Kiss, of course, was the opposite of a faceless band. Since the mid-1970s the fire-breathing, blood-spewing New York showmen parlayed the Alice Cooper brand of shock rock to even greater fame and fortune, while simultaneously serving the same symbolic role as designated outrages for their spectators. "In the Deep South, people loved us when we were onstage," recalled Starchild Paul Stanley in a memoir, *Face the Music.* "We had a license to be freaks on-stage and were welcomed as entertainers. But offstage, people wanted to kill us. As soon as we left the venues we were just guys with platform boots and big hair, wearing scarves, jewelry, and women's blouses, we felt hunted. . . . When we ran into people outside the show calling us names, I wanted to say, 'Hang on a minute—I'm the same guy you were clapping for. I put down my guitar and you want to lynch me?'"[41]

As with so many other rock 'n' roll bands of those years, Kiss had taken to the road with a range of other groups whose packaged bookings suggested that despite the performers' requisite claims to musical uniqueness and creative individuality, promoters knew just how discriminating the audiences were—and were not. The trademarked songs and stage shows might have differed from each other, but, product-wise, it was all loud white guys' electric guitar boogie. Thus in their early sojourns Kiss opened for ZZ Top, Black Sabbath, and Nazareth, then subsequently headlined over Uriah Heep, Slade, Styx, Journey, and AC/DC. On the boards, Stanley had appropriated the proselytizing fervor he'd seen in the favorite shows of his youth. He was pushing his band, but the overall cause was something bigger. "I saw Humble Pie, Slade, and Grand Funk Railroad, who all created a churchlike atmosphere, a religious connection to their audience," he testified. "A frontman like Humble Pie's Steve Marriott was leading a congregation, evangelizing for rock and roll."[42] For the churchgoers, the itinerant preachers came, delivered their sermons, and went on to the next town; the religious devotion stayed behind.

So even Kiss, dressed and painted as bisexual demonic feline outer space superheroes, somehow connected with the I-want-my-money's-worth mentality of shift workers and their teenage kids, which they acknowledged through old Jim workin' hard in "Deuce," the titular heroine out on the streets for a livin' in "Black Diamond," the sailor's only daughter in "Hard Luck Woman," and the

fake radio news intro to "Detroit Rock City," reporting that legislators were expected to rally to the aid of striking longshoremen (listen closely). "From the
beginning, the people of Detroit took us in as one of their own," Stanley said
about the locale of the latter number, the first cut on 1976's *Destroyer*. "While
we were still an opening act in most parts of the country, we were headlining
there—and I wanted to write a song about that."[43] Detroit's Cobo Hall was also
the site where most of the raw tracks on their landmark 1975 album *Alive!* were
recorded (other tape sources were Davenport, Iowa, and Cleveland, Ohio);
bassist Gene Simmons also had fond memories of Kiss's appearances there.
"Detroit, being the home of the auto industry, was antifashion, much more
meat-and-potatoes. . . . It's very blue-collar—a real middle-American metropolis. . . . People in New York and Los Angeles misread us—they affected a certain sophistication and felt that we weren't up to their standards. But Detroit
understood our mix of fun and energy from the start."[44] Conversely, Simmons
often put down pop music's critical elites who fawned over acts with far fewer
committed fans than the massed ranks of the Kiss Army. "The rock press was
always attracted to the Talking Heads, Television, the Ramones, the New York
Dolls, the Sex Pistols—bands who couldn't sell out a stadium or even an arena,"
he said. "There is a side to that media completely devoid of connection to the
people who make up most of the rock audience . . . as if they are telling kids
that they and they alone know what's important."[45] Every Kiss concert was
introduced with their trademarked declaration of rock 'n' roll populism, in
Cleveland, Davenport, Detroit, and a hundred other latter-day Colosseums
across the provinces of the new empire: *You wanted the best, you got the best!
The hottest band in the land!*

And where did Rush belong? The Canadian hard rock threesome was al-
ways in their own category: more musically and conceptually advanced than
just about all the acts they opened for or toured with, including Uriah Heep,
Mountain, Aerosmith, Mott the Hoople, Thin Lizzy, Lynyrd Skynyrd, Styx,
Ted Nugent, ZZ Top, Kiss, AC/DC, and, on one surreal date, Sha Na Na, yet
rarely compared to art rockers like Genesis or Van Der Graaf Generator.
"When you talk to metal people about Rush," mused vocalist and bass player
Geddy Lee, "eight out of ten will tell you that we're not a metal band. But if you
talk to anyone outside of metal, eight out of ten will tell you we *are* a metal
band."[46]

Rush's self-titled debut album, from 1974, was rife with guitarist Alex
Lifeson's Zeppelin-style guitar lines and featured one of the great clock-
punching anthems, "Working Man," which even enshrined Canada's national
beverage of ice-cold beer. When the original drummer John Rutsey bailed and
was replaced by Neil Peart, however, the band took on the sui generis identity

of literate headbangers that they would hold on to for the rest of their career. Peart was a reader and a writer who incorporated into his own lines a syllabus of J. R. R. Tolkien, Ayn Rand, and Ernest Hemingway, among others, for Rush's run of intricately arranged and conceived albums *Fly By Night* (1975), *2112* (1976), *A Farewell to Kings* (1977), and *Hemispheres* (1978). Between the unusually wordy lyric sheets and the musicianship, which blended the interplay of jazz fusion with the power of arena rock, Rush grew into the thinking wasted teenager's favorite group as they spent several years establishing a devout following in middle America and its equivalent in the mid-size burgs of their home country (this was the same audience that would boo new wavers Blondie off the stage when they opened for Rush in 1979). "The strategy was, 'There's a gig. We'll go play it,'" Lee looked back. "If you look at our routing plans for those first four years, it was totally nonsensical. One time we went from Gainesville, Florida, straight up to Allentown, Pennsylvania."[47] A key locale in their rise was the rust belt capital of Cleveland, Ohio, whose supportive local DJ, Donna Halper of WMMS, was name-checked on the back of their first record. Though Rush eventually became international stars over several decades, it had been the North American heartland that first welcomed their idiosyncratic, intellectual character. On 1982's *Signals*, the debt was repaid in the dystopian cityscape of "Subdivisions," where countless Rush fans were then spending their youths in the rat race, the basement bars, the shopping malls, and the mass production zone.

AC/DC were then leading a very competitive field of hard rock acts—but Bon Scott was not around to celebrate. On February 19, 1980, he was found dead in a car in London, after another of his long nights of drinking. This time a hanger-on had left him to sleep off his bout in the vehicle; it was cold, and the singer was too inebriated to properly regurgitate when his dental plate came loose. The official verdict cited both "Acute Alcoholic Poisoning" and "Death by Misadventure," though persistent theorists maintain he overdosed after a characteristically reckless dabble in heroin. Scott's death was a particular tragedy not only for the human loss but also because he and AC/DC had finally made it to the brink of the international rock stardom they had spent several years crisscrossing three continents to attain. *Highway to Hell* had become a big hit in North America, packed with the monolithic title track, as well as the rapacious "Girl's Got Rhythm" and "Shot Down in Flames," and even the album's closer, "Night Prowler," which was later claimed as a supposed inspiration of the American serial killer Richard Ramirez (he left an AC/DC hat at a crime scene).

Highway to Hell was produced by Robert John "Mutt" Lange, after Atlantic Records insisted the band bring in an outsider to replace the established team of Harry Vanda and George Young. Manager Michael Browning rational- ized, "As much as I think Vanda and Young were totally crucial in the role of creating the sound . . . they weren't switched on to what American radio was sounding like. You had to be in America to really understand what the men- tality of the kids was, the listeners and the programs. You can have all the atti- tude and all the vibe, but you've got to disguise it as something slicker with a more full production."[48] So the record had a sweeping, spacious ambience and massed vocal refrains behind Scott, conveying a mood of a rock 'n' roll bar- racks room that was to accompany untold numbers of high school and after- work beer busts. The quintet's first works had been rowdy and raunchy, but *Highway to Hell* packed their music into a sonic wallop that was more com- mercial than anything they'd done before. After Scott expired, Malcolm and Angus Young could only soldier through their grief, and they kept Lange on to produce their next work, with replacement singer Brian Johnson. Its title announced both AC/DC's short period of mourning and their swaggering re- turn to hard rock contention: *Back in Black*.

When *Back in Black* was issued in July 1980, many casual fans marveled that AC/DC had managed to find a voice identical to their late frontman's, although discerning ears picked out tonal differences that would become more obvious in later albums. Brian Johnson got the job after the band audi- tioned numerous substitute vocalists in England (unsubstantiated reports named the Easybeats' Stevie Wright as a possible appointment); Johnson was from Newcastle and had fronted a Slade-like act named Geordie, which Bon Scott himself had seen and praised. "I was brought up in a council house, or government housing, just like all the other kids," Johnson said describing his background. "Our dads were hardworking, hard-drinking Geordies: miners, steelworkers, shipbuilders, and turners."[49] *Back in Back* may well be AC/DC's masterpiece, as well as Johnson's tour-de-force, where the bluesy SG bends and clanging Gretsch open chords of the Young brothers were distilled into an audio signature of huge presence and di- mension. The irreducible E–D–A title song, the collective bender of "Have a Drink on Me," the solemn A-minor arpeggio struck home by Phil Rudd's drums in "Hells Bells," and the ready-made stadium chants of "You Shook Me All Night Long," all bedrock for Johnson's penetrating yowl, were man- datory trials by decibel for teenage car radios and home stereos in the first months of the new decade. *Back in Black* eventually sold over twenty mil- lion copies in America alone and is ranked as one of the best-selling discs of popular music ever made, among Michael Jackson's *Thriller*, the Eagles' *Hotel California*, *Led Zeppelin IV*, and Fleetwood Mac's *Rumors*. Today a hardcore contingent of fans insist the record's lyrics were in fact taken from

Bon Scott's notes, pilfered from his residence by the AC/DC organization soon after he died.

There was another side to the resuscitated version of AC/DC, though, which foretold a newer strain of rock and popular culture then rising out of the industry. It wasn't so much the music itself, which was still distinctly the Australian roadhouse rock of Malcolm and Angus Young, rather than the more recent flamboyant pop metal of Hollywood acts like Van Halen or Mötley Crüe. "They all want to run from one end of the fretboard to the other," Angus said, criticizing the new generation of guitarists. "They want to practice their scales. I mean that's all very good, so long as they do it at home."[50] But the *Back in Black* songs "Shoot to Thrill," "What Do You Do for Money Honey," "Given the Dog a Bone," and "Let Me Put My Love into You"—whoever actually wrote the words—anticipated the ever-more juvenile misogyny that was infesting the entire medium, while material from AC/DC's 1981 follow-up, *For Those about to Rock We Salute You*, like "Inject the Venom," "Put the Finger on You," and "Let's Get It Up" strayed further and further away from the winking wit of Bon Scott and more toward the bathroom wall. Later AC/DC titles included "Deep in the Hole," "Sink the Pink," "Hard as a Rock," and "Cover You in Oil." In a 1984 review of Mötley Crüe's *Shout at the Devil*, *Rolling Stone*'s J. D. Considine conceded that the record "boasts enough sexual innuendo to amuse the average thirteen-year-old boy until the next issue of *Penthouse*."[51] This was the lyrical direction hard rock had taken with the mammoth success of *Back in Black* and its derivatives.

In 1985, the spouses of numerous national politicians in the United States (including Tipper Gore, wife of then-Senator Al Gore, and Susan Baker, wife of Ronald Reagan's treasury secretary, James Baker), formed the congressional lobby group Parents' Music Resource Center (PMRC) to highlight the dangers of what they called "porn rock." The next year, feminist advocates Andrea Dworkin and Catherine MacKinnon took their own antipornography campaign to the US government, testifying before the Attorney General's Commission on Pornography on the public harm represented by magazines like *Playboy* and *Penthouse*. *Back in Black*'s "Let Me Put My Love into You" made the PMRC's "Filthy Fifteen" list, along with Madonna's "Dress You Up," Prince's "Darling Nikki," Sheena Easton's "Sugar Walls," and Judas Priest's "Eat Me Alive." Such political and social division—between the increasingly outraged conservatives and women's groups and the increasingly explicit publications, videos, and music that outraged them—was the background against which AC/DC's legend solidified.

For a long time, the band continued to tour and put out new albums every few years, even while records like *Flick of the Switch* (1983), *Fly on the Wall*

(1985), and *The Razor's Edge* (1990) never moved the units of *Back in Black*. Like Iron Maiden, Motörhead, Judas Priest, and other groups with the same clientele, AC/DC was gradually obligated to live up to the image fixed in the ears, hearts, and minds of their first generation of followers. "We've always tried to stick by what we are," Angus said in a 1995 interview to promote the latest disc, *Ballbreaker*. "Our art is that there's no art. It's the same approach it's always been."[52] At that point established rock groups of AC/DC's stature no longer gave shows to sell a record; they put out records to announce their current itinerary of shows, where the real money was. AC/DC concerts were dominated by "You Shook Me All Night Long," "For Those about to Rock," and then all the numbers the crowds had really come for: "Highway to Hell," "Whole Lotta Rosie," "TNT," "Let There Be Rock," "Live Wire," and "Shot Down in Flames." Even posthumously, no one did dirty deeds like Bon Scott.

For most adult American leaders and citizens, rock music and the entertainment industry still mattered little. In bids to quell the inflation and unemployment crises of the late 1970s, first Jimmy Carter and then, more forcefully, Ronald Reagan had started the long, slow dismantling of Franklin Roosevelt's New Deal policies of state regulation and social welfare. One by one, the airline, rail, trucking, electricity, financial, and other industries were loosed from government controls or oversights implemented generations prior. A collateral casualty of these efforts was organized labor: 27 percent of American workers were unionized in 1973, but the figure had dropped to 19 percent in 1986 and, for private-sector employees, went below 7 percent in 2011. Already battered by technological change and foreign competition, the cities of the North American foundry—Toledo, Milwaukee, Pittsburgh, Gary, Dayton, Hamilton, Windsor, and many others big and small—slid further into unemployment and depopulation. During the same period, increased numbers of unskilled nonnative arrivals joined the US workforce after the overturning of discriminatory immigration quotas in the mid-1960s, and more and more women of all backgrounds also entered the labor market. Next to such historic developments, the commercial durability of AC/DC, the multiplatinum sales of *Back in Black*, or the eternal bawdiness of "The Jack," "Big Balls," and "Go Down" were but footnotes.

Or maybe not. Obviously the band, whether in its Bon Scott or the Brian Johnson edition, still reached far more people than the relative few who might still have called themselves "working class." In the United States, it was long seen that even those with not much or a lot of money nevertheless claimed a middle-class station, and nothing so peripheral as an Australian rock group would shake such convictions. But for a vast audience, the sounds and messages of AC/DC and the bands that copied them became totems of working-class instincts—for prizing team solidarity, for appreciating the value of a dollar, for chafing under the manager's orders, for taking full advantage of a sexual dynamic where men were men and women were women (most of the time)—in a political arena that increasingly ignored working-class identities and an economy that increasingly shed secure working-class occupations. "Blue-collar culture permeated the heavy metal subculture," Deena Weinstein theorized in her 1991 analysis *Heavy Metal*. "The separation of the sexes, the boisterous, beer-swilling, male camaraderie, among other features, are rooted in blue-collar folkways."[53] The lyrics of "What Do You Do for Money Honey" and "Girl's Got Rhythm" were among the last expressions of blatant sexism that could go unchallenged in the public sphere; the shouted backing vocals to "Hells Bells" and "Have a Drink on Me" were echoes of an era when drunken pals sang rude ditties together; to crank *Highway to Hell* or *High Voltage* was to experience a vestige of a shared shop floor or neighborhood bar sensibility that most young fans would never know directly. AC/DC was rallying music for populations that no longer had much else to rally around.

Today there are no less than three public monuments to Bon Scott in two hemispheres: in his Scottish birthplace of Kirriemuir, in his adoptive home of Fremantle, and a larger-than-life bas-relief likeness built into a street wall in Melbourne, ceremoniously unveiled in 2018. AC/DC tribute bands like Bonfire, Bon but Not Forgotten, Bon Scotch, TNT, and Highway to Hell concentrate on material from Scott's tenure with the group, while all-female homages like AC/DShe and Hell's Belles put buxom "Bonnie" Scotts at the microphone, adding an extra layer of kink to songs already as rude and racy as their original author. A sleeve note for Journey's 1981 live album, *Captured*, dedicated the record to "the memory of Bon Scott, a friend from the highway." In death, Scott and the music he made with AC/DC are alive as vital avatars of rock 'n' roll manhood in a digitized, globalized, postindustrial society where his attitudes toward work, women, and the world are scarcely tolerated in mere mortals. Only a Bon Scott might still proudly boast of being dirty, mean, and mighty unclean. Only a Bon Scott might still warn us to lock up our daughter, our wife, and our back door. Only a Bon Scott might dare to remind us how it's poor man last, rich man first, and why can't the businessmen ever learn to pay? But even though he might be the only one still complaining about how you drown in debt while the upper-upper class drown in bars, even the late great Bon Scott might have to show due respect for the Boss.

8

Youngstown

In the evening a strange thing happened: the twenty families became one family, the children were the children of all. The loss of home became one loss, and the golden time in the West was one dream. And it might be that a sick child threw despair into the hearts of twenty families, of a hundred people; that a birth there in a tent kept a hundred people quiet and awestruck through the night and filled a hundred people with the birth-joy in the morning. . . . In the evening, sitting about the fires, the twenty were one. They grew to be units of the camps, units of the evenings and the nights. A guitar unwrapped from a blanket and tuned—and the songs, which were all of the people, were sung in the nights. Men sang the words, and women hummed the tunes.

John Steinbeck, *The Grapes of Wrath*

It was once remarked of the American illustrator Norman Rockwell that it was a good thing he became a liberal. Famed for his *Saturday Evening Post* covers idealizing wholesome white Americana, in the later part of his career the painter moved toward more charged representations of racial tensions and high-minded social values. The man who once rendered cozy barber shops and kids' summer baseball games was making pictures of a little Black girl escorted to school by federal agents and a multihued vision of the Golden Rule. Had Rockwell's gifts been put to the service of right-wing philosophies to idealize segregation or militarism, his admission with and influence over millions of ordinary Americans might have led to frightening ends.

The same might be said for Bruce Springsteen. Like Rockwell, Springsteen acquired an early stature as a sympathetic chronicler of the common man, whose work gradually confronted the common man's vulnerability to wealth and power. Himself one of the wealthiest and most powerful artists in the global music industry, Springsteen did not have to take a stand on behalf of the little guy. He could have justified his own enormous success and glorified the system in which only a very fortunate few, like himself, would ever

Takin' Care of Business. George Case, Oxford University Press (2021). © George Case.
DOI: 10.1093/oso/9780197548813.003.0009

come out on top. He could have gone for the cheap adulation that came with rah-rah jingoism and Supporting the Troops. Yet so honest had been his musical descriptions of regular young men and women from the mill towns and seaside getaways of New Jersey, there was nothing to diminish his integrity when his characters began to age and settle down, when his mill towns fell on hard times and his seaside getaways looked to be going nowhere, and when he started to question the very overseers of the system in which he was already adulated. Springsteen never turned his back on the poor and unknown, even when he became stratospherically rich and famous.

Unlike Bob Dylan, to whom he was initially often compared, Springsteen's words seemed to have been based on actual people and settings he had walked among rather than the surreal world of a young rock star's imagination. Dylan had probably never been to Desolation Row or been stuck inside of Mobile with the Memphis blues, but Springsteen wrote and sung as if he had truly met her in a Kingstown bar, built a '69 Chevy straight out of scratch, and sat with the last of the Duke Street Kings. And though Kiss or Ted Nugent or AC/DC themselves enlisted substantial followings among America's threatened working class, their records and concerts tended to offer more escapism than engagement—safety-valve music to captivate a mostly adolescent fandom with visions of superhuman sexual potency, chemical tolerance, or tribal strength that went unrealized in the fans' daily lives. If rock 'n' roll was a religion, as Paul Stanley believed, hard rock risked turning into an opiate of the masses. Springsteen was different. Not only did he personally abstain from drugs, but his songs addressed the sober realities of growing older and wiser in a blue-collar cohort where there were no simple ways up or out. He was not afraid to admit his vulnerability in changing times or a changing world. Past a certain stage of life, the shocks of Alice Cooper and the spandex of Judas Priest became irrelevant to people starting families or paying bills on a biweekly paycheck. Springsteen, in contrast, gave his listeners the opportunity to mature with him, rather than remain their permanent madman, starchild, or schoolboy.

He had taken a hard path. Raised in the New Jersey manufacturing town of Freehold, roughly equidistant from New York City, Philadelphia, and the Atlantic resort of Asbury Park (mother employed in a law office, father mostly occupied at a Ford plant in nearby Edison), Springsteen had been a working musician since his teens and had scarcely held anything resembling a real job. He honed his guitar skills and stagecraft in hundreds of low-paying bookings in juke joints and dance halls around the touristy Jersey "Riviera," and by 1969 he was leading a heavy blues act called Steel Mill, who had the distinction of once opening for Grand Funk Railroad and another time for Black Sabbath.

Springsteen had strong potential as a guitar hero, perhaps an American Jeff Beck or a New England Nugent, but he was also writing his own pieces and wanted to direct a band, not serve in one. He signed to Columbia Records as a solo act in 1972.

As he assembled and reassembled his backup team over his first albums *Greetings from Asbury Park, The Wild, the Innocent, and the E Street Shuffle* (both 1973), and *Born to Run* (1975), Springsteen's musical definition became apparent. For all the leader's ability on six strings, Bruce Springsteen and the E Street Band were not really a guitar-based group. With a piano, keyboards, and saxophone in the ensemble, the sound harked back to pre–British Invasion rock 'n' roll, an emulation of Motown acts, Roy Orbison, Junior Walker and the All-Stars, Gary U. S. Bonds, the Kingsmen, and other performers better known for delivering kick-ass live entertainment in small clubs rather than lip-syncing trendy pop on the small screen. As a lyricist, Springsteen was heavily influenced by the elaborate, Beat-colored verses of Dylan and Van Morrison, but as an orchestrator he was not much into the self-indulgence of so many rockers from the 1960s and early 1970s. He had marked out his home audience when he was still hustling the waterfront circuit at seventeen, as he later explained in his memoir, *Born to Run*: "Except for their Top 40 hits, the bohemian poses of the Stones or their other sixties brethren held little relevance to these kids' experience. Who could afford that? You had to fight, struggle, work, protect what was yours, remain true to your crew, your blood, your family, your turf, your greaser brothers and sisters and your country."[1]

Onstage and on camera, Springsteen and his crew again crafted their own character. He didn't have epic hair like Led Zeppelin's Robert Plant, nor did he sport a wardrobe of glitter wear like David Bowie, billowing flares like Rush, or hippie castoffs like the Grateful Dead. Most of the time, in fact, he was seen dressed and (un)shaved like any skinny drifter from the Jersey boardwalks. His familiar Fender Telecaster-Esquire hybrid was as scuffed and scavenged as its owner. In various formations the E Street Band resembled an infantry platoon or bomber crew from a war movie, featuring, behind the Catholic Irish-Italian Springsteen himself, a jumble of guys named Federici, Van Zandt, Lopez, Tallent, Weinberg, and Bittan, plus Black keyboardist David Sancious and Black sax player Clarence "Big Man" Clemons. The entire tableau of Bruce Springsteen and the E Street Band on the job made for an unusually hopeful cross-section of an integrated America that was echoed by the music itself.

As he had doggedly climbed the ladder of exposure and airplay, Columbia Records and concert promoters had tried scheduling him with boogie bands like Mountain and Black Oak Arkansas, sensitive rockers Jackson Browne and the Eagles, and even the nostalgia showcase Sha Na Na; he was a bit like each of them, but no one was quite like him. He contracted to Frank Barsalona's Premier Talent agency in 1977, by which time he was a certified headliner and a live performer of mythic passion. In the beginning Springsteen wrote about the gallery of freaks he'd hung around coming of age between the big city, the neighborhood, the barrooms, and the backstreets. They happened to be rough or perhaps desperate—wounded, not even dead—as in "Meeting Across the River" or "Jungleland," but they were dropouts more by choice than any broader economic circumstance. Girls were named Kitty, Wendy, Cherry, and Sandy, and cars were Dodges, Cadillacs, and Chevrolets. Other songs, like "Rosalita (Come Out Tonight)," "It's Hard to Be a Saint in the City," or "Thunder Road," could have been 1950s doo-wops or hot-rod sagas done up to operatic scale. *E Street Shuffle*'s "New York City Serenade" evoked *West Side Story*.

When *Born to Run* broke Springsteen wide open, critics seized on his working-class roots and image, only partly in admiration. In 1975 the middle class was still the default tier where most Americans lived, earned, and thought, and a rock singer whose music (and publicity) linked him so strongly to a lower, less advantaged strata was thought at best a self-restricting oddity and at worst a gimmicky contrivance. *Time* magazine's cover story in October of that year called him a "glorified gutter rat from a dying New Jersey resort town,"[2] not sensing that towns would soon be dying across Ohio, Pennsylvania, and upstate New York as well; after all, the lovers of "Born to Run" still enjoyed an opportunity to get out, presumably to somewhere more prosperous, while they were young. But John Sinclair, who'd managed the Motor City Five back in the revolution-fixated 1960s, took some shots at Springsteen and admiring rock journalists Dave Marsh and Jon Landau (soon to be Springsteen's manager) in a piece for the *Ann Arbor Sun*: "Springsteen's are not songs of direct experience compellingly told as acts of cathartic artistic release. They are tales of a mythic urban grease scene. . . . It is easy to fool persons such as Landau and Marsh regarding the authenticity of such a fantastic proposition, since the streets are not where they feel most comfortable."[3] No one doubted Springsteen's background as a poor kid from a tough local culture—the question was, was he writing about it or exploiting it?

This issue was put to rest with Springsteen's next records, wherein he displayed a starker, less romanticized picture of his heritage. The Dylanesque floridity of *Asbury Park* and *E Street Shuffle* subsided as the songwriter began to investigate the simpler rhymes of Hank Williams and the biography of Depression troubadour Woody Guthrie. By 1978's *Darkness on the Edge of Town* and 1980's *The River*, his subjects were no longer willing exiles on the frayed fringes of city nightlife but from a now unmistakably expanding sector of underemployed Americans clinging to domestic security one day at a time. There were fewer vagabond buddies like Eddie, Terry, and Spanish Johnny and more regular Joes like the workers in "Factory," the poor man and rich man of "Badlands," the no longer quite so young drag strip couple of "Racing in the Streets," the desperate suitor of "Prove It All Night," and the narrator of "The River," who got a union card and Mary pregnant at nineteen. Touring to promote *The River*, Springsteen was encountering in his audience the living inspirations for his songs. "We were at that very moment out and engaged with people who were on the other end of the stick,"[4] he remembered.

In 1982 he made a solo record, *Nebraska*, without the E Street Band and put to tape on a then-novel home cassette recorder. A raw suite of lonesome ballads performed only with harmonica and acoustic guitar and sung with convincing Guthrie- or Williams-like resignation, *Nebraska* further marked the emergence of Springsteen's social conscience. "Mansion on the Hill," "Reason to Believe," and the hopeless petty criminals of "Johnny 99," "Highway Patrolman," "State Trooper," and "Atlantic City" dealt with contemporary issues of joblessness, poverty, family breakdown, the legacy of Vietnam, and the widening American income gap. "The record was basically about people being isolated from their jobs, from their friends, from their families, their fathers, their mothers—just not feeling connected to anything that's going on—your government," Springsteen said. "And when that happens, there's just a whole breakdown."[5] No other rock 'n' roll star of Springsteen's renown was taking on these subjects. His next work went even further into them, but to a very different reception. *Nebraska* sold about a million copies. *Born in the USA* sold twenty-five million. *Nebraska* won Springsteen thoughtful plaudits from music reviewers. *Born in the USA* won him the scripted approval of the president of the United States.

The album that launched Bruce Springsteen into superstardom was developed as an electric companion to the unaccompanied material the artist had been essaying in his home studio, but the might of the E Street Band chugging on all cylinders threatened to drown out the composer's intended messages. In a couple of crucial instances, it did. Released in June 1984, *Born in the USA* was a huge seller and generated several hit singles and inescapable music videos in "Dancing in the Dark," "Cover Me," "Glory Days," "My Hometown," "I'm Goin' Down," and the title song. The album cover featured Springsteen's backside against the backdrop of an American flag, while promotional shots and the constant clips on MTV showed a newly buffed, cleancut figure who contrasted with the scruffy Asbury Park reprobate depicted on his older records. This brought Springsteen a new and unexpected breed of fan. On September 13, 1984, the conservative *Washington Post* columnist

George Will, who'd recently attended a concert and met Springsteen back-stage, authored a widely syndicated essay, "Bruce Springsteen, USA," extolling the musician's all-American optimism. "I have not got a clue about Springsteen's politics, if any, but flags get waved at his concerts while he sings songs about hard times," Will enthused. "He is no whiner, and the recitation of closed factories and other problems always seems punctuated by a grand, cheerful, affirmation: 'Born in the USA!' "[6] The lyrics of "Born in the USA" were actually a depressing mini-history of post-Vietnam America, with a returning vet losing a brother at Khe Sanh and then being denied help at the Veteran's Affairs office and employment at the town refinery. Will's column seemed a clueless middle-aged man's attempt to claim Springsteen for Ronald Reagan's Republicans, but just a few days later the clueless Reagan himself, in New Jersey while campaigning for a second term, invoked Springsteen at a rally: "America's future rests in a thousand dreams inside our hearts," the president intoned. "It rests in the message of hope so many young people admire, New Jersey's own Bruce Springsteen. And helping you make those dreams come true is what this job of mine is all about."[7] Despite GOP press agents' claims to the contrary, no one believed the seventy-three-year-old Reagan actually listened to Springsteen's music. In the long run, though, the president's New Jersey speech (and Will's column) meant less to the Republicans than to Springsteen himself. Reagan went on to handily defeat Democrat Walter Mondale in November, but Bruce Springsteen remained pissed.

Shortly after Reagan mentioned him on the stump, Springsteen spoke about the incident at one of his own gigs, in Pittsburgh. "I don't think [Reagan's] been listening to this one," he said, before playing *Nebraska*'s saga of an unemployed outlaw, "Johnny 99." He added, "It's a long walk from the government that's supposed to represent all the people to where it seems like . . . there's a lot of stuff being taken away from a lot of people that shouldn't have it taken away."[8] It was the Reagan-appointed chairman of the Federal Reserve, Paul Volcker (first hired on by Jimmy Carter in 1979), whose policies of high interest rates had badly hurt the American export market, where the harshest effects were felt in the industrial towns of middle America that Springsteen sang to and about. In a subsequent *Rolling Stone* interview, Springsteen was more direct, referencing Creedence Clearwater Revival: "You see the Reagan reelection ads on TV—you know, 'It's morning in America.' And you say, well, it's not morning in Pittsburgh. It's not morning above 125th Street in New York. It's midnight, and, like, there's a bad moon risin.'"[9]

Yet because Springsteen and *Born in the USA* had become so popular, his unsought association with honest-to-goodness American values died hard during the Reagan presidency. Television jingles for Chrysler belted out *The pride is back—born in America!* over a seismic backbeat echoing E Street drummer Max Weinberg's, while numerous other acts of the Just Say No era tried to capitalize on Springsteen's athletic, drug-free image: John Eddie, John Cafferty and the Beaver Brown Band, and New Jersey's Bon Jovi, a kind of hair-metal version of the E Street Band, whose hit 1986 album *Slippery When Wet* hailed the working-class hopes and dreams of young Tommy and Gina in "Livin' on a Prayer."

There were several reasons why Springsteen had become so sanitized. In the first place, he was the only major pop celebrity of his time—Black or white, male or female—who might have walked unnoticed through a mall while wearing his stage outfit. His commercial peers, from Madonna and Michael Jackson to Prince and Boy George of Culture Club, apparently dressed and undressed to scandalize, with Jackson's glove, Madonna's underwear, Prince's and Boy George's androgyny, plus Cyndi Lauper's pastels, and Ozzy Osbourne's orally administered bat decapitations. Next to them, Springsteen was perhaps the sole contemporary rock idol who still resembled a regular person. On top of this he also became a favorite cover subject of *Rolling Stone*, as publisher Jann Wenner's editorial focus moved away from rock 'n' roll toward media hotness generally, however acquired and whatever signifying; the elegist of "Backstreets," the electrifying guitar player of "Adam Raised a Cain," and the patrilineal poet of "Independence Day" had his likeness splashed across nationwide newsstands, in company with geniuses like Daryl Hannah, Michael J. Fox, and Don Johnson.

Although Springsteen and his saxophonist and *Born to Run* cover partner Clarence Clemons were genuinely close, and though the singer addressed racial tensions in *Born in the USA*'s troubled "My Hometown," observers couldn't help noticing that there were usually more Black people in Springsteen's shows than in his audiences. This too might have endeared him to the pundits of the American right, as a maker of reassuringly white music for white fans, where minorities filled visible but secondary roles. As well, "Born in the USA" and songs including *Nebraska*'s "Highway Patrolman" considered the postwar trauma of Vietnam, just when Vietnam had become a hot cultural commodity—notably in action star Sylvester Stallone's movies *First Blood* (1982) and *Rambo* (1985), wherein a muscular, headband-sporting veteran takes on unfeeling cops and then goes back to vanquish his former Communist foes in Southeast Asia. Here again Springsteen's biography was just safe enough for Republican strategists and voters to admire: as a young man Springsteen had bid farewell to New Jersey friends and bandmates sent off to Vietnam, some of whom did not return, while Springsteen himself (like Ted Nugent) had assiduously disgraced himself out of the US draft. As a rock star he was introduced to disabled Vietnam veterans, including *Born on the Fourth of July* writer Ron Kovic, and played benefit concerts for vets' organizations—covering CCR's "Who'll Stop the Rain," among other tunes—but Springsteen never really voiced an opinion on the war itself.

If *Born to Run* had made working-class lives palatable for middle-class tastes (the protagonists were just colorful failures who'd more or less volunteered to live on the margins), then *Born in the USA* made the working-class experience palatable for conservatives (the characters were wholesome men who put patriotism ahead of paycheck). Neither perception was what Springsteen intended with his songs, but the praises of Ronald Reagan and George Will had arisen from natural misunderstanding rather than cynical exploitation. For listeners in Canada or Europe, especially, the flag and country Springsteen wrote of were what they saw and heard first; his political meanings were only taken in later. *Born in the USA* may have expressed Springsteen's bitterness over the erosion of the US industrial base and its unionized workforce, but the songs did not yet lay blame on any specific official or agenda, like Paul Volcker's artificially devised recession or, indeed, Reagan's deflective geniality. None of the Republican whitewash was Springsteen's fault, yet it was an enormous stigma for a fundamentally humble and sensitive rock artist to bear. To his credit, he eventually dealt with it in his own way.

The terminal trajectory of America's manufacturing centers, of course, was not just source material for musicians to write about or inconvenient data for politicians to gloss over. It was uprooted families and homeless ex-servicemen, addiction and crime, destitution and hopelessness. And in the 1980s, Springsteen's subjects of plant closings and boarded-up downtowns were not the only miseries inflicted on America's working people. During the decade, the country's smaller but historically resonant agricultural economy—farmers—was itself convulsed by a fateful coincidence of high indebtedness, falling commodity prices, rising interest rates, a global recession, international trade policies, and outdated or unresponsive federal programs, which together made the nation's traditional family growers an endangered species. In 1984, US farmers collectively owed $215 billion in private or government loans. Small farms, once worked and lived on by several generations of homesteading clans, were being foreclosed, abandoned, or sold to large agribusinesses at disastrous rates. Premature deaths, domestic violence, divorce, alcoholism, suicides, and murder-suicides were increasingly reported throughout the American breadbasket. The crisis over the plains was a rural relation to the industrial crisis decimating the cities.

This was not Bruce Springsteen's beat, but it was John Mellencamp's. Mellencamp had been making records since 1976, at first under the name

Johnny and then John Cougar, to scant public interest in the first few years. He was hyped as both a rock 'n' roll bad boy and a streetwise urban bard, but few bought into his image, until 1982's *American Fool* and 1983's *Uh-Huh* delivered several hit singles and heavily rotated videos capitalizing on Mellencamp's husky timbre and bantamweight attitude and the hooky simplicity of his songs: "Hurts So Good," "Jack & Diane," "The Authority Song," and "Crumblin' Down." Though dogged by friendly and unfriendly comparisons to Springsteen, the singer-guitarist had a distinctly qualified patriotism that predated *Born in the USA*, and the Indiana native was more forward than his New Jersey counterpart in talking celebrity and talking politics. In a 1984 *Creem* profile he said simply, "This is just my job. This whole rock star trip and the image people create around it is bullshit."[10] Mellencamp also made it clear that, despite *Uh-Huh*'s popular track "Pink Houses" and its ain't-that-America chorus, he was no George Will Republican: "[The song's] saying the American Dream and all that shit is propaganda," he explained. "It's not rah, rah, rah America at all, and I think it puts America in its place . . . [but] the majority of the public is going to fall right in line with the way Reagan wants them to think."[11]

Mellencamp's 1985 album *Scarecrow* was his most successful and his most topical, clearly addressing the US farm crisis from the perspective of one who knew what he was singing about. "The farm crisis . . . is real for me," Mellencamp acknowledged. "Drive around my town [Bloomington, Indiana] and you see that it's closing down. Are all the grain stores in town going to go out of business? Are all the farm implement companies going to go out of business? Are the small Chevrolet dealers going to go out of business? These corporate farms are taking over and buying up everything directly. It destroys the look of this country."[12] Recorded in Belmont, Indiana, *Scarecrow*'s radio-friendly tracks "Small Town," "Lonely Ol' Night," and "The Face of the Nation" had the crack and drive of the 1960s-period Rolling Stones but added new lyrical themes of home, roots, and pride just when each was under siege by the impersonal forces of an unrestrained market. "Small Town" was an unabashed statement of local loyalty in a globalizing world, and even the uptempo hit "R.O.C.K. in the USA" name-checked the first generation of homegrown American bands to humbly stand up to the British Invasion: the Young Rascals, Mitch Ryder, Bobby Fuller, and others. The record's opener, "Rain on the Scarecrow," was a minor-key rocker about farm foreclosures that fingered banks as the chief villains and quoted the artist's grandfather lamenting the loss of his own land, which had once fed the nation but which was now just memories. Critics acclaimed Mellencamp for taking on a sense of responsibility unheard in the music of his younger self. "When Mellencamp sings that he can't recognize the face of the nation anymore, he's not grandstanding—he's articulating for a growing underclass that's being stripped of everything, starting with its voice,"[13] wrote Jimmy Guterman in *Rolling Stone*, while Jon Pareles in the *New York Times* appreciated how the artist "wants to pay tribute to the heartland's workers, to stick up for the unglamorous life and to counsel grit and steadfastness."[14] Soon Mellencamp made his words into deeds.

On July 15, 1985, the all-star, two-continent televised concert of Live Aid drew millions of viewers in a fundraising benefit for Ethiopian famine relief. As the last performer of the show's American half, Bob Dylan muttered a vague preamble that a similar effort could be made on behalf of America's farmers, whose own hardships were already well known. This provided the impetus for John Mellencamp, along with Willie Nelson and Canadian folk rocker Neil Young, to organize a comparable charity event of popular musicians soliciting an audience's donations for strapped agricultural families in the United States. "What it really amounts to is we are going to call some attention to the farmers' situation and raise some money and see where it can be spent,"[15] Willie explained to the press. "The family farm is dwindling away," Mellencamp put in. "That's unhealthy and we thought some attention should be paid to the problem."[16] The first Farm Aid took place in Champaign, Illinois, on September 22, 1985, and more Farm Aid affairs were staged in 1986 (Austin, Texas), 1987 (Lincoln, Nebraska), 1990 (Indianapolis, Indiana), 1992 (Irving, Texas), and beyond. Mellencamp figured prominently in each, as an act and as a leading voice offstage.

Meanwhile, he solidified his stature as a representative of embattled farm people with his 1987 album, *Lonesome Jubilee*. The music of this album went further into a folky, front-porch flavor that incorporated the traditional acoustic instruments of Appalachia while keeping the AM rock 'n' roll appeal that was Mellencamp's bread and butter: "Cherry Bomb," "Paper in Fire," "We Are the People," "Down and Out in Paradise," and the gospel-style singalong "Hard Times for an Honest Man," whose title alone summed up Mellencamp's politics. "Once I heard the violin and the accordion playing a line together," the singer recalled, "I knew that was a sound that nobody'd really heard, and it was still in the vein of what we wanted to do. Guys had been doing it for years, but we were the first band that was able to bring it to the general public."[17] "John related to the hardworking underdog," remembered Mellencamp's longtime drummer, Kenny Aronoff, whose smart, snappy backbeats were defining features of the songs. "This was a deep part of who John was, and I think these new instruments had the sounds of what he was feeling in his soul as the voice for those small, struggling family farmers."[18] *Lonesome Jubilee* was another major seller and forever erased Mellencamp's slick Johnny Cougar past.

But as an ongoing cause, meanwhile, Farm Aid consistently fell short of fundraising goals. There was never much clear plan for how the donated funds should be distributed, or if the real objective was only the vague aim of "awareness." Willie Nelson later suggested his visibility as a proponent of cannabis legalization and farm relief may have led to his investigation by the Internal Revenue Service for millions of dollars in unpaid taxes. "The men in charge didn't like how Farm Aid, the yearly event I'd cofounded, led to discussions about how the government continued to fuck the farmers,"[19] he opined. By 1992 Mellencamp admitted that viewers were not opening up their wallets as much as had been hoped: "I could tell you something that might make everything seem rosy, but I find that a lot people are having a hard enough time paying their own bills. They're questioning—'I can't even make my own payments anymore, you really expect me to donate money?' It's tough out there."[20]

Many of the first Farm Aid spectacles were broadcast live on the new cable channel of TNN (The Nashville Network), and the roster of performers—besides the fixtures of Willie Nelson, John Mellencamp, and Neil Young—were a colorful assortment of pop, rock, and blues artists. Country and country rock were Farm Aid's anchors, though, and whether the diverse assembly of musicians had previously imagined themselves playing to a stadium of cowboy hats and John Deere baseball caps, they often gained exposure to a different public than they were used to. In 1985 Billy Joel, Joni Mitchell, Bob Dylan, B. B. King, and the Beach Boys ran through their songs in between sets by Loretta Lynn, Waylon Jennings, Charlie Daniels, Glen Campbell, Roger Miller, and Merle Haggard. Just under the surface of Farm Aid's mission was a midwestern populism that stood in quiet rejoinder to the global spectacle of Live Aid, as something staged in support of Black Africans was remade as smaller-scale gatherings to mark the plight of mostly white Americans. Within the arena of pop culture, it was a rare occasion for white people to be presented as a hard-done-by group, a role some may have inhabited more readily than others. At the 1992 Farm Aid in Texas, Black activist Jesse Jackson received a scattering of boos when he spoke to the crowd about the farm crisis.

During this era the entertainment business, as always, spotted potential profits a long way off; even Hollywood had produced pious treatments of farmers' problems in *Country* and *The River* (both 1984). So for several years an expansive acreage of new musical acts were signed, promoted, and reviewed as "roots" or "heartland rock" in hopeful emulation of Bruce Springsteen's and John Mellencamp's popularity as truth-telling guys from the Rust and Corn Belts, including Omar and the Howlers, the Long Ryders, the Beat Farmers, the Bo Deans, the Georgia Satellites, the Kentucky Headhunters, Bruce

Hornsby and the Range, and Dave Alvin, formerly of the Blasters. Proven stars who'd ventured into the same musical or lyrical regions, such as Tom Petty and the Heartbreakers (*Southern Accents*, 1985) and Billy Joel (*The Nylon Curtain*, 1982), were themselves sometimes placed in the category. Heartland rock was defined as straightforward tunes about average people just getting by, performed by acts coiffed and dressed as ordinary Americans. "Our look and the way we acted was actually who we were," recalled Kenny Aronoff of Mellencamp's band. "We were all pretty down-to-earth guys from the Midwest."[21] The music was distinct from its commercial rivals of hard rock and heavy metal—no million-note guitar solos in the songs, and no pentagrams on the album covers or bikinied babes in the videos—reaching a slightly older audience that had moved on from the titillations of AC/DC or Iron Maiden.

How or to what extent this audience resembled the actual human subjects of the heartland rockers' material was anyone's guess. Earnest ballads about pressing social issues, along with causes like Live Aid, Farm Aid, and the Artists United against Apartheid organization (whose 1985 fundraising single "Sun City" was written by Steve Van Zandt of the E Street Band) became something of a media stereotype by the end of the decade, and some of the work could veer dangerously close to a liberal sanctimony that flattered the consciences of comfortably virtuous fans more than it achieved tangible good for the disadvantaged. In 1987 Jon Pareles of the *New York Times* described the evident formulae of the genre Mellencamp led: "Commercial rock radio stations have become increasingly conservative; they're looking for songs that won't sound out of place next to early-1970s 'classic rock' from the Rolling Stones or Lynyrd Skynyrd, so there's a powerful incentive for bands to take up three-chord blues-rock," he wrote. "Heartland rock isn't traditional, it's neo-traditional, self-conscious about seeking roots; it's not a local, home-grown style but one that wishes it were. While its storytelling lyrics stem from folk and country music and its back beat from rock and rhythm-and-blues, its sound and attitude are strictly from the 1980s—scruffy but respectable."[22] Even at their angriest, moreover, heartland songwriters seldom mounted direct us-versus-them mobilizations against an economic or political elite. Populism, for the most part, was channeled into pop.

This was a problem that confounded Steve Earle. A strong singer and guitarist with Nashville roots, and a natural heir to the hell-raising spirit of outlaw country, Earle and his band the Dukes emerged in the mid-1980s with a trio of volatile country rock records on the MCA label, *Guitar Town* (1986), *Exit 0* (1987), and the big hit *Copperhead Road* (1988). The albums were dominated by Earle's electric and acoustic picking and by his old-before-his-time songs about the ongoing rural exodus ("Hillbilly Highway"), thwarted small-town ambitions ("No. 29"), farm foreclosures ("The Rain Came Down"), and a Vietnam vet turned to crime ("Copperhead Road"). He performed a cover of Bruce Springsteen's *Nebraska* standout "State Trooper" at live gigs. It was quintessential heartland rock, dour and dangerous, and Earle was soon a regular at the Farm Aid concerts. But he also seemed to take his characters' resentment and alienation to heart, racking up a series of marriages, arrests, incarcerations, and addictions that nearly destroyed his career and ended his life. "I just saw that lifestyle as an inevitability of the job," he said years later. "If you were going to be a singer-songwriter with any integrity, it seemed to me you worked harder and died a lot younger than other performers. That just seemed to be a fact of that kind of life."[23] In time, a clean and sober Earle would manage to keep his integrity and still make openly political music that made no bones about what he stood for and against.

George Thorogood, on the other hand, had few serious messages to impart, but that may have been his most powerful message of all. Thorogood and his band, the Delaware Destroyers, were contracted to the obscure Rounder Records label when his eponymous debut album of 1977 and its follow-up the next year, *Move It on Over*, started selling in numbers to match bigger companies' most hyped acts. In his case, doggedly working a steady schedule of roof-raisers at small venues around the United States and Canada paid off in a cult reputation as a certified good time on Saturday night. A slate of gigs opening for the Rolling Stones in 1981 put him before a much larger market, after which his music was released through EMI. Thorogood made no claims of being a poet or a prophet; most of what he recorded and played live were covers of old blues, honky-tonk, or rock 'n' roll classics. "Why should I write songs when Chuck Berry already wrote them all?"[24] he was quoted in a 1979 *Rolling Stone* profile. At most he was a proselytizer for a timeless juke-joint art form many new converts weren't aware they'd been missing—small guitar, bass, sax, and drum combos laying down party music like Earl Hooker's "You Got to Lose," Bo Diddley's "Who Do You Love?," and Hank Williams's "Move It on Over."

This simplicity of style—proudly branding himself as a purveyor of solid saloon entertainment, nothing more—won Thorogood a legion of admirers greater than any tavern could accommodate. Like many full-time showmen, he found that a full program of bookings was more fulfilling as an honest day's labor (and a surer source of revenue) than cutting albums. His rare self-composed songs, including "Bad to the Bone," "I Drink Alone," and the trucker escapade "Gear Jammer," fit well into his implacably gutbucket sound, built around Thorogood's authentic slide guitar tributes on Gibson semiacoustic instruments, plus longtime Destroyers Jeff Simon's drums, Billy Blough's bass, and Hank Carter's saxophone. He could sometimes show off subtler techniques, as in his takes on the minor blues chestnut "As the Years Go Passing By" and Bob Dylan's jaded American travelogue "Wanted Man," first performed by Johnny Cash on *Live at San Quentin*, but more character-istic were 80-proof sprees like "If You Don't Start Drinkin' (I'm Gonna Leave)" and his signature appropriation of John Lee Hooker's "One Bourbon, One Scotch, and One Beer." It all added up to a reliable package of earthy blues rock that was as popular with college kids celebrating the end of exams as with shift workers celebrating a three-day weekend, and he wasn't above playing small cities well off the stadium circuit either. "The people go to the Rolling Stones," he said. "George Thorogood and the Destroyers go to the people."[25] If John Mellencamp was heartland rock, George Thorogood was heartland boogie.

Unlike the Texan Strat picker Stevie Ray Vaughan, whose first albums came out a little after his, Thorogood was not an obvious virtuoso; the two appeared with Chuck Berry at the 1984 Grammy Awards, both played versions of Elmore James's "The Sky Is Crying," and each was credited with reviving the commerciality of electric blues, but there were subtle differences in their playing and their audiences. Vaughan covered Jimi Hendrix's "Little Wing" and "Voodoo Chile (Slight Return)" and had a short residence in David Bowie's band, becoming a sensation among six-string fans in the 1980s. In contrast, George Thorogood remained at a folk level, squawking rockabilly blasts over the cheers of rowdy crowds, instead of being spotlighted as the next guitar god. That status aggravated Stevie Ray's drug and alcohol habits, which eventually landed him in rehab, while the clean-living Thorogood (he had been a pro baseball prospect in his youth) weathered the industry's pressures and temptations for a decades-long career. "In our country, we've got Budweiser, we've got Chevy and Ford trucks," he told a Canadian inter-viewer in 2012. "When people ask, 'Where you been, George,' I tell them we've never been away like Ford or Chevy have never been away. We may not be big news but, like Budweiser, we are still stocked on the shelves."[26]

It was telling, though, that George Thorogood and Stevie Ray Vaughan were both white guys reaching a mostly white public, even as they offered catalogs whose source lay largely with Black musicians. Of course, 'twas ever thus with rock 'n' roll, but in the beginning Thorogood and others in his cat-egory were sometimes chastised as pretenders to a throne rightfully occu-pied by African Americans. There was no question of racial insensitivity on Thorogood's part: once asked who might play him in a movie, with a straight face he named the Black actor Sidney Poitier. Ironically, his first records on Rounder came as unexpectedly big sellers for a specialty label hitherto based around folk and blues traditionalists, and one historian of Rounder sniffed that "Thorogood was merely one more in a long line of white performers who mined a black-originated repertoire, even as many of the artists who created that repertoire were still working, generally with less success. Viewed cynically, his growling approach . . . barely rose above the level of caricature."[27] Yet the fact that modern blues music was gradually associated with the likes of Thorogood, Vaughan, Bonnie Raitt, the blind Canadian wonder Jeff Healey, or even comedy stars John Belushi and Dan Ackroyd as the Blues Brothers, at least as much as a current Black act like Robert Cray, was an indication of demographic and cultural shifts bigger than any one player's appeal.

Bob Seger, as Barbara Mandrell might have put it, was heartland when heartland wasn't cool. Born in Michigan in 1945 (older than Bruce Springsteen and John Mellencamp by a few years), Seger was performing throughout the US interior since the mid-1960s, first with his Motor City–formed groups the Last Heard and the Bob Seger System, then as a soloist and the leader of the Silver Bullet Band. "I used to go out and play 250 nights a year," he recalled. "Drove all over the country in a station wagon from '65 to '75."[28] It was with the Silver Bullet Band and his 1976 records *Live Bullet* and *Night Moves* that Seger vaulted into real stardom, but he had earned his way to the top. "My father left us when I was ten, so I had to make enough money for us to be able to live in a house because my brother went in the service during Vietnam and I was sole support of my mother," said Seger;[29] he even did short stints on the assembly lines of Ford and GM. Very gradually he acquired a following around Detroit—he signed as a Capitol artist in 1968—which expanded outward to the young jean-clad hordes of the central states. He and the Silver Bullet Band opened for brother rockers Bachman-Turner Overdrive, Kiss, Thin Lizzy, and Black Oak Arkansas, while Rush opened for Bob Seger and the Silver Bullet Band. Another Detroit artist, Ted Nugent, heard Seger's potential as early as the System's regional hit of 1969, "Ramblin' Gamblin' Man": "Young Bob and his killer band were animals. He is a world-class representation of our soulful Michiganiac legacy."[30] Seger eventually attributed his lengthy career to a steady work ethic next to that of volatile Great Lakes state contemporaries like the Stooges and the MC5. "I think those [other] bands came and went because they just didn't have the stamina to go all the way. Either that or, in some cases, it was drugs. . . . You can't just go out there and piss people of and expect to be superstars. . . . Whereas Nugent would go out there and sweat, and so would I."[31]

Bob Seger's music with the Silver Bullet Band was a slow-burning prairie fire of rock 'n' roll, where the hot energy of drums, keyboards, and saxophone smoldered behind Seger's windswept vocals and acoustic guitar. His

best-known songs introduced a motif of nostalgia unusual in the medium—
the recollections of teenage rites of passage in "Night Moves," "Like a Rock,"
"Fire Lake," and "Against the Wind"; the importance of permanence and
continuity in "Mainstreet," "Still the Same," "Rock and Roll Never Forgets,"
and "You'll Accomp'ny Me"; the open preference for the past in his signature
track, "Old Time Rock and Roll." The last tune, from 1978's *Stranger in Town*,
was further popularized by its inclusion in the 1984 Tom Cruise movie *Risky
Business* and marked an early expression of an embryonic affinity within the
rock culture for the simpler, somehow more honest standards of yesteryear.
Since when had there been anything old time about rock 'n' roll? Yet Seger
was no reactionary. There was no race-baiting in "Old Time Rock and Roll,"
which took a shot at disco and the soullessness of today's music while still
extolling the virtues of blues and funky old soul, and Seger's inclination toward traditionalism was qualified by the young longhair's appetites described
in "Hollywood Nights," "Her Strut," and "The Horizontal Bop" and by the itinerant rock musician's occupational hazards of always feeling outnumbered by
the straights and not daring to make a stand against them, in his mother of all
road epics, "Turn the Page."

The enduring FM radio ballads "Night Moves," "Against the Wind," and
"We've Got Tonight" were Seger's heartland cousins of the Allman Brothers
Band's "Ramblin' Man," Lynyrd Skynyrd's "Free Bird," and even the Eagles'
"Desperado"—jaded musings and cautionary tales from hirsute guys who'd
won sexual and other liberties their fathers and grandfathers had never known
yet who found them to be a mixed blessing in real relationships, wishing they
didn't know now what they didn't know then. (Members of the Eagles contributed backing vocals to the *Against the Wind* album of 1980, and Eagle Glenn
Frey was a Detroit-born friend of Seger's.) His songs had captured the outlook of decidedly average young men grappling with existential opportunities
for which they'd had little emotional preparation. "I try to write about other
people's lives," he explained, "people I'm close to, people in the band, a guy in
the crew, or someone I've just met."[32] When Seger sang about looking back,
he wasn't necessarily endorsing better times or conservative values but just
reminding the listener that those times and values would inevitably change.
He and the Silver Bullet Band put out hard-hitting barroom rock on an arena
scale, but the underlying messages were often reflective, somber, and intimate.

Seger's Detroit roots (and he remained based in Michigan even after making
several platinum-selling records) were also evident in his songs of work and
routine, as in "Makin' Thunderbirds," "I've Been Working," "The Fire Down
Below," "Beautiful Loser," and his broadside against employers, teachers, the
IRS, Ma Bell, and the rest of the contemporary technocratic order, "Feel Like

a Number." He never focused on economic problems to the extent that his peers had, although in 1986 he too issued a state-of-the-nation album, *Like A Rock*, which opened with the single "American Storm" and closed with a cover of CCR's class-conscious "Fortunate Son." Asked if he was a representative of the American Midwest, he responded, "Well, only in the sense that I've stayed there, you know. Maybe because my songs are a little more direct. They're not vague or anything. I think people pretty much understand it's a pretty plain speaking."[33] Nor did Seger really turn his commercial success into major celebrity stature, which also endeared him to his audience as a regular dude. "I've always considered myself an antistar,"[34] he said. In the same years that Springsteen and Mellencamp got famous depicting the struggling jobbers and family men of the mill towns and the farm communities, the more anonymous Bob Seger's lyrics were portraying the post-counterculture generation coming of age in the small cities and down the long interstates of America's flyover longitudes: more free but more frustrated than their elders, more open but more exposed, more experienced but more aware of what they had lost along the way.

Though heartland rock had enjoyed its greatest prominence in the 1980s, it was not until the next decade that the lasting consequences of the conditions originally addressed by *The River*, *Nebraska*, *Scarecrow*, *Lonesome Jubilee*, *Exit 0*, *Against the Wind*, or Farm Aid could be discerned. Farm foreclosures and factory shutdowns, it came to light, were only the initial symptoms of a much broader set of domestic and global shifts affecting the United States and countries across the developed world. The collapse of the USSR and the Communist bloc over 1989–1991 transformed the international economic system, whereby the formerly closed societies of Eastern Europe entered a worldwide market for goods and labor; at the same time, the modernizing economies of populous nations such as China, India, and Brazil also began to compete for trading revenues that had for decades been exclusively shared between North America, Western Europe, and Japan.

More upheaval was to come. Technological advances in computers and communications hugely accelerated the convenience and pace of the expanded trade networks, while also revolutionizing measures of productivity. Observers began to characterize the United States and its allies as "knowledge economies," with the majority of workers employed in clerical or service jobs—fewer and fewer of them unionized—rather than doing manual labor on factory floors, down mine shafts, or on oil rigs. Treaties established under neoliberal political programs also meant the livelihoods of employees in Sheffield or Cleveland or Windsor might instantly be handed over to citizens of Bangalore, Buenos Aires, or Tianjin. While billions of people in once

impoverished continents saw their standards of living rise, millions accus-
tomed to relative prosperity in Canada, America, or Britain found themselves
rivals for wealth circulating not in the next big city but in other hemispheres.
In the 1960s, children in rich countries were warned to eat their vegetables and
think of the starving poor overseas; by the 1990s, their own kids were told to
study their homework and think of the Indian computer engineering students
who might be hired ahead of them. Competitiveness became a watchword
among social scientists and urban planners, as municipalities that had long
relied on the stable occupations and taxes provided by the local plant or transport hub now had to promote themselves over and above similar places on the
other side of the country, or the planet.

The two-term presidency of Bill Clinton in the United States also saw the
repeal or relaxation of restrictions on banking and finance in place since the
Great Depression. Combined with the new momentum of globalization and
the Internet, capitalism was unleashed into what appeared to be a new Gilded
Age: the rewards of such unprecedented growth disproportionately went to
CEOs and investors rather than anything resembling the old working class.
As the income gap between the richest and poorest Americans widened,
politicians hailed the virtues of "meritocracy," asserting that those who fared
well under the new economic regime had simply tried harder or graduated
from better schools than those who didn't. The ideal of a lifelong job was a
thing of the past, it was said, and anyone negotiating the labor market should
strive to be a lifelong learner, maintaining and adding skills over the course
of a career, lest they fall off the shrinking life raft of job security or through
the weakening social safety net. It was in this context of headlong change that
Bruce Springsteen made his 1995 album, *The Ghost of Tom Joad*.

Following the historic success of *Born in the USA*, Springsteen had mostly
turned his attention inward. Uneasy with the level of fame he'd achieved and
smarting from the misappropriation of his lyrics and image by conservatives,
his next records, *Tunnel of Love* (1987), *Lucky Town*, and *Human Touch* (both
1992), chronicled his short first marriage, his personal history, and his newfound status as a more contented husband and father. There were also live
albums and continued performances, but he had chosen to disengage from
the E Street Band, whose members contributed only separately or not at
all to the latest studio tracks and who did not back him on a world tour in
1992–1993. He had not completely forsaken his social awareness, though—
the 1992 piece "57 Channels and Nothin' On" was a funny, pungent indictment of the expanding entertainment-industrial complex, and his Academy
Award-winning single, "Streets of Philadelphia," was featured in the 1994 film
Philadelphia, one of the first mainstream productions to deal with the AIDS

epidemic; Springsteen's song was a haunting and compassionate gesture toward AIDS victims from someone who could easily have distanced himself from their cohort.

Though Springsteen had watched the geopolitical evolution of the United States and the world from the rarefied perspective of an international traveler and a wealthy pop icon, he did not insulate himself from the news or reality. With little formal education beyond an indifferent record in New Jersey's public schools in the 1950s and 1960s, he had taken to reading serious studies like Howard Zinn's *A People's History of the United States* and Henry Steel Commager's *A Pocket History of the United States*, and as far back as *Darkness on the Edge of Town* he was influenced by the work of *Grapes of Wrath* author John Steinbeck. In the early 1990s he was aware of how the hard-hit workers of America's rust belt had their counterparts in many other countries, all affected by the same tides of capital and debt washing through the global system. This knowledge began to seep into his songwriting. He eventually stated in his memoir, "*The Ghost of Tom Joad* chronicled the effects of the increasing economic division of the eighties and nineties, the hard times and consequences that befell many of the people whose work and sacrifice created America and whose labor is essential to our everyday lives."[35]

Sonically, *Tom Joad* took shape with the same spare production as *Nebraska*, with little to augment Springsteen's storytelling against his subdued acoustic guitar. The E Street Band was not on the record. The singer's voice, a stadium-shaking instrument at full power, was turned way down to a laconic balladeer's drawl, telling of a Vietnam vet's making peace with a Vietnamese refugee in "Galveston Bay," of Mexican migrants reduced to cooking methamphetamine instead of harvesting orchards in "Sinaloa Cowboys," of the latest wave of homeless families sleeping in cars or under bridges throughout new world order America in "The Ghost of Tom Joad." Springsteen's current reading material directly inspired the album's "Youngstown" and "The New Timer," after he pulled from his living room shelf the 1985 nonfiction book *Journey to Nowhere*. Subtitled *The Saga of the New Underclass*, it captured through reporting and photojournalism of authors Dale Maharidge and Michael Williamson the unforgiving landscape of the postindustrial United States, as an internal diaspora of the unemployed and indigent roamed train yards, relief shelters, and work camps across the land. These were not voluntary dropouts. *Journey to Nowhere*, Springsteen wrote in the foreword to a 1995 reissue of the book, "put real lives, names, and faces on statistics we'd all been hearing about throughout the Eighties. People who all their lives had played by the rules, done the right thing, and had come up empty, men and women whose work and sacrifice had built this country, who'd given their sons to its wars and whose lives were marginalized or discarded."[36]

"Youngstown" was a minor-key dirge about the eponymous Ohio city, whose chief employers of Republic and US Steel had shut down for good the previous decade, leaving thousands of citizens out of jobs. Other local factories joined the exodus, until the area's familiar horizons of smoke and flame guttered out. Unemployment in the area soared to almost 25 percent, while violent crimes, domestic violence, divorce, suicide, and substance-related health issues also climbed. "If a plague had taken away this many people in the Midwest," observed John Russo, a professor of labor studies at Youngstown State University, "it would have been considered a huge historical event."[37] Springsteen worked the real musings of laid-off Youngstown steelworkers, as quoted by Maharidge and Williamson, into his verses—quietly embittered thoughts of men returned from fighting and winning World War II only to have their bosses defeat them as Adolf Hitler never could—and cited the locale as one of many in its region where the story was always the same: honest men laboring years in hellish blast furnaces just so other men could grow rich enough to forget them. With *The Ghost of Tom Joad*, Springsteen called out the illusions proffered by the political and business classes in a way no one could misinterpret. Touring for the record in 1995, he for the first time performed his concerts alone, equipped only with his acoustic guitar while delivering the recent material and revisiting rousing fan favorites as somber one-man meditations. Springsteen was no longer a rock 'n' roll Rambo but an open conscientious objector. Even "Born in the USA," in a sullen, solo version, was restored to its original purpose of decrying the owners, managers, and national leaders who turned their backs on the people who'd worked and fought on their behalf.

Like the cussedly independent Texan Willie Nelson, the politicized Springsteen was a tricky character for conservatives to challenge: he had once had the approval of the sainted Ronald Reagan, after all, and had been almost literally wrapped in the American flag in his previous incarnation on the *Born in the USA* jacket. In 1984 the rightist *National Review* magazine had extolled him as "one of the few rockers capable of writing intelligent lyrics" who had "led the rightward tide. . . . He still writes about the working-class victims of the Rust Belt, but on his two albums—Nebraska and Born in the USA—his heroes are invested with a cowboy libertarianism."[38] But sixteen years later, *New York Times* editorialist John Tierney wrote that Springsteen was "no longer the poor Jersey kid singing about his blue-collar neighbors. He is a millionaire who doesn't have to hitchhike on Route 9 anymore. The singer who once defended Vietnam veterans and Middle American values has lately been focused on conventional liberal causes, like homelessness and AIDS."[39] Others sneered at one more world-famous rock musician pontificating on Big Issues, implying that Springsteen's activism was a calculated career move, or the sanctimony of a privileged dilettante.

Criticism such as John Tierney's was occasioned by Springsteen's 2000 song "American Skin (41 Shots)." The piece was written, recorded, and issued as a single in the aftermath of the police killing of an unarmed Black African immigrant, Amadou Diallo, in New York City the previous year; Diallo had been reaching for his identification when suspicious and agitated white patrolmen blasted a barrage of bullets into him. The cops were later acquitted of second-degree murder. "American Skin" depicted the incident from the point of view both of the innocent minority stopped for little other reason than his race and of the police making instant life-or-death decisions about whether suspects were pulling a knife, a gun, or a wallet on them. No verdict was rendered in the lyrics, which merely noted that being killed for being dark was a fact of American life. When the song was played live with a reunited E Street Band in New York, Springsteen was booed by some in the audience, and NYPD rank and file refused to escort the act from Madison Square Garden, while Mayor Rudolph Giuliani commented, "There are still people trying to create the impression that the police officers are guilty, and they are going to feel strongly about that."[40] Resentment from the men in blue simmered long after. "On one of my motorcycle forays through western New York," Springsteen remembered, "I stopped at a little roadhouse and ran into a few local officers with a few beers under their belt who were thoroughly displeased with my editorializing."[41]

Yet as much as opponents and skeptics tried to cast Bruce Springsteen as a phony or a lefty do-gooder cushioned by wealth and renown, the fundamental decency of the man and his message never stopped coming through. His history as an alert and ambitious young rock 'n' roller raised among the stoic, tight-knit networks of New Jersey's lower classes could not be unwritten by the fame and fortune he'd since secured for himself through rock 'n' roll. In 1995 Dale Maharidge, author of *Journey to Nowhere*, met Springsteen, who'd sought him out as an admirer of his book. Maharidge went with him to the skeletal remains of the Jeanette blast furnace in Youngstown, Ohio, the two trespassing together on the abandoned yard of scrap and rubble where thousands of working men had once earned their living. Springsteen had used his music to describe the place and its meaning in "Youngstown"; now he had gone to see it for himself. Silently they wandered the empty, dilapidated structures, each lost in thought, and it was then that Maharidge appreciated Springsteen's true qualities. "Up to that point at the Jenny furnace, I had never truly felt at ease around Bruce because of my discomfort with celebrity," the journalist wrote. "But that day he was not a big rock star. He was just a guy standing in a dead steel mill wondering and worrying about the future of the United States of America, a guy creating art to help make us understand and ask questions about what the future might be like."[42]

9
One in a Million

> But the country's tectonic plates had shifted. Politics was no longer simply a pocketbook issue but a moral issue as well, subject to moral imperatives and moral absolutes. . . . Accordingly, liberalism and conservatism were defined in the popular imagination less by class than by attitude—the position you took toward the traditional culture and the counterculture. What mattered was not just how you felt about the right to strike or corporate taxation, but also how you felt about sex, drugs, and rock and roll, the Latin mass or the Western canon.
>
> **Barack Obama,** *The Audacity of Hope*

In November 2004, reporter Dexter Filkins was embedded with the US military outside the besieged Iraqi city of Fallujah. Thousands of American, British, and Iraqi troops were poised to retake Fallujah from its insurgent occupying forces, in what promised to be the climactic battle of the entire Iraq war, begun early the previous year. Most of the city's civilian inhabitants had already fled. The impending action was codenamed Operation Phantom Fury. Fighting was anticipated to be heavy and would be conducted house to house as the soldiers moved in. In his 2008 book *The Forever War*, Filkins recalled how the battle began: "And then, as if from the depths, came a new sound: violent, menacing, and dire. I looked back over my shoulder to where we had come from, into the vacant field at Falluja's northern edge. A group of marines were standing at the foot of a gigantic loudspeaker, the kind used at rock concerts. It was AC/DC, the Australian heavy metal band, pouring out its unbridled sounds. I recognized the song immediately: 'Hells Bells,' the band's celebration of Satanic power, had come to us on the battlefield."[1]

Filkins bore witness to what by then had become a supreme irony of rock music's admission with several generations of fighting men: a genre long associated with insubordination, dissent, and outright pacifism was often deployed by highly organized military forces as a morale booster, and as a psychological weapon. Outside Fallujah, the sounds of AC/DC booming over the desert were used to signal a widely spaced roster of combat units that the

Takin' Care of Business. George Case, Oxford University Press (2021). © George Case.
DOI: 10.1093/oso/9780197548813.003.0010

engagement was about to begin and to distract and intimidate the entrenched Iraqi enemies inside the city. Contrary to some cinematic depictions, troops were not to be accompanied by songs during actual firefights, much less listen to personal playlists through earbuds, at moments when hearing superiors' commands or the gunshots of concealed snipers was all-important. Before moving in to an opposing stronghold, however, the ominous tolling of "Hells Bells," Angus Young's slow arpeggios, and Brian Johnson's announcement that he would take no prisoners and spare no lives were potent parts of the arsenal. A spokesman for the American forces explained, "It's not so much the music as the sound. It's like throwing a smoke bomb. The aim is to disorient and confuse the enemy to gain a tactical advantage."[2] Music had always been part of warfare, of course, with everything from trumpets and drums to bagpipes and human battle cries used to stimulate soldiers and terrify their enemies—but rock 'n' roll was different, wasn't it?

Not much, in fact. In the same way that the medium had already proven as appealing to the silent majority as to the student demonstrators, and to the southern crackers as much as the northern cosmopolitans, rock 'n' roll could be enjoyed by hawks as well as doves. When Elvis Presley was drafted into the US Army in 1958, rebellious pop singers were proven perfectly amenable to the dictates of the Cold War. Elvis did his hitch and won the respect of his fellow servicemen for doing ordinary recruit duty instead of opting for detail as camp entertainment. A young Jimi Hendrix served as an Army paratrooper; one-hit R&B act the Essex ("Easier Said Than Done," 1963) had formed as Marines stationed in Okinawa; country outlaw Kris Kristofferson had trained as a helicopter pilot for US forces in Germany; Johnny Cash served in the US Air Force, and both Everly Brothers joined the Marine Corps reserves in 1961; Rolling Stones bassist Bill Wyman did two years in the Royal Air Force in the 1950s; John Fogerty and Doug Clifford each trained as Army reservists before forming Creedence Clearwater Revival. There was nothing inherently incompatible about rock musicians toting guns and marching on parade.

Wide opposition to the Vietnam war among young people had skewed the popular perception of their lingua franca of rock 'n' roll as anti-military. Rock-listening young men who grew their hair long in 1967 were obligated to have it shorn if they were conscripted; presumably their musical tastes were to be likewise severely trimmed. Classics like Dylan's "Masters of War," the Beatles' "All You Need Is Love," Joni Mitchell and CSNY's "Woodstock," the Original Caste's AM success "One Tin Soldier," and John Lennon's "Give Peace a Chance" solidified the music's status as inspirational hymns for protesters, deserters, and draft dodgers. Yet many more willing recruits brought their civilian entertainment with them and saw no contradiction between cranking tunes and carrying out orders. In Vietnam and wherever American and other Western nations' troops were deployed afterward, rock became a staple element of R & R, and its philosophies—and sometimes its actual recordings—saw operational duty. Draftees in rice paddies in the late 1960s brought tapes of psychedelia with them, as recounted by Michael Herr in *Dispatches*: "I suddenly heard an electric guitar shooting right up in my ear and a mean, rapturous black voice singing, coaxing . . . and when I got it all together I turned to see a grinning black corporal hunched over a cassette recorder. 'Might's well,' he said. 'We ain' goin' *no*where till them gunships come.' "[3] US warplanes and helicopters flew over Indochina bearing customized nose art like "Good Vibrations," "The Crystal Ship," "In a Gadda da Vida," and "Iron Butterfly," while in subsequent decades attack aircraft over the Persian Gulf were painted with the "War Pig" insignia.

During the 1970s and 1980s, large contingents of NATO troops were on permanent standby in Western Europe, squaring off against the armies of the Warsaw Pact, and while there they and their families formed a ready-made audience for rock 'n' roll acts touring Britain, France, West Germany, Italy, and the Netherlands. Alex Lifeson of Rush remembered the lucrative market of the era: "Britain was always the main thing, and in Germany, you know, there were so many American and Canadian troops stationed there—even British troops—that you could play a place like Frankfurt and do good business and have good crowd of ten thousand, eleven thousand people."[4] No incongruity between guarding freedom and banging heads was detected; teenage military brats grew up with tandem role models in the martial honor of their parents and the guitar heroism of Lifeson, Angus Young, or Jimmy Page. Later in the 1980s, syndicated North American radio shows *High Voltage* and *Metal Shop* were sponsored by recruiters from the US Army, so that adolescent fans heard slick ads touting the adventure and male bonding of the military in between the latest cuts by Ozzy, Priest, or the Crüe. Over the years, the messages of the music and the promotional drives blurred into each other.

In 1968 Godfather of Soul James Brown became the only really hip musical act to perform for soldiers in Vietnam through the United Service Organization, when most self-respecting rock and soul artists were opposed to everything military as a matter of course. Times had changed by 2010, though, when the USO brought prominent nu-metal bands Five Finger Death Punch and Avenged Sevenfold to Iraq for the entertainment of men and women in uniform. "I think everyone in the band has had someone that's served in their family," Avenged Sevenfold's vocalist M. Shadows told an interviewer. "Both of my grandfathers were in the military. But I also have a lot of friends who, out of high school, went into the Navy, some went into the

Marines, some went into the Army. . . . Those men and women over in Iraq and Kuwait and different parts of the world, defending our country, they're people we grew up with. They're from *our* generation. So we figured we could go over there and entertain them. It's the least we could do while they're in harm's way."[5] Armed Forces Entertainment, a branch of the US Air Force, also solicited lesser-known rock acts to perform in bases outside the secure Green Zone of Baghdad. Niki Barr of Baltimore's Niki Barr Band told *Rolling Stone* that her experience playing to scared service personnel, where sounds of explosions and low-flying aircraft accompanied the music, "has definitely made me more patriotic to go over there and see these guys. Politics aside, they're just serving."[6] In Iraq during the first years of the millennium, young soldiers had the same assumptions of unlimited access to private stocks of entertainment as any young American civilian back home. "Back in Vietnam you had those doing recreational drugs on one side and the heavy drinking on another," Sgt. Daniel Kartchien was quoted in the press. "Here [in a Muslim nation] there's no alcohol involved. And drugs aren't the thing anymore. Everybody has their own MP3 player to pass the time."[7] Country, rap, hip-hop, pop, heavy metal, rock 'n' roll—all of it was picked and played by warriors carrying out Operation Iraqi Freedom.

Conflict in the Persian Gulf occurred as a new set of perceptions of popular music came into play. The end of the US-led Cold War against a superpower adversary and the consequent loss of at least a vague national purpose uniting ages, classes, and political persuasions ushered in an era of "culture wars": internal fissures between societal groups whose superficial differences had hitherto been mostly discounted but who now stood in stark demographic contrast to each other. Rock 'n' roll was suddenly in the unfamiliar position of being an established folkway rather than a controversial fad. Testifying before a US Senate committee on "obscene" pop records in 1986, Frank Zappa had declared, "Rock music is not written or performed for conservative tastes. It was not designed for easy listening for mom and dad."[8] As America's baby boom generation matured into parental or governmental responsibility, though, its preferred music began to win official sanctions inconceivable thirty or forty years earlier.

In 1988 Democratic presidential candidate Michael Dukakis had used singer-songwriter Neil Diamond's 1980 piece "America" as a campaign theme, while his Republican opponent, George H. W. Bush, employed the inflammatory race-baiting tactics of strategist Lee Atwater, who'd performed as a semiprofessional blues guitarist. In 1992 President Bush was defeated at the polls by Bill Clinton, who carefully sidestepped questions about his 1960s youth, when he'd tried marijuana but did not inhale and avoided conscription in the

US draft; candidate Clinton played a saxophone rendition of Elvis Presley's "Heartbreak Hotel" during a talk show appearance and blared Fleetwood Mac's bubbly 1977 hit "Don't Stop" at rallies. From then on rock music was certified patriotic. Clinton's 1996 rival Bob Dole, although a World War II veteran, adopted Sam and Dave's 1967 groove "Soul Man" as "Dole Man" to play at his own events, and Al Gore supporters were rocked by Bachman-Turner Overdrive's crunching "You Ain't Seen Nothing Yet" during the 2000 race, against George W. Bush appropriating "I Won't Back Down" by Tom Petty (in another precedent, Petty soon denied permission for the song's use as an implicit endorsement). Into 2008, GOP vice presidential hopeful Sarah Palin was stirring her own campaign stops with recordings of Heart's Zeppelinesque "Barracuda"—once again, the band issued a legal objection.

One of the most important political figures to spread a message through rock 'n' roll was not even running for office. Talk radio host Rush Limbaugh, who'd once worked as a regular platter-spinning DJ, had by the early 1990s built a major broadcast audience pontificating on the evils of big government, feminism, environmentalism, the welfare state, and all things supposedly liberal, while playing a variety of rock tunes as intros and segues during his weekday program. According to a rock legend that should be true if it isn't, Limbaugh was the first to broadcast Alice Cooper's frustrated-youth anthem "I'm Eighteen" in the United States, twenty years prior; now he was inserting snatches of T. Rex's "Bang a Gong (Get It On), Jimi Hendrix's "Purple Haze," Bob Seger's "The Fire Inside," and other tracks to fire up his diatribes against the sex, drug, and rock 'n' roll ethos. Some of the musicians were dismayed to hear their songs bolstering right-wing opinion, notably Chrissie Hynde, the songwriter of the Pretenders' "My City Was Gone," adapted into the show's theme. The radio provocateur knew what he was doing when he picked the Pretenders cut, which lamented the transformation of Hynde's Ohio home town by shopping malls and parking lots. "It is anti-development, anti-capitalist," he chortled. "Here I am going to take a liberal song and make fun of [liberals] at the same time."[9] Hynde, for her part, was an animal-rights activist on the other side of most positions held by Limbaugh and his audience, yet she understood that there was little to be gained by blocking the host's use of her work. "Rock music was once political and countercultural," she conceded. "Now music is music. The whole of popular culture has gone more mainstream. And even conservatives want to be hip."[10]

That politicians and pundits, even conservative ones, were basking in the reflected coolness of rock 'n' roll represented a major victory in the culture wars. But a victory for whom? From the 1980s onward the worldwide entertainment industry had grown into a vast economic driver in which the spontaneity of the artists' inspirations and the unpredictability of the audience's responses had been meticulously plotted out of the business. Rock and its variants could be as edgy or "alternative" as the market allowed, but the demands of the market were more paramount than ever. This was especially true with the advent of music videos, as recordings became only one piece of the overall product line. "Gangsta rappers think they are using rock to take on the official culture," wrote Benjamin Barber of pop's edgiest genre in 1995's *Jihad vs. McWorld*. "But of course the official culture owns them rock, stock, and barrel and it is they who are being used. The point is neither the words nor even the music, but the pictures as they image the music and the big sell that goes with the pictures. . . . It is hard to know exactly what, beyond simple consumption, the impact of selling ambience by promoting rock music will be either in America or on the hundred cultures whose youth are now tuned in to it."[11] In 1997 it was estimated that most popular music (and related television programming) in the world was owned, produced, and distributed by just six multinational corporations. Bruce Springsteen's label of Columbia was an asset of the Japanese firm Sony; John Mellencamp's *Lonesome Jubilee* made profits for Mercury, a subsidiary of Polygram, itself a division the Dutch conglomerate Philips Electronics.

This postindustrial realignment of makers and consumers was reflected in the leanings of rock 'n' roll's public constituency. For one thing, the numerical buying power of the baby boomers meant that acts from the 1960s and 1970s continued as viable attractions long after their creative and physical primes. In the 1990s the Rolling Stones, Pink Floyd, the Grateful Dead, and other bands who'd been making discs for a quarter century, were competing strongly against new performers and styles; adult fans with secure incomes were sustaining the music through purchasing tickets to see the surviving members in huge, expensive concerts and tuning in to the widespread FM radio format of classic rock. In the same way that golden oldies stations and Rock 'n' Roll Revival tours had defanged the formerly menacing implications of Bill Haley or Little Richard, classic rock was, in its turn, tamed by the passage of time. The technological development of compact discs also boosted sales of recordings first issued during the Summer of Love or Watergate, as scratchy vinyl copies were replaced with sleek plastic editions of the same albums. Middle-aged musicians (or their legal beneficiaries) were living off fortunes generated by flashes of brilliance they'd experienced at twenty-four. The human instinct to relive one's past was a big part of all this, but more so was the mindset of perennial youth that rock 'n' roll had itself encouraged in its initial followers. Nostalgia was for old folks, said nostalgic baby boomers.

Yet the younger generations ensuring the commerciality of classic rockers, and in some cases extending their artistic influence, were themselves growing up in very different circumstances than those of the legends. People who'd been children when Lynyrd Skynyrd's plane went down or Bon Scott passed out for the last time had access to an almost limitless range of entertainment in various convenient media but far fewer hopes of attaining lifelong jobs or single-family homes. Statistics revealed sharp declines in income among young American white males between 1973 and 1986, with especially precipitous drops for those without college or high school degrees. Though many millionaire rock stars of the baby boom had been raised among scarce material comforts, they had nonetheless lived in a comparatively wealthy era of postwar growth—their latest followers, in contrast, were surrounded by stuff but scrambled for meaningful employment in a remade service economy. It was indicative of the changes in labor and industry that whereas Tony Iommi and Ozzy Osbourne had each held positions in Birmingham factories before forming Black Sabbath, Metallica, Sabbath's heirs apparent of the 1980s, were fronted by James Hetfield, who'd worked in fast-food restaurants in his native California. Metallica eventually paid tribute to their common-man forefathers by releasing covers of Sabbath's "Sabbra Cadabra," Thin Lizzy's "Whiskey in the Jar," Budgie's "Breadfan," Bob Seger's "Turn the Page," and even Skynyrd's "Tuesday's Gone." "All the equipment I ever got, I had to pay for, through really bad jobs like working in Burger King and washing dishes,"[12] Hetfield recalled. Of his main inspiration, the Metallica leader spoke for many fans of his age and wage slot: "Sabbath was everything that the Sixties weren't. Their music was so cool because it was completely anti-hippie. I hated the Beatles, Jethro Tull, Love, and all that other happy shit."[13]

The disparity between more- and less-credentialed young citizens was manifested in their favorite music. The pre-Internet 1990s were the peak years of the "alternative" sound, as acts who had descended from punk's first wave were sold as smarter, more socially aware artists distinct from the Neanderthal fist-pumpers of heavy metal or the bland crooners of pop. Jane's Addiction, the Cure, the Jesus and Mary Chain, Belle and Sebastian, the Pixies, PJ Harvey, and the platinum-selling Pearl Jam and Nirvana were for the bright kids; Metallica was for the burger flippers. But like the original punks of an earlier time, alternative performers became associated with an educated elite rather than the truly disenfranchised they claimed to come from and sing for. The popular MTV show *Beavis and Butt-Head*, creator Mike Judge's cartoon series about two dimwitted adolescents whose main activity was lying around commenting on rock videos, had the boys deriding what they called "college music." In the show, which ran from 1993 to 1997, Beavis wore a

Metallica logo on his clothes, while his friend Butt-Head's touted AC/DC. College rock—Archers of Loaf, the Flaming Lips, and others whose works were critiqued by the pair—was the cerebral, ostentatiously underground music played on campus radio stations by student DJs who were by definition destined for better careers and lives than—well, than Beavis and Butt-Head. "College music sucks," Beavis says when an Oingo Boingo video appears. "I think it's only cool if you, like, go to college," Butt-Head agrees. The joke was that teenagers like Beavis and Butt-Head were too stupid to recognize their own stupidity, but on another level the episodes satirized the widening socio-economic gap between television-dazed suburbanites who held unskilled jobs at Burger World and the smaller strata of citizens who could afford to cultivate an appreciation for Oingo Boingo or the Flaming Lips. College music may have sucked, but the prospects of its listeners didn't.

Pop music articulated still another division in American society from the 1980s and beyond, this one even more revealing than the one exposed by Beavis and Butt-Head. It was not without precedent. Since rock 'n' roll had come to dominate the industry, there had been a handful of well-known songs espousing, unusually, conservative principles: in 1966 alone there was the Beatles' fiscally libertarian "Taxman," the Rolling Stones' quietly threatening assertion of male prerogative "Under My Thumb," and Paul Revere & the Raiders' anti-drug "Kicks," and Staff Sergeant Barry Sadler of the US Army Special Forces had a surprise no. 1 American hit with the patriotic "Ballad of the Green Berets," in praise of the Special Forces soldiers serving in the increasingly fraught Vietnam War. By the end of the decade the specialized genre of Christian rock was also purveying religious messages in the youthful idiom of guitars and drums, after the release of Larry Norman's influential *Upon This Rock* album in 1969 and the Explo '72 gathering in Dallas, characterized as a Christian Woodstock. Christian rock and eventually even Christian metal won over a small but viable slice of the record-buying public thereafter. Frank Zappa's 1986 argument that rock was never meant for conservatives rang more hollow every year. So the 1994 release of the single "Get Over It," a denunciation of political correctness and the cult of victimhood by reunited folk rockers the Eagles (of all people), was hardly the first time opinions held mostly on the right had been expressed in a medium assumed to be mostly by and for the left.

The most dramatic example of rock's upended politics, however, was heard from Guns n' Roses. A Los Angeles–based outfit that was at first just one of many Sunset Strip hair metal bands, GNR parlayed a series of media provocations into massive commercial success from their 1987 debut *Appetite for Destruction*, to *G N' R Lies* the following year, and then the hugely hyped two-disc event of 1991, *Use Your Illusion I* and *II*. Musically, Guns n' Roses were closer to the bluesy riffing of classic Thin Lizzy or AC/DC, or even the acoustic departures of Queen or Led Zeppelin, than they were to the modern gothic densities of Megadeth or Slayer. "Nighttrain," "You Could Be Mine," the epic ballads "Don't Cry" and "November Rain," the radio staple "Sweet Child O' Mine," and the feed-the-rich, bury-the-poor accusations of "Civil War" were finely chiseled hard rock. But their real distinction was in how they and their overseers at the Geffen label exploited contemporary content standards to generate publicity through their scandalous album art (*Appetite* showed an illustration of a semi-nude ravaged woman), profane lyrics ("You're Crazy," "It's So Easy," "Mr. Brownstone," "Out ta Get Me," "Get in the Ring," "Bad Obsession," and "Reckless Life" each contained variations on the word *fuck*), and relatively open enjoyment of alcohol and hard drugs (backstage at some shows they were obliged to keep their bad influence quarantined away from freshly sober headline act Aerosmith). Calculated though the danger plainly was, it was all "controversial" and thus lapped up by the rock and mainstream press. Other GNR material conveyed a bitch-slap misogyny uglier than any older rockers', like "Welcome to the Jungle," "Anything Goes," "Rocket Queen," "Nice Boys," "Back Off Bitch," "Locomotive," "Pretty Tied Up," and the infamous "Used to Love Her," wherein vocalist Axl Rose recounted murdering a female partner and burying her in his backyard, where he could still hear her complain. The records sold tens of millions of copies. Guns n' Roses broke down a lot of barriers, but there was nothing progressive about them.

The band's most inflammatory song was "One in a Million," the closing track on *Lies*. Ostensibly a story of Rose's arrival in LA from his Indiana home, where he was harassed in the bus terminal by an assortment of big-city denizens, the piece voiced the singer's equal resentments toward "police and niggers" and "immigrants and faggots" and his admission that he was but a small-town white boy trying to make ends meet. *Billboard* later called "One in a Million" "a piece of racist, gay-bashing garbage,"[14] and for journalists, activists, and sociologists, GNR and "One in a Million" became the go-to examples of popular music's conclusive turn away from the communitarian values of the 1960s. Rap music also used racist, anti-Semitic, homophobic, and quasi-pornographic language, with acts such as Public Enemy and Heavy D and the Boyz cited alongside the Gunners in the news furor. In 1989 the Simon Wiesenthal Center's Canadian division ran advertisements denouncing the "growing manifestation of racist lyrics" in works by rappers and Guns n' Roses, with director Sol Littman commenting, "Any oppressed group certainly has a right to sing about their wants and their needs, but it's another thing to sic one group of Americans on another group of Americans."[15]

In an article titled "There's a New Sound in Pop Music: Bigotry," the *New York Times* referenced the Guns n' Roses song and quoted Bard College professor Joel Kovel: "The need in our society to express identity by excluding others has always been very, very strong. With the decline of the cold war, demonizing the Soviets doesn't carry the symbolic weight it used to, and there's a resurgence of more old-fashioned nativism and racism."[16] Media consultant John Parikhal of Joint Communications suggested "One in a Million" and its like were merely symptoms of a much wider set of problems that dated back to the winding down of the postwar boom in the mid-1970s. "It used to be that if you put your head down and were a good person, you got a good job and were assured of a roof over your head. Nothing's certain any more. Popular music is only reflecting the world around it. Something close to two thousand years of tradition have fallen apart in a fifteen-year span with nothing to replace it."[17]

Such coverage, of course, fed Guns n' Roses' popularity and thus indulged more affronts to civility. Bryn Bridenthal of Geffen Records admitted, "Guns n' Roses have a lot of power because they've sold a lot of records."[18] The group's label head, David Geffen, was gay, its lead guitarist Slash (Saul Hudson) was of mixed Black and white parentage and an immigrant from Britain, and bassist Duff McKagan's brother was married to a Black woman. "There's a line in that song, 'police and niggers,' that I didn't want Axl to sing," Slash said later. "But Axl's the kind of person who will sing whatever it is that he feels like singing."[19] In a 1989 *Rolling Stone* interview at the height of his fame, Axl Rose denied any deep-seated prejudices and said "One in a Million" was based on his real experiences with predatory men and African Americans. At the Los Angeles Greyhound depot, he said, "There are a large number of black men selling stolen jewelry, crack, heroin and pot, and most of the drugs are bogus. . . . Trying to misguide every kid that gets off the bus and doesn't quite know where he's at or where to go, trying to take the person for whatever they've got. That's how I hit town." His use of racial slurs? "Why can black people go up to each other and say, 'nigger,' but when a white guy does it all of a sudden it's a big put-down?" he asked. "I used the word 'nigger' to describe somebody that is basically a pain in your life, a problem. The word 'nigger' doesn't necessarily mean black." His anti-immigrant lines? "I've been chased out of a store with Slash by a six-foot-tall Iranian with a butcher knife because he didn't like the way we were dressed. Scared me to death." The word "faggots"? "I've had some very bad experiences with homosexuals. When I was first coming to Los Angeles, I was about eighteen or nineteen. On my first hitchhiking ride, this guy told me I could crash at his hotel. I went to sleep and woke up while this guy was trying to rape me. . . . That's why I have the attitude I have."[20] In a subsequent explanation he said that the verses were "a way for me to express my anger at how vulnerable l felt in certain situations that had gone down in my life."[21] On the mock-tabloid cover copy of *Lies*, Rose offered preemptive contrition for his song's take on cops, Blacks, gay people, and new Americans: "Ever been unjustly hassled by someone with a gun and a badge? . . . Been to a gas station or convenience store and treated like you don't belong here by an individual who can barely speak English? Hopefully not, but have you ever been attacked by a homosexual? . . . This song is very simple . . . my apologies to those who may take offense."[22] "One in a Million," in its hick midwestern perspective, anticipated America's future as a minority-majority nation, where even decadent blond rock singers like Axl Rose were no more advantaged than vast numbers of other citizens unlike and unimpressed with them.

Substance issues and personal clashes gradually undermined Guns n' Roses' stature as the biggest hard rock act of their time—Axl Rose himself became notorious for concert no-shows and was arrested for inciting a riot at an appearance in St. Louis—but they continued to stir sensational press into their twilight. A 1993 album, *The Spaghetti Incident?* consisted mostly of cover songs, including the Stooges' "Raw Power" and a knockout version of Nazareth's "Hair of the Dog," but it was the bonus track, "Look at Your Game, Girl," which attracted the most condemnation: the piece was written by Charles Manson in 1968, back when Manson was just a hopeful singer-songwriter and not yet convicted of conspiracy to commit mass murders. Copies of Manson's demo tape for "Look at Your Game, Girl" had circulated underground for years, but its appropriation on *The Spaghetti Incident?* raised the possibility that the incarcerated killer might be entitled to substantial royalties from sales of Guns n' Roses' latest record. It was around this time that Rose also appeared at GNR concerts wearing a T-shirt illustrated with Manson's instantly recognizable image, and it was hard to forget that Manson was a white supremacist who had instigated his slaughters in a bid to precipitate a Black-white race war. Some fans spread rumors that Rose's chosen initials, W. A. R., did not represent William Axl Rose (his original name was actually William Bruce Bailey) but White Aryan Resistance. Given the flurry of shocks and outrages contrived around the brief career of Guns n' Roses, the story seemed more than plausible.

Insofar as rock 'n' roll was now exhibiting an intolerance or a chauvinism that would once have seemed out of place in its canon, country music was well ahead of it. Where only the most emboldened country acts had just started to venture political views across a left-right spectrum a few years earlier, many artists had become proudly right-wing from the 1980s onward. Country singers were trumpeting their social alignment with no apologies, in Hank

Williams Jr.'s "A Country Boy Can Survive" in 1982, the Bellamy Brothers' "Redneck Girl" the same year, Lee Greenwood's "God Bless the USA" in 1983, Charlie Daniels's "(What the World Needs Is) A Few More Rednecks" in 1985, Billy Ray Cyrus's tribute to American veterans "Some Gave All" in 1992, Joe Diffie's "Honky Tonk Attitude" in 1993, Sammy Kershaw's gently joking "Queen of My Double-Wide Trailer" in 1993, and Brooks & Dunn's "Redneck Rhythm & Blues" in 1996. Red State righteousness was now a prime lyrical (and in music videos visual) ingredient of the genre, the old themes reduced to flags, bumper stickers, and T-shirt slogans. Any complicated sentiments about nationalism, freedom, and class that had ever been sung by outlaws Merle Haggard, Johnny Cash, Kris Kristofferson, or Waylon Jennings were all but inaudible in the corporatized, televised, digitized lifestyle accessory country music had become.

Yet in deteriorating into just another consumer trinket, country was merely ahead of the cultural wave. The other great American musical forms of the twentieth century, jazz and blues, had themselves decisively ceded commercial primacy to rock 'n' roll by the late 1960s and had survived less by evolving organically than by preserving and amplifying the broadest stylistic elements people already expected from them. In the case of country, so many acts had borrowed from rock's artistic and career devices that the medium became barely recognizable as country: superstar Garth Brooks said he'd been influenced by the grandiose concert spectacles of Kiss, and Shania Twain's multiplatinum records *The Woman in Me* (1995) and *Come On Over* (1997) were produced by her then-husband, Mutt Lange, who'd had comparable successes producing AC/DC's *Highway to Hell* and *Back in Black*. Typical hit country singles like Twain's "Any Man of Mine" or "Man! I Feel Like a Woman" were arranged less and less like the Nashville pop of Patsy Cline or Ray Price and more like Lynyrd Skynyrd or 38 Special, meshing electric guitars and heavy drums with pseudo-rural dialects and the clomp of cowboy boots. What remained, then, was not so much a particular order of popular song but a self-identifying subculture of which particular popular songs were only one component. Evangelical Christianity, college football, and NASCAR racing were no less part of the subculture's spending and voting patterns, all of which demarcated it with equal obviousness. Country music had been made freshly relevant by the outlaws in the 1970s, but the fans who responded to it in later decades were made relevant—whether they realized it or not—by a nexus of money, opinion polls, and exploitation that was anything but outlaw.

Even in rock 'n' roll, it was not just music like Guns n' Roses' "One in a Million" or the Eagles' "Get Over It" but some musicians who were tenuously linked to a hodgepodge of conservative positions. Detecting a political message that could be extrapolated from song lyrics was one thing; the songwriters themselves demonstrating their politics in public was another. In the Just Say No era a few rock stars had contributed to anti-drug promotional campaigns—among them Gene Simmons of Kiss, Jon Bon Jovi of Bon Jovi, Belinda Carlisle of the Go-Gos, and Dee Snider of the pop-metal act Twisted Sister—and the Beach Boys accepted an invitation to Ronald Reagan's White House after Reagan's secretary of the interior, James Watt, gracelessly banned the group from performing at the Washington Mall's Fourth of July events. In 1996, Geri Halliwell, "Ginger Spice" of pop sensations the Spice Girls, said that Margaret Thatcher had been a role model for their trademarked Girl Power. "We Spice Girls are true Thatcherites," she was quoted as saying. "Thatcher was the first Spice Girl, the pioneer of our ideology."[23] The next year a comment from Phil Collins before a British national election ("If they put up taxes, I'd consider going abroad")[24] was taken as a criticism of the Labor Party's platform, and Collins subsequently did emigrate to Switzerland for a time.

But easily the most prominent of the right-wing rockers was the Motor City Madman, Ted Nugent. Though his most memorable music was well behind him by the 1990s, Nugent maintained a consistent career with a short spell in the supergroup Damn Yankees (featuring guitarist Tommy Shaw of Styx and bassist Jack Blades of Night Ranger) and regular concert appearances in his old stomping grounds of the North American heartland. In a 1987 profile in *Guitar World* magazine, he described himself as "an uninhibited Chuck Berry devotee who has experimented with and broke a lot of ground in the area of feedback and solid variations in tonal and dissonant utilizations. I'm one of the best guitarists in the world, and I play with great emotion."[25] With the Damn Yankees, part of his live routine included using for target practice a cardboard cutout of America's latest archenemy, Iraqi dictator Saddam Hussein, with the archery gear he toted onstage. Nugent's staunch refusal of the drugs and alcohol that had destroyed or debilitated many other performers of his generation also aided his longevity, a point on which he did not hesitate to boast. "I was ridiculed and outcast by some of the people that I had great respect for in music," he said. "They made fun of me because I wouldn't smoke their dope, and because I carried a gun and went hunting. They thought it was dangerous to carry a gun but cool to get high. Now they're dead, and I'm still Ted. I never needed their kind of danger."[26] That he was healthy and well-spoken enough to present his views in public made him an amusing figure on talk shows and in music magazines—the long-haired, sex-obsessed rock performer who had the political leanings of Rush Limbaugh—until the views began to go from eccentric to unsettling.

Nugent had authored a first book, *Blood Trails: The Truth about Bowhunting*, in 1991, a short manual in which he told stories of his outdoor experiences and offered technical tips to fellow sportsmen. His 2000 title, however, capitalized on the confrontational persona he had developed outside of his concerts: *God, Guns, and Rock 'n' Roll*. With gun control now a major wedge issue in American debate, especially after mass shootings in California, Oklahoma, and Texas and at Columbine High School in Colorado shocked the country, Nugent's position on the right to bear arms made him a natural spokesman for the pro-gun lobby. In this role he started to lose some fans who liked his music but not his values, yet he was hardly fazed by the desertions. Ever since his song "Stormtroopin'" in 1975, he had cast himself as a defiant fighter against intrusive governments bent on taking away law-abiding citizens' weapons, and so his appearances on CBS, CNN, and particularly the renegade cable network of Fox News invariably delivered a compelling few minutes of TV—Nugent was already a professional entertainer, so he was adept at going on air and hogging the microphone to promote his brand of personal liberty, drowning out and rolling over any guests who happened to be booked against him. In *God, Guns, and Rock 'n' Roll* his messages even carried coded appeals as yet too harsh for television: "I grew up in the shadows of Detroit City, for God's sake," the book read. "What kind of spineless dolt would dare venture forth virtually incapable of wiping his or her nose or surviving the vicious predator mentality of the paroled masses on the planet of the apes? Not I, sayeth the guitarboy. Want my car? Come and get it, Cornelius."[27] Nugent later authored a sequel to *Blood Trails*, plus *Kill It and Grill It: A Guide to Preparing and Cooking Wild Game and Fish*, and a 2010 work, *Ted, White, and Blue: The Nugent Manifesto*, all of which played well to the specialty market he'd attracted beyond the music store and the arena.

Indeed, so devoted were fans to Nugent's political spiels that some floated the possibility that he could mount a successful election campaign—for governor of his home state of Michigan, perhaps, or New Mexico. Nugent demurred, citing his continued schedule of outdoor expeditions, charity work, and performances. Being Ted Nugent had become something of his full-time business, including retailing branded merchandise at gigs and on his website and making himself available for meet-and-greets and as a paid leader of celebrity trophy hunts. Of course, there was also the 1977 *High Times* article in which he claimed to have dodged the US draft through shitting his pants that dogged his latter-day reputation, as well as his confirmed paternity of nine children by several different women over the course of marriages and short liaisons from his years as a touring rock 'n' roller. "It was a source of such hysterical outrage, and the guy interviewing me was such a stoned inept idiot,"[28] Nugent said, explaining that his confessions to *High Times* were all a big gag. One ex-partner, Pele Massa, came forward to assert that Nugent had signed on to be her legal guardian when she was seventeen years old and he was thirty, allowing them to lawfully cohabitate *Lolita*-style. "I'm a human being and in fact I'm a perfect human being because I stumble perfectly," the guitarist said of his affairs and unexpected offspring. "And if you're going to stumble, you know what I recommend? Stumble sexually."[29] How much the Republican faithful—let alone Democrat opponents—could have accepted such indiscretions in Ted Nugent the candidate, rather than Ted Nugent the outrageous aging rock star and conservative pundit, remained unknown.

The flux of politics and pop music grew yet more bewildering with the rise of white rappers Eminem and Kid Rock. Since its emergence in the late 1970s and commercial breakthrough the next decade, rap had been generally heard as an African American medium, communicating the experience of urban Black youth in an improvised sonic and lyrical language exclusive to the culture. Like jazz, blues, and rock 'n' roll before it, however, soon enough rap was adapted and further popularized by white acts—in 1986 the Beastie Boys' *Licensed to Ill* became the first rap album by artists of any color to reach the no. 1 *Billboard* sales rank, and the Black act Run-DMC's hit collaboration with Aerosmith on a rap version of "Walk This Way" the same year both boosted Run-DMC's career and revived Aerosmith's. But rap had also been specified as the music of the belligerent, criminal subset of Black males, a form of expression white listeners might freely enjoy but could never authentically duplicate. The successes of Eminem and Kid Rock undermined this truism.

Born Marshall Mathers in Missouri but raised in the Rust Belt wastelands around Detroit, Eminem became the most controversial music star of the era, following the release of his albums *The Slim Shady LP* (1999), *The Marshall Mathers LP* (2000), and *The Eminem Show* (2002). There was no denying his talent and his passion for hip-hop, which he'd learned as a white kid growing up in a mostly Black environment. "As soon as I grabbed the mike, I'd get booed," he said of his early appearances at local amateur competitions. "Once motherfuckers heard me rhyme, though, they'd shut up."[30] Even in a category known for offensive lyrics, Eminem's corrosive raps on murder, rape, and hatred drew the ire of conservative politicians and liberal activists: "Kim" (about killing his wife), "'97 Bonnie and Clyde" (about burying her corpse), "Kill You" (about killing everyone else, including bitches, sluts, whores, and faggots) were typical thematic explorations. Eminem's millions of fans justified his work as cartoon scenarios whose extremes of mayhem and vulgarity were themselves the underlying joke; others pointed out how his squalid background of family trauma, minimum-wage employment, and pharmaceutical abuse had made him a representative white American of his generation, a perspective he confronted in *The Slim Shady LP*'s "Rock Bottom" and "If I Had," and *The Eminem Show*'s "White America." "Just seeing the cycle of dysfunction in our family—my little brother went through a lot, court systems and being taken away by the state and child-protective services coming out—and I just wanted to do good to pull him out of it," he reflected on the ambitions that launched him. "Like if I don't do something now, I'm gonna be caught in the same sort of cycle of dysfunction that the rest of my family is in."[31] Comedians compared Eminem to fairway phenomenon Tiger Woods, cracking that times had definitely become strange when the biggest golfer in the world was Black and the biggest rapper was white.

"When I say, 'I've got love for my honkies' in my songs, I'm not saying I don't have love for anybody else," said Kid Rock in 1999, quoting his rap on the title track from his 1998 *Devil Without a Cause* album. "I'm just saying, 'Hey, man, it's all right to be white.'"[32] Kid Rock, who'd gone by the deeply ordinary name Bob Ritchie until his teens, was another Michigan Caucasian who, like Eminem, rode a wave of bad-good publicity to become another hoe-cursing and homophobic hip-hop star defying the genre's racial conventions. Unlike Eminem, though, Kid Rock's background was relatively prosperous—his father owned a car dealership—and his music often borrowed from styles outside rap. In concert he interspersed measures of "Fortunate Son" and Grand Funk Railroad's "We're an American Band" in and between his familiar hits "Bawitdaba" and "Cowboy," and in his "American Badass," from 2001's *Cocky*, he specified that he liked AC/DC, ZZ Top, Bob Seger, and Johnny Cash as much as he liked Grandmaster Flash. Kid Rock came by his African American influences honestly, as recounted in his autobiographical teen story "Black Chick, White Guy," from 1996's *Early Mornin' Stoned Pimp*, but he also exemplified the outlook of young white Americans for whom coexistence didn't mean capitulation. Over time his songs integrated rock and country elements more freely with those of rap, peaking with 2007's worldwide hit "All Summer Long," which sampled the D–C–G chord progression shared by Warren Zevon's "Werewolves of London" and Lynyrd Skynyrd's "Sweet Home Alabama." In Kid Rock's wake his formula of blending the lyrical bluster and vocal cadences of hip-hop with the instrumentation of heavy metal brought success to several other white acts, including Linkin Park, Limp Bizkit, and Detroit's Insane Clown Posse.

Again, white rappers weren't catering to a sense of racial solidarity; plenty of non-Black kids like the young Marshall Mathers had gotten into NWA, for instance, the way their older siblings had taken to Michael Jackson or their parents to Stevie Wonder. Eminem himself was often compared to Elvis Presley, as a breakout star from the sticks who desegregated one form of popular culture by doing it as well as its originators in the inner city. Kid Rock, too, was realistic enough to claim that he hadn't come straight outta Compton but straight outta the trailer. Rap's acceptance by white fans and appropriation by white artists, rather, meant that there was a white population who related to rap's anger and its underclass affectations. The popular 1998 single "What It's Like," a brooding acoustic rap-rock hybrid by Everlast aka Whitey Ford aka Erik Schrody, described a series of contemporary victims whose color was irrelevant to their problems: a homeless beggar at the liquor store, a pregnant girl braving the protesters outside the abortion clinic, a young man caught up in the thug life of drugs and guns. This was not the same as when university students took to folk music in the early 1960s or when sci-fi buffs from the suburbs discovered prog rock in the 1970s, or for that matter when flappers danced to Louis Armstrong in 1928 or sock-hoppers twisted to Chubby Checker in 1960. Rap's acceptance across racial lines was both a testament to social progress (it doesn't matter what you look like, the rhymes are for everyone) and an indictment of social decline (the same landscape of violence, crime, poverty, and amorality that rap charted was now occupied by a rainbow coalition).

The decline accelerated with the historic crises that beset the United States and the world from the first months of the new millennium. George W. Bush was awarded the American presidency despite a bitterly contested ballot count; Islamic militants destroyed New York City's World Trade Center on September 11, 2001, killing thousands and spurring a potentially endless international War on Terror; President Bush launched an ill-considered US invasion of Iraq in 2003; a global financial meltdown in 2008 provoked the worst economic contraction since the Great Depression; and the election of Barack Obama as the first Black president of the United States in 2008 revealed the profound and sometimes ugly depths of polarization within American society. Rock 'n' roll figured in the catastrophes early on. At the Concert for New York City on October 20, 2001, an all-star lineup of show business and political celebrities played in tribute to the dead office staffers and emergency personnel; among the performances were John Mellencamp and Kid Rock's duet on "Pink Houses" and Mick Jagger and Keith Richards doing the great Stones number of 1968, "Salt of the Earth," honoring the common foot soldiers, the uncounted heads, and the lowly of birth, many of whose bodies were then lying under tons of rubble in lower Manhattan. And it later emerged that Bruce Springsteen had privately approached numerous survivors of the first responders killed on 9/11, large numbers of whom lived in New Jersey and had been eulogized as identifying with Springsteen's songs of regular working people carrying on with their jobs, up to and including sacrificing their lives in the line of duty. The widow of a New York fireman reported gratefully, "After I got off the phone with him, the world just felt a little smaller. I got through Joe's memorial and a good month and a half on that call."[33] In 2002 Springsteen and the E Street Band put out a well-received album, *The Rising*, a redemptive vision of hope and endurance in the aftermath of the country's most shattering defeat; the catchy, simple song "Waitin' On a Sunny Day" offered a joyful uplift as only an artist of Springsteen's stature could then deliver.

But the national cohesion the Concert for New York City and *The Rising* celebrated was short-lived, and soon pop musicians and their audiences became more politically fragmented than ever before. Average rock fans, or at least surprising numbers of them, saw no disconnect between the countercultural origins of their favorite bands and their own newly conservative leanings. Online forums devoted to Aerosmith or Iron Maiden often grew tangential discussion threads where posters debated gun laws, immigration, climate change, and other hot-button topics from across an ideological spectrum. A shared love for "Sweet Emotion" or "Run to the Hills," it turned out, didn't mean one listener wouldn't call another a libtard or promote conspiracy theories about mass shootings or Barack Obama's birthplace. In 2015 Sam Rapallo, the administrator for the official Led Zeppelin website, was obligated to prohibit any posts on political or religious topics that divided followers of the legendary English Satan-worshipping, groupie-ravaging drug addicts. "Many forums have adapted a 'no political / religious topics' rule, as they always quickly result in fighting, insults, etc.," he wrote in a comment he pinned to the chat boards. "So, we'll have to update the rules here too."[34] Reflecting later, Rapallo put it diplomatically: "There's several generations of fans since the hippie days, from all parts of the world, with varying political and religious beliefs. Today's political climate is so divisive, it's nice to have a place with the LZ forum where fans participate in a community and those personal differences don't matter."[35]

With a deeper tradition of conservatism, many country singers and devotees embraced the bellicose policies of the George W. Bush government or bluntly declared their cultural loyalties, as in Toby Keith's "Courtesy of the Red, White and Blue (The Angry American)" (2002), Gretchen Wilson's "Redneck Woman" (2004), and Blake Shelton's "Kiss My Country Ass" (2011). In 2003 Darryl Worley's "Have You Forgotten" was a no. 1 country hit, generally heard as a martial call to arms in the leadup to the US invasion of Iraq, tying the 9/11 attacks to Americans' patriotic obligation to fight the War on Terror. Only a few backed away from the rhetoric. "This country doesn't need to be incited with 'The Fightin' Side of Me,' " an aging Merle Haggard demurred to his fans shortly after September 11, 2001. "It needs to know we're together, but it sure doesn't need to be incited."[36] The Dixie Chicks, an all-female country act from Dallas, were boycotted by fans and their songs were dropped by some country radio stations after singer Natalie Maines told punters at a gig in London,

England, in March 2003, "Just so you know, we're ashamed the president of the United States is from Texas."[37]

Meanwhile, even before 9/11, some rock acts had already gone off in the exact opposite direction. Fatally distressed by drugs, inner demons, and the unexpected fame he achieved with Nirvana, Kurt Cobain had confided to a journal his sad and eventually unrealized hopes for the opportunities success might bring: "We can pose as the enemy to infiltrate the mechanics of the system to start its rot from the inside. Sabotage the empire by pretending to play their game . . . littering the floors of Wall Street with revolutionary debris."[38] Nirvana's grungy peers Pearl Jam played spoken-word excerpts from the writings of dissident academic Noam Chomsky at concert stops. Since the quartet's self-titled debut in 1992, Rage Against the Machine had packed unambiguous messages of Marxist revolution into their volatile rap-metal fusion, distinguished by Tom Morello's shock-to-the-system guitar effects and vocalist Zack de la Rocha's hoarse harangues against Western imperialism, racism, capitalism, and consumerism. RATM songs "Killing in the Name," "Bombtrack," "Bulls on Parade," "People of the Sun," and others were the most politically radical music to have come out on a major record label (theirs was Epic) to major sales since the Clash back in the first punk era; their harrowing recitation of the Allen Ginsberg poem "Hadda Be Playing on the Jukebox" distilled their worldview into a planetary attack on conspiratorial money and power that played well to young recruits to the growing antiglobalist "culture jamming" movement. Quotations from living and legendary leftist icons like Chomsky, Michael Moore, and Che Guevara were presented onstage. The followers of RATM were not necessarily the wage slaves or indigenous casualties of corporatism featured in de la Rocha's lyrics—Morello himself was a Harvard graduate—but it was obvious that the old markers of class were now defined by something more than just occupation or income. "Right now, the biggest employer in the United States is a temp agency, and I got to experience that firsthand," Morello said in a 1997 *Guitar World* interview. "People tend to think that if the worker and boss enjoy the same TV shows, or own some of the same commodities, then that represents the disappearance of class antagonism. But the splendor of Beverly Hills could not exist without the sweat shops of Indonesia, and without the layoffs in Flint, Michigan. Or, for that matter, without centuries of black slavery, the genocide of Native Americans, numerous imperialist wars, foreign death squads, fascist dictators supported with our tax money."[39]

If acts such as Rage Against the Machine had played against the simmering tensions between American conservative and progressive values during the 1990s, the next decade's War on Terror vastly exacerbated those tensions, and rock 'n' rollers like Tom Morello were subject to instant with-us-or-against-us judgments from commentators and listeners alike. Popular songs and popular singers took on new significance. On the one hand, there was AC/DC's "Hells Bells" blared at the gates of Fallujah in 2003, as Avenged Sevenfold and Five Finger Death Punch were joined by Toby Keith and Kid Rock entertaining troops in and around Baghdad. On the other, antiwar protesters in the US and elsewhere often invoked Creedence Clearwater Revival's "Fortunate Son," as another generation of poor Americans went off to a battle directed by men who had themselves avoided combat in Vietnam through family and economic advantage—President George W. Bush and Vice President Dick Cheney foremost among them. In 2007 that song's author, John Fogerty, did not hesitate to blame the Iraqi quagmire on the same motivations of greed and deceit he had originally denounced back in 1969: "I just happen to feel that in this case, with this administration, it's not simply bad judgment. . . . I can't remember such a group of people in power and taking the entire country to a place that makes their close friends so wealthy, so quickly,"[40] he said. Then again, Ozzy Osbourne, the singer of Black Sabbath's similarly reproachful "War Pigs," accepted an invitation to the White House Correspondents' Association dinner in 2002. "Y'know, ever since I went to that dinner, people ask me what I think of Bush," Ozzy put it in a memoir. "But I can't say I have an opinion, because I don't know enough about all that political stuff."[41] Talk about brainwashed minds.

Rock stars who took an audible stand against the War on Terror or Bush, or who dared find fault with anything in the contemporary American condition, were often turned on by people who might once have praised them or sought the artists' approval. Steve Earle's 2002 song "John Walker's Blues" considered the plight of the young American convert to Islam John Walker Lindh, captured while fighting for Taliban forces in Afghanistan. A first-person, almost claustrophobically intimate prisoner's ballad that attempted to humanize the Californian jihadist, Earle's piece came under heavy fire from the US right wing. "This puts him in the same category with Jane Fonda . . . and all those who hate America,"[42] thundered Nashville radio host Steve Gill. In 2003 some Pearl Jam fans booed singer Eddie Vedder when he tromped on a George W. Bush mask onstage in Denver, Colorado. "I love Pearl Jam, but that was just way over the edge,"[43] an audience member said. John Mellencamp's 2003 album of folk and blues standards, *Trouble No More*, featured a reworking of Woody Guthrie's "Baltimore to Washington" called just "To Washington" that took on Bush's rush to invade Iraq; played on the radio in his home state of Indiana, it prompted one listener to call in, "I don't know who I hate worse, John Mellencamp or Saddam Hussein."[44] Longtime Bloomington neighbors gave Mellencamp and his family dirty looks and left rude messages on his wife's car. "Wait a minute," the singer thought to himself. "You guys have known me for thirty years. You don't know who George Bush is. This guy just showed up. You're going to take his word over mine?"[45] Holding forth as a guest on Fox News in 2008, *Wall Street Journal* editor Dan

Henninger dismissed the views of Bruce Springsteen, who that year campaigned on behalf of Bush's Democratic opponent, John Kerry, in the presidential contest. "I have long felt that *Born to Run* in 1975 was his last truly great album," Henninger sniffed. "Because after that he sort of transformed himself into this rock 'n' roll Woody Guthrie, the world's last concerned man. . . . We listen to people like Bruce Springsteen for fun, not to have our faces rubbed in politics."[46] And in 2014 Ryan L. Cole, a contributor to the conservative *Weekly Standard*, wrote that "Springsteen's songs, in fact, often overlook how dynamic this land truly is. . . . But isn't the Boss's success—he is, after all, the son of a working-class father, as his admirers never tire of pointing out—evidence against the inevitability of his own narrative?"[47]

But as support for the Iraq war declined with steadily mounting US casualties and no clear victory, protest music won partisan approval from the anti-Bush bandwagon. *American Idiot*, a 2004 album by the California pop-punkers Green Day, sold over five million copies in its first year of release, with its title song disavowing the redneck agenda in a nation deceived by paranoid propaganda, and "Holiday" giving a mock Sieg Heil to the president. "American Idiot" was reportedly conceived by Green Day guitarist and songwriter Billie Joe Armstrong after hearing one of Lynyrd Skynyrd's 2003 tributes to red state living, either "That's How I Like It" or "Red, White & Blue," on his car radio. "It was like, 'I'm proud to be a redneck,' " was as much as Armstrong could remember of the track. "And I was like, Oh my God, why would you be proud of something like that? This is exactly what I'm against."[48] Him and a whole side of the American electorate. *American Idiot* won several major awards in 2005, including a Grammy for Best Rock Album. To friends and fans, Green Day was speaking truth to power; to foes and citizens of Skynyrd country, they were just another pawn of the mainstream liberal media. "It's one thing when you're in California and you're saying, 'Fuck George Bush,' " Armstrong said of his song's reception when performed live. "But when you're in Texas . . . It was a mixed response. That's a weird noise, man. Half the crowd cheering and half the crowd booing."[49] Over Bush and Iraq, rock was as disunited as its public.

Some rock musicians caused surprise and dismay across the ideological spectrum when they spoke up. At the 2002 Rock and Roll Hall of Fame induction ceremony, guitarist Johnny Ramone of the punk trailblazers the Ramones closed his acceptance speech by saying "God bless President Bush, and God bless America."[50] Kiss's Gene Simmons, the fire-breathing, tongue-waving demon born Chaim Witz to Holocaust survivors in Israel, supported the removal of Saddam Hussein. "I don't often agree with the Republican Party's stance on air, water, big business, Roe v. Wade, ad infinitum. But in time of war, it's time to cut it out, or we're not here," he asserted. "I'm alive because my mother is alive, and my mother is alive because America liberated her from the Nazi German concentration camps. I'm living proof that there's a country out there that really cared enough to risk its lives."[51] In a 2012 coup for Mitt Romney, Kid Rock joined Ted Nugent in his endorsement of the candidate at the head of the GOP ticket. That year even Nugent was pushing the envelope by predicting that if Barack Obama won reelection, "I will be either dead or in jail because I'm on his enemies list"[52] (a comment that prompted a visit from the US Secret Service to Nugent's home), and in 2014 the Nuge, still alive and at large, offered further thoughts on the election victor: "I have obviously failed to galvanize and prod, if not shame, enough Americans to be ever vigilant not to let a Chicago Communist-raised, Communist-educated, Communist-nurtured subhuman mongrel like the ACORN community organizer gangster Barack Hussein Obama to weasel his way into the top office of authority in the United States of America."[53]

The strange symbiosis between rock 'n' roll and politics was not always quite so dire. In 2006 Keith Richards, recovering from a head injury sustained on a trip to Fiji, received a get-well message from British prime minister Tony Blair that began, "Dear Keith, you've always been one of my heroes." "England's in the hands of somebody who I'm a hero of?" Richards marveled. "It's frightening."[54] Elsewhere, rock acts continued to protest candidates' unauthorized use of their music at public events or even apparent enjoyment of their music in private. Representatives for Journey told Republican Newt Gingrich to stop playing "Don't Stop Believin'" in 2011, and GOP vice presidential candidate Paul Ryan's admitted appreciation for Rage Against the Machine's "sound" in 2014 drew a scathing response from Tom Morello in *Rolling Stone*: "Paul Ryan's love of Rage Against the Machine is amusing, because he is the embodiment of the machine that our music has been raging against for two decades."[55] Rush objected to Senator Rand Paul's invoking of "The Trees," "Tom Sawyer," and "The Spirit of Radio" as inspirations for his libertarian views—ostensibly over copyright issues, although lyricist Neil Peart distinguished himself from Paul's neo–Ayn Randian platform to write, "I define myself as a 'bleeding-heart libertarian' . . . So I am repelled by the cold-hearted and crypto-racist attitudes of the so-called 'Christian' right."[56] The cease-and-desist notices, whether legally effective or not, showed that some vestige of rock 'n' roll rebelliousness persisted, but the fact that certain elected leaders might cast themselves as the rebels showed something else. This was no longer Rush Limbaugh using the Pretenders' "My City Was Gone" to spite Chrissie Hynde; this was legislators of one philosophy (and their supporters) being honestly energized by musicians who held very different ones. As ever, there was no accounting for taste. Unlike the old days when antiestablishment rock stars offended politicians, now it was antiestablishment politicians offending rock stars.

The players were embattled in other ways. As rock's baby boom and Gen X markets were displaced by millennials who preferred newer music accessed through newer media, various artists hitherto distinct from each other discovered an unsuspected compatibility. In some cases it just made commercial or contractual sense to pair up, but in others there was a genuine admiration and empathy between performers who'd never before shared a studio or stage—and between the remaining audiences they could pool together. Aerosmith and Kiss ran a co-headlining tour in 2003, while ZZ Top and Lynyrd Skynyrd played gigs together in 2010–2011, with Skynyrd promoting their latest album, *God and Guns*, featuring the song "That Ain't My America." ZZ Top and CCR's John Fogerty also made the same bills in 2018. Guns n' Roses' Axl Rose replaced Brian Johnson in AC/DC in 2016, fronting several concerts. And Rage Against the Machine's Tom Morello served as an intermittent member of Bruce Springsteen's band for several years after 2008, doing "The Ghost of Tom Joad" (which RATM had already covered) and other Springsteen favorites. Always a gracious guest and a class act, Springsteen led Morello and the group through customized versions of "Highway to Hell" and the Easybeats' "Friday on My Mind" in Australia and the Clash's "Clampdown" in Britain. If the fan base for classic rock acts was slowly dwindling with time, the base was also coalescing around unified themes and hardened survivors.

By the mid-2010s rock stars, or the lower ranks of them, had become more like generic pop product placements than electric troubadours of social change. They did talk shows; had cameos in movies, television series, or video games; wrote autobiographies; and appeared at awards galas, charity benefits, and other pseudo-events. While some rock 'n' rollers were still strongly tied in the popular mind to staunch positions from populist left (Springsteen's "We Take Care of Our Own" was a 2016 campaign theme of Democrat Bernie Sanders) to populist right (Skynyrd and Kid Rock performed private shows during the 2016 Republican National Convention in Cleveland), others served more to lend a very small bit of rock 'n' roll glamour to otherwise mainstream bread-and-circus entertainment. Ozzy Osbourne, Gene Simmons, and hair metal vets Vince Neil, Tommy Lee, Bret Michaels, Sebastian Bach, and ex-GNR drummer Steven Adler each had their own reality TV programs or were featured in them. One long-running series had guest spots from the still somewhat famous and formerly outrageous Simmons, Michaels, Sharon Osbourne (wife of Ozzy), Twisted Sister's Dee Snider, Sugar Ray's Mark McGrath, and Meat Loaf, all of them making rock music just a little bit more palatable to stupefied channel-surfers and making stupefied channel-surfing just a little bit more susceptible to fame and outrage. That show was *The Celebrity Apprentice*, starring Donald Trump.

Conclusion

Subdivisions

> The counterculture got most of the nation's attention during the 1970s and the underclass got most of the attention during the 1980s. But during those decades—quietly, gradually, without creating obvious social problems for America as a whole—the population of white Americans who defied traditional American expectations grew in size. By the 1990s and 2000s, the new lower class was a shaping force in the life of working-class Americans.
>
> **Charles Murray,** *Coming Apart*

The US election of 2016, the Brexit referendum the same year, and a widespread revival of far-right nationalism in many countries have put increased focus on populations whose stated values and voting preferences have at least temporarily upset presumptions that they were passing from political significance. Rural populations—people living outside of big cities and cultural capitals, people with notions of home inherited from the many generations that preceded them on the same geography. Ethnic populations—people conscious of ancestry and tribe in ways that could never be wholly extinguished by longstanding orthodoxies of melting pots and mosaics. Economic populations—people still reliant on precarious week-in, week-out routines of jobs and compensation for their security. These groups, overlapped with each other to varying degrees in various societies, now form a discrete bloc measurably impacting everything from public health and immigration to education, employment, and democracy itself.

And rock music has impacted them. In subtle but substantial changes, the legacy of rock 'n' roll and the fate of the postindustrial working classes have been intertwined for several decades. What happens in one realm shapes the other. As an art form and as a business, pop music has always responded to conditions of labor and living standards, but never so directly as over the

Takin' Care of Business. George Case, Oxford University Press (2021). © George Case.
DOI: 10.1093/oso/9780197548813.003.0011

twentieth century's second half. As national, regional, personal, and socio-economic identities, citizens' perceptions of their own civic characters have often been shaped by the entertainments they consume, but never as persuasively as by Creedence Clearwater Revival, Lynyrd Skynyrd, Black Sabbath, AC/DC, Bruce Springsteen, and the other talents whose stories have been told here. Not all the people who enjoy their music are white working-class conservatives, and not every working-class white conservative enjoys high-energy, unpretentious rock music. Yet the two groups undeniably correlate.

Some contemporary results of this correlation are apparent. One is that guitar-bass-drums rock 'n' roll has become almost entirely the preserve of white males. Notwithstanding a historic list of Black performers, from Chuck Berry, Little Richard, Jimi Hendrix, and Sly Stone to Prince, Lenny Kravitz, Ben Harper, Vernon Reid, and Gary Clark Jr., the standard image conjured by the phrase "rock musician" is of a young white person, just as a cross-section of his fans will look pretty monochromatic. Such a generalization should be no more problematic today than assumptions that a typical reggae singer is Jamaican or a typical yodeler is Swiss. Despite its uniquely African origins, the formal genre of rock music seems to have become overwhelmingly associated with people of European descent. Indeed, to aficionados of K-pop, techno, trap, or other more recent styles, there may be little to differentiate a Motörhead from a Merle Haggard: both feature white guys with electric stringed instruments, backed by acoustic drums and other accompanists, delivering three- or five-minute arrangements of verses and choruses about their personal experiences or opinions in 4/4 time. Rock 'n' roll began with a melding of Black and white styles that, depending on the observer, was either promising or provocative, but most of the music's course covers a racial retrenchment. Though the coming of rock foretold Black Americans' march to legal equality, most subsequent pop music has reinforced identity politics more than it has surmounted them. In real life, people of all backgrounds are still mixing and marrying, but on the platforms of electronic media increasingly perceived as real, they remain starkly divided. It was the African American blues guitarist B. B. King who had the most dispassionate perspective on the phenomenon, in his 1996 autobiography *Blues All Around Me*: "I hold no grudges. . . . Elvis didn't steal any music from anyone. . . . I've heard blacks ask, 'Why couldn't the first big rock star be black, since rock came from black music?' The commonsense reason is in the numbers. Blacks are a small minority. The white majority, whether in movies or music, want their heroes and heroines to look like them. That's understandable."[1] The demographics King described have changed, but their influence on rock 'n' roll has lasted.

It should also be clear that old-fashioned social conservatism now has little remaining place in what is generally considered the right wing. In some crucial ways, rock definitely had the last laugh on the old elites. Men could wear long hair; pop songs could be loud, raw, and rude; casual sex could be a staple topic on radio and record; idioms of poor Blacks and whites could filter up to higher classes; the impulses of youth warranted adult accommodation; commercial entertainment could be made to serve explicit political purposes—such concessions signified major defeats for the parties of Dwight Eisenhower, Barry Goldwater, or Harold Macmillan. But rock 'n' roll lost some important battles as well. Electric guitars could be played by sober, law-abiding grown-ups; hard partiers could still support an established social system; colorful show business personalities could hold the same convictions as anonymous ordinary folks; and white racists could still enjoy music with distant roots in sub-Saharan Africa. When Ted Nugent and Gene Simmons are considered effective spokesmen for gun rights or military intervention, the Republican stereotypes of hard-hatted Archie Bunker or uptight Richard Nixon are obsolete. The politics of rock 'n' roll, in turn, are no longer tied to the vaguely socialist visions of John Lennon's "Imagine," Buffalo Springfield's "For What It's Worth," or the Sex Pistols' "Anarchy In the UK," but more to the ain't-nobody's-business independence of AC/DC's "Highway to Hell," CCR's "Bootleg," Skynyrd's "Sweet Home Alabama," Grand Funk Railroad's "We're an American Band," and Nugent's "Stormtroopin'." In some ways this is just a consequence of time: the principles of any individual or institution almost seventy years old, however radical they might once have been, will eventually appear conventional next to the principles of younger people and younger movements. Popular views of sex, race, courtship, duty, and the self that rock promoted with such verve are taken for granted, or are outright scorned, in 2021. Musical messages that once shocked parents and grandparents for their vulgarity or their sedition now shock children and grandchildren for their un-wokeness. Yesterday's libertine is tomorrow's prude. Rock music hasn't evolved nearly as much as the attitudes surrounding it.

As well, although the growth and artistic triumph of rock happened in tandem with the post–World War II economic boom, the better part of its work coincides with a long economic decline. The Rolling Stones' 1965 breakthrough "(I Can't Get No) Satisfaction" was an attack on the empty materialism of a surfeited society; just a generation later, Springsteen's "Racing in the Streets" and Judas Priest's "Breaking the Law" attacked the empty promises of a straitened one. Born out of rising affluence and expectations, most rock actually soundtracks their diminution. The transition from a manufacturing economy to one based around service and communications—a transition in which the billion-dollar pop music business played no small role—meant that rock 'n' roll players were to some degree unwittingly responsible for the very slowdown that informed their art. Fans felt better having Alice Cooper to distract them with grotesquery or John Mellencamp to remind them of what really mattered, but in a better world, fans might not have needed Alice Cooper or John Mellencamp at all.

It's arguable, too, that rock contributed more directly to the downturn, inasmuch as its steady celebrations of adolescent drives and desires created an international psychology forever arrested at around age twenty-one, cheapening the disciplines of planning, deferred gratification, and respect for maturity on which the infrastructures of the Industrial Age were built. As the background for the baby boomers' fixation on extending the span of active, sexually desirable human biology, rock was ideal, but as motivation for productivity it was music much better suited for Saturday nights than Monday mornings. Some commentators have suggested the crises of serial relationships, drug addiction, single-parent families, and cross-generational poverty affecting midwestern America can be ascribed in part to the five-decade primacy of rock 'n' roll. After all, while many fans heard the work of brilliant poets and composers, others just saw—and tried to emulate—a pantheon of stoned, piratical groupie ravagers jet-setting around the world in limousines and luxury planes, dodging record company suits, ex-partners, taxes, and police. An itinerant career of heedless sex and constant intoxication looked great on Bon Scott or Ronnie Van Zant, but it didn't wear as well on the assembly lines of Michigan or the English Midlands. In this reading, it was not remote public officials or corporate leaders who devastated cities like Youngstown, Ohio, but the region's own residents. "Even the economic changes of the past few decades do very little to explain the dysfunction and negligence—and the incomprehensible malice—of poor white America," wrote Kevin D. Williamson in the *National Review*, in May 2016. "The truth about these dysfunctional, downscale communities is that they deserve to die. Economically, they are negative assets. Morally, they are indefensible. Forget all your cheap theatrical Bruce Springsteen crap."[2]

Whatever caused the evisceration of the middle class in the United States and elsewhere, it may be more accurate to say rock 'n' roll did not accelerate the process so much as provide a language for coping with it. Rock music has become so successful and so established in American life that it is no longer just about escape, protest, and youth but about acceptance, resilience, and hard-earned wisdom. Indeed, for many who now hear it as such, the orthodox venerations of singer-songwriters and psychedelic, soul, punk, or alternative artists has only felt like more elite condescension, as every other pop category but their favorite wins critical credit and scholarly appraisal. To be told over decades that Steppenwolf, then Grand Funk Railroad, then Lynyrd Skynyrd, then Iron Maiden, then Styx, then George Thorogood, then Metallica, then Guns n' Roses are strictly for rubes or racists is no more than a musical variation of the messages they've long received from arbiters of every other kind of prestige. The generations rock first reached have grown middle-aged and old as the songs scored the arc of their working (or nonworking) lives. Rock has today become what country music was sixty years ago: a quaint, categorically isolated folk aesthetic whose admission is limited to a single shrinking cohort, which in its original form will one day be of more interest to purists and curators than active audiences. Rock did not become its own opposite; it became its own heritage.

Has rock stretched or torn the social fabric of the Western world? No more so than a thousand other products that flatter their users' sense of separateness from people with whom they otherwise share faiths, or neighborhoods, or ages, or income levels, or humanity. Instead, rock 'n' roll has reflected the gathering tensions felt between differing peoples inhabiting a planet at once more pluralistic and more polarized than ever before. Young and old, Black and white, male and female, gay and straight, liberal and conservative, rich and poor: all have been presented with a panoply of information and entertainment that has been endlessly modified for more and more narrow castes of insiders. The popular music that best assuaged the anxieties of the North Americans and Europeans most sensitive to loss of status, or the popular music which that explained how those anxieties arose—the blue-collar boogie—was the entertainment of one such caste. It was only one, and the people within it may not have always been just, or wise, or deserving in how they held their status or denied the status of others. They were exploited and abused by chieftains of finance and politics; they were themselves sometimes guilty of abuse and exploitation. They may well be rendered extinct by the technological, demographic, and cultural advances that have slowly overtaken them. They are probably passing into history. But they sure left some good tunes.

Notes

Introduction

1. Destination Cleveland, "2016 RNC Convention Logo Unveiled," *This Is Cleveland*, November 23, 2015, https://www.thisiscleveland.com/media/news-releases/november-2015/2016-rnc-convention-logo-unveiled.

Chapter 1

1. David Szatmary, *A Time to Rock: A Social History of Rock 'n' Roll* (New York: Schirmer, 1996), 57.
2. Jon Savage and Hanif Kureishi, *The Faber Book of Pop* (London: Faber & Faber, 1996), 46.
3. Glen Jeansonne, David Luhrssen, and Dan Sokolovic, *Elvis Presley, Reluctant Rebel: His Life and Our Times* (Santa Barbara, CA: Praeger, 2011), 122–123.
4. Reebee Garofalo, *Rockin' Out: Popular Music in the USA* (New York: Prentice Hall, 2008), 154.
5. Jeansonne et al., *Elvis Presley*, 123.
6. Linda Martin and Kerry Segrave, *Anti-Rock: The Opposition to Rock 'n' roll* (New York: Da Capo, 1993), 31.
7. Ibid., 37.
8. Jeff Greenfield, *No Peace, No Place: Excavations along the Generational Fault* (Garden City, NY: Doubleday, 1973), 36.
9. Jonathan Cott, *Dylan: The Essential Interviews* (New York: Wenner, 2006), 13.
10. Roy Carr and Tony Tyler, *The Beatles: An Illustrated Record* (London: New English Library, 1981), 20.
11. Paul Johnson, "The Menace of Beatlism," *New Statesman*, February 1964, available online at https://www.newstatesman.com/culture/2014/08/archive-menace-beatlism.
12. Barney Hoskyns, *Hotel California: The True-Life Adventures of Crosby, Stills, Nash, Young, Mitchell, Taylor, Browne, Ronstadt, Geffen, the Eagles, and Their Many Friends* (Hoboken, NJ: John Wiley, 2006), 63.
13. Stephen Davis, *Hammer of the Gods: The Led Zeppelin Saga* (1986; repr., New York: Ballantine, 2008), 104.
14. Robbie Robertson, *Testimony: A Memoir* (New York: Alfred A. Knopf, 2016), 357.
15. Jefferson Cowie, *Stayin' Alive: The 1970s and the Last Days of the Working Class* (New York: New Press, 2012), 186.
16. John A. Farrell, *Richard Nixon: The Life* (New York: Vintage, 2018), 335–336.

Chapter 2

1. Bruce Miroff, "Green River," *Rolling Stone*, October 19, 1973, available online at https://www.rollingstone.com/music/music-album-reviews/green-river-249393/.
2. John Lennon and Jann Wenner, *Lennon Remembers* (London: Verso, 2000), 136.
3. Joe Smith and Mitchell Fink, *Off the Record: An Oral History of Popular Music* (New York: Warner Books, 1989), 248.
4. Anthony DeCurtis, James Henke, and Holly George-Warren, *The Rolling Stone Illustrated History of Rock & Roll: The Definitive History of the Most Important Artists and Their Music* (New York: Random House, 1992), 450.
5. John Fogerty, *Fortunate Son: My Life, My Music* (New York: Little, Brown, 2016), 190.
6. Jefferson Cowie, *Stayin' Alive: The 1970s and the Last Days of the Working Class* (New York: New Press, 2012), 187. Bottom of Form.
7. Fogerty, *Fortunate Son*, 190–191.
8. Fogerty, *Fortunate Son*, 137.
9. Fred Goodman, *The Mansion on the Hill: Dylan, Young, Geffen, Springsteen, and the Head-On Collision of Rock and Commerce* (New York: Vintage Books, 1998), x.
10. Nancy Hardin and Marilyn Schlossberg, eds., *Easy Rider: Original Screenplay by Peter Fonda, Dennis Hopper, [and] Terry Southern, Plus Stills, Interviews and Articles* (New York: New American Library, 1969), 22.
11. John Kay and John Einarson, *Magic Carpet Ride: The Autobiography of John Kay and Steppenwolf* (Kingston, ON: Quarry Press, 1994), 200.
12. Kay and Einarson, *Magic Carpet Ride*, 220–221.
13. Joan Didion, *The White Album* (New York: Pocket Books, 2017 [1979]), 101.
14. Philip Norman, *Symphony for the Devil* (New York: Dell, 1985), 336.
15. Johnny Rogan, *Ray Davies: A Complicated Life* (London: Vintage Books, 2016), 377.
16. Tom Beaujour, "The Kinks: Arthur (or the Decline and Fall of the British Empire)," *Guitar World*, June 1999, 93.
17. John Ivan Simon, *Movies Into Film: Film Criticism, 1967–1970* (New York: Dell, 1972), 95.
18. Charles R. Cross, *Room Full of Mirrors: A Biography of Jimi Hendrix* (New York: Hyperion, 2005), 271.
19. Scott Laderman, *The "Silent Majority" Speech: Richard Nixon, the Vietnam War, and the Origins of the New Right* (New York: Routledge, 2020), 141.

Chapter 3

1. Steve Miller, *Detroit Rock City: The Uncensored History of Rock 'N' Roll in America's Loudest City* (New York: Da Capo, 2013), 79.
2. Billy James, *An American Band: The Story of Grand Funk Railroad* (London: SAF, 1999), 9–10.
3. Ibid., 16.
4. Miller, *Detroit Rock City*, 79.
5. James, *An American Band*, 24.
6. Ibid., 31.

7. John Lennon, Peter McCabe, and Robert D. Schonfeld, *John Lennon: For the Record* (Toronto: Bantam, 1984), 117.

8. Timothy Ferris, "Grand Funk Railroad: Is This Band Terrible?," *Rolling Stone*, August 19, 1971, available online at https://www.rollingstone.com/music/music-news/grand-funk-railroad-is-this-band-terrible-41111.

9. Robert Christgau, "Consumer Guide Album: Grand Funk Railroad, *Closer to Home*," on Robert Christgau's website, https://www.robertchristgau.com/get_album.php?id=6927.

10. Ellen Willis, Nona Willis Aronowitz, Sasha Frere-Jones, Daphne Carr, and Evie Nagy, *Out of the Vinyl Deeps: Ellen Willis on Rock Music* (Minneapolis: University of Minnesota Press, 2011), 113.

11. Miller, *Detroit Rock City*, 36.

12. Gary Graff, "Grand Funk Railroad: On Time," *Guitar World*, June 1999, 74.

13. Stephen Davis, *Hammer of the Gods: The Led Zeppelin Saga* (New York: Ballantine Books, 2008 [1986]), 179.

14. Songfacts, "We're an American Band," https://www.songfacts.com/facts/grand-funk/were-an-american-band.

15. Miller, *Detroit Rock City*, 70.

16. Robert Matheu and Brian J. Bowe, *Creem: America's Only Rock 'n' Roll Magazine* (New York: Collins, 2007), 30.

17. Dean Budnick and Josh Baron, *Ticket Masters: The Rise of the Concert Industry and How the Public Got Scalped* (New York: Plume, 2012), 44.

18. Michael Walker, *What You Want Is in the Limo: On the Road with Led Zeppelin, Alice Cooper, and the Who in 1973, the Year the Sixties Died and the Modern Rock Star Was Born* (New York: Spiegel & Grau, 2013), 152.

19. "Something Must Happen," *Billboard*, November 14, 1970, R-63.

20. Ann Powers, "The Male Rock Anthem: Going All to Pieces," *New York Times*, February 1, 1998.

21. Fred Goodman, *The Mansion on the Hill: Dylan, Young, Geffen, Springsteen, and the Head-On Collision of Rock and Commerce* (New York: Vintage Books, 1998), 193.

22. John Einarson and Randy Bachman, *Takin' Care of Business* (Toronto: McArthur, 2000), 249.

23. Ibid., 252.

24. Gordon Fletcher, "Not Fragile," *Rolling Stone*, October 24, 1974, available online at https://www.rollingstone.com/music/music-album-reviews/not-fragile-203061/.

25. Cameron Crowe, "Bachman-Turner Overdrive: A Canadian Mormon Tabernacle Rock & Roll Band," *Rolling Stone*, January 16, 1975, available on the Cameron Crowe fan website The Uncool at http://www.theuncool.com/journalism/rs178-bachman-turner-overdrive/.

26. Einarson and Bachman, *Takin' Care of Business*, 256.

27. Joe Perry, *Rocks* (New York: Simon & Schuster, 2015), 135.

28. Jon Bream and Robert Alford, *Whole Lotta Led Zeppelin: The Illustrated History of the Heaviest Band of All Time* (Minneapolis: Voyageur, 2010), 247.

29. Perry, *Rocks*, 136.

30. Steven Tyler and David Dalton, *Does The noise in My Head Bother You?: A Rock 'n' Roll Memoir* (New York: Ecco Press, 2011), 121–122.

31. Jefferson Cowie, *Stayin' Alive: The 1970s and the Last Days of the Working Class* (New York: New Press, 2012), 401.

32. "Midwest Report Ho Hum Attitude," *Billboard*, November 14, 1970, R-12.

33. Irene Clepper, "Promotion Man's Firm Focuses on 'Vitality,'" *Billboard*, December 15, 1973, 13.

34. Anthony DeCurtis, James Henke, and Holly George-Warren, *The Rolling Stone Illustrated History of Rock & Roll: The Definitive History of the Most Important Artists and Their Music* (New York: Random House, 1992), 461.

35. Simon Reynolds, *Shock and Awe: Glam Rock and Its Legacy from the Seventies to the Twenty-First Century* (New York: Dey Street Books, 2016), 134.

36. Dave Thompson, *Alice Cooper: Welcome to My Nightmare* (London: Omnibus, 2012), 102.

37. Walker, *What You Want Is in the Limo*, 85.

38. Thompson, *Alice Cooper*, 103.

39. Walker, *What You Want Is in the Limo*, 85.

40. Ibid., 13.

41. Thompson, *Alice Cooper*, 118.

42. Dennis Dunaway, Chris Hodenfield, and Alice Cooper, *Snakes! Guillotines! Electric Chairs! My Adventures in the Alice Cooper Group* (New York: Thomas Dunn Books, 2018), 145.

43. Miller, *Detroit Rock City*, 62.

44. Reynolds, *Shock and Awe*, 146.

45. Ted Nugent, *Ted Nugent*, Epic PE 33692, 1975.

46. Miller, *Detroit Rock City*, 56.

47. "Classic Rock Rules," *Guitar World*, October 1993, 44.

48. Steve Hendrix, "Ted Nugent, Guitarist and Gun-Lover, Rocks the Political World," *Washington Post*, July 5, 2013.

49. "Classic Rock Rules," *Guitar World*, October 1993, 44.

50. John Spong, "Ted or Alive: How a Foulmouthed Rock Star Became the Country's Most High-Profile Advocate for Hunting, Personal Liberty, and the Right to Bear Extremely Large Arms," *Texas Monthly*, July 2009, 82

51. Matheu and Bowe, *Creem*, 139.

52. Fred Schruers, "Ted Nugent: The Ted Offensive," *Rolling Stone*, March 8, 1979, available online at https://www.rollingstone.com/music/music-news/ted-nugent-the-ted-offensive-84814/.

53. Alice Cooper, Keith Zimmerman, and Kent Zimmerman, *Alice Cooper, Golf Monster: A Rock 'n' Roller's Life and 12 Steps to Becoming a Golf Addict* (New York: Random House, 2008), 41.

54. David Mikkelson, "Ted Nugent Dodged [*sic*] the Draft?," *Snopes*, April 20, 2012, https://www.snopes.com/fact-check/the-artful-dodger/.

55. Miller, *Detroit Rock City*, 40.

56. Hendrix, "Ted Nugent," 2013.

57. Mark Crispin Miller, *Boxed In: The Culture of TV* (Evanston, IL: Northwestern University Press, 1991), 175.

58. Gary Herman, *Rock 'n' roll Babylon* (London: Plexus, 2008 [1994]), 65.

59. Philip Kamin and Peter Goddard, *The Rolling Stones: Live* (Toronto: Musson, 1982), 115–117.

Chapter 4

1. Robert Matheu and Brian J. Bowe, *Creem: America's Only Rock 'n' Roll magazine* (New York: Collins, 2007), 262.

2. David Cantwell, *Merle Haggard: The Running Kind* (Austin: University of Texas Press, 2013), 155.

3. George Case, *Out of Our Heads: Rock 'n' Roll before the Drugs Wore Off* (New York: Backbeat Books, 2010), 82.

4. Randy L. Schmidt, *Dolly on Dolly: Interviews and Encounters with Dolly Parton* (Chicago: Chicago Review Press, 2017), 5.

5. Pamela Des Barres, *I'm with the Band: Confessions of a Groupie* (London: Helter Skelter, 2011), 186.

6. Ibid., 263.

7. Michael Streissguth, *Outlaw: Waylon, Willie, Kris, and the Renegades of Nashville* (New York: It Books, 2013), 153.

8. Chet Flippo, *Everybody Was Kung-Fu Dancing: Chronicles of the Lionized and the Notorious* (New York: St. Martin's Press, 1991), 286–290.

9. Jessi Colter and David Ritz, *An Outlaw and a Lady: A Memoir of Music, Life with Waylon, and the Faith That Brought Me Home* (Nashville: Nelson Books, 2017), 159.

10. Robert Ward, "Redneck Rock," *New Times*, June 25, 1976.

11. Raymond Obstfeld, *Twang! The Ultimate Book of Country Music Quotations* (New York: H. Holt, 1997), 129.

12. Case, *Out of Our Heads*, 84.

13. Willie Nelson and David Ritz, *It's a Long Story: My Life* (New York: Little, Brown, 2016), 229–230.

14. Ralph Emery and Patsi Bale Cox, *The view from Nashville* (New York: Morrow, 2000), 159.

15. Joe Nick Patoski, *Willie Nelson: An Epic Life* (New York: Little, Brown, 2009), 266.

16. Ibid., 315.

17. Obstfeld, *Twang*, 116.

Chapter 5

1. Alan Paul, Butch Trucks, and Jaimoe, *One Way Out: The Inside History of the Allman Brothers Band* (New York: St. Martin's Press, 2014) , 65.

2. Ibid., 65.

3. Ellen Mandell, "The Georgia Peach," *Guitar Legends* 106, 19.

4. Alan Paul, "The Allman Brothers Band," *Guitar World*, June 1999, 54..

5. Paul, Trucks, and Jaimoe, *One Way Out*, 183.

6. Ibid., 19.

7. Ibid., 34.

8. Gregg Allman and Alan Light, *My Cross to Bear* (New York: William Morrow, 2013), 128.

9. Mark Kemp, *Dixie Lullaby: A Story of Music, Race, and New Beginnings in a New South* (New York: Free Press, 2004), 29.

10. Allman and Light, *My Cross to Bear*, 266.

11. Gene Odom and Frank Dorman, *Lynyrd Skynyrd: Remembering the Free Birds of Southern Rock* (New York: Broadway Books, 2002), 118.

12. Kemp, *Dixie Lullaby*, 77–78.

13. Alan Paul, "Gimme Three Chords," *Guitar Legends* 106, 66.

14. Kemp, *Dixie Lullaby*, 78.

15. Jaan Uhelszki, "Lynyrd Skynyrd: A Southern Ghost Story," *Guitar Legends* 106, 26.

16. Al Kooper, *Backstage Passes and Backstabbing Bastards: Memoirs of a Rock 'n' Roll Survivor* (New York: Backbeat Books, 2008), 181.

17. Alan Paul, "Hell Raisers," *Guitar Legends* 106, 60.

18. Ibid., 59.

19. Odom and Dorman, *Lynyrd Skynyrd*, 108.

20. Kemp, *Dixie Lullaby*, 155.

21. Mark Ribowsky, *Whiskey Bottles and Brand-New Cars: The Fast Life and Sudden Death of Lynyrd Skynyrd* (Chicago: Chicago Review Press, 2018), 123.

22. Referenced in Ribowsky, *Whiskey Bottles and Brand-New Cars*, 122.

23. Kemp, *Dixie Lullaby*, 155.

24. Ribowsky, *Whiskey Bottles and Brand-New Cars*, 120.

25. Paul, "Hell Raisers," 62.

26. Paul, "Gimme Three Chords," 66.

27. Ibid.

28. Neil Young, *Waging Heavy Peace: A Hippie Dream* (New York: Plume, 2013), 417.

29. "Tough Times, Still Merry," *Record Collector*, https://recordcollectormag.com/articles/tough-times-still-merry.

30. Merry Clayton promotional interview for *Twenty Feet from Stardom*, June 6, 2013, available on YouTube at https://www.youtube.com/watch?v=Zj7KrKsW6Q.

31. "Classic Rock Rules," *Guitar World*, October 1993, 49.

32. Tim Stegall, "ZZ Top: Tracking the Beards," *Austin Chronicle*, December 27, 2013, available online at https://www.austinchronicle.com/music/2013-12-27/zz-top/.

33. Steven Rosen, "Billy Gibbons" (interview), *Guitar World*, July 1990, 74.

34. Paul, "Hell Raisers," 59.

35. Uhelszki, "Lynyrd Skynyrd," 30.

Chapter 6

1. Ray Davies, *X-Ray* (London: Duckworth, 2008), 74.

2. Charles Dickens, *The Old Curiosity Shop* (London: Penguin Classics, 2001 [1841]), 340.

3. Tony Iommi and T. J. Lammers, *Iron Man: My Journey Through Heaven and Hell With Black Sabbath* (New York: Perseus Books Group, 2011), 7.

4. Brad Tolinski, with Alan Paul, "Iron Men," *Guitar World*, August 1992, 48.

5. Ozzy Osbourne and Chris Ayres, *I Am Ozzy* (New York: Grand Central, 2011), 5–6.

6. Steven Rosen, *Black Sabbath* (London: Sanctuary, 2002), 24.

7. Dan Epstein, "Black Magic," *Guitar World*, July 2001, 64.

8. Osbourne and Ayres, *I Am Ozzy*, 46.

9. Ibid., 53.

10. Iommi and Lammers, *Iron Man*, 105.

11. Lester Bangs, "Master of Reality," *Rolling Stone*, November 25, 1971, available online at https://www.rollingstone.com/music/music-album-reviews/master-of-reality-102188/.

12. Lester Bangs and John Morthland, *Mainlines, Blood Feasts, and Bad Taste: A Lester Bangs Reader* (New York: Anchor Books, 2003), 227.

13. Rosen, *Black Sabbath*, 38.

14. Simon Reynolds, *Shock and Awe: Glam Rock and Its Legacy from the Seventies to the Twenty-First Century* (New York: Dey Street Books, 2016), 165.

15. Turner, Alwyn W. 2013. *Glam rock: dandies in the underworld*. London: V & A Publishing, 35.
16. Reynolds, *Shock and Awe*, 286.
17. Ibid.
18. Anthony DeCurtis, James Henke, and Holly George-Warren, *The Rolling Stone Illustrated History of Rock & Roll: The Definitive History of the Most Important Artists and Their Music* (New York: Random House, 1992), 460.
19. Dominic Sandbrook, *State of Emergency: The Way We Were; Britain, 1970–1974* (London: Allen Lane, 2010), 594.
20. Paul Trynka, *David Bowie: Starman* (New York: Little, Brown and Company, 2011), 304.
21. Leah Collins, "For Nazareth Veterans, Touring Is 'a Natural Thing,'" *Times-Colonist* (Victoria, BC), July 5, 2007, D6.
22. Jim Windolfe, "Nick Lowe on Songwriting," *Vanity Fair*, March 20, 2009, available online at https://www.vanityfair.com/news/2009/03/nick-lowe-on-songwriting.
23. Jon Savage and Johnny Marr, *England's Dreaming: Sex Pistols and Punk Rock* (London: Faber & Faber, 2016), 114–115.
24. Barry J. Faulk and Brady Harrison, *Punk Rock Warlord: The Life and Work of Joe Strummer* (Farnham, UK: Ashgate, 2016), 89.
25. Ibid., 85.
26. Martin Popoff, *Beer Drinkers and Hell Raisers: The Rise of Motörhead* (Toronto: ECW, 2017), 85.
27. Ibid., 49.
28. Ibid., 173–174.
29. Ibid., 102.
30. Ibid., 118.
31. Graham Murdock, Guy Phelps, and Schools Council (Great Britain), *Mass Media and the Secondary School*, Schools Council Research Studies (London: Macmillan, 1973), 100.
32. Linda Martin and Kerry Segrave, *Anti-Rock: The Opposition to Rock 'n' Roll* (New York: Da Capo Press, 1993), 266.
33. Stephen Duncombe and Maxwell Tremblay, *White Riot: Punk Rock and the Politics of Race* (London: Verso, 2011), 133.
34. David Pilgrim, *Elvis Costello and Thatcherism: A Psycho-Social Exploration* (London: Taylor & Francis, 2016), 93.
35. Ibid., 95.
36. Eric Clapton, *Clapton: The Autobiography* (New York: Broadway Books, 2007), 94.
37. Jon Wiederhorn and Katherine Turman, *Louder than Hell: the Uncensored, Unflinching Saga of Forty Years of Metal Mayhem* (New York: It Books, 2012), 95.
38. Gary Herman, *Rock 'n' roll Babylon* (London: Plexus, 2008 [1994]), 202.
39. Bruce Dickinson, *What Does This Button Do?: An Autobiography* (New York: Dey Street Books, 2017), 80.
40. C. Burns and J. D. Considine, "Metal Mania," *Rolling Stone*, November 1990, 100.
41. David Simonelli, *Working Class Heroes: Rock Music and British Society in the 1960s and 1970s* (Lanham, MD: Lexington Books, 2013), 180.
42. Robert Matheu and Brian J. Bowe, *Creem: America's Only Rock 'n' Roll Magazine* (New York: Collins, 2007), 232.
43. Robert Walser, *Running with the Devil: Power, Gender, and Madness in Heavy Metal Music* (Hanover, NH: Wesleyan University Press, 1993), 106–107.

44. Wolf Marshall, "Euro-Metal Special," *Guitar One*, August 1997, 27.

45. Wiederhorn and Turman, *Louder than Hell*, 90.

46. Liam Lacey, "Heavy Metal: A Bluffer's Guide," *Globe and Mail*, March 31, 1984, E1.

47. Amy Langenberg, "Heavy-Metal Kids: 'Rock-till-You-Die' Metal Heads Are Energetic— and Desirable—Group" *Adweek's Marketing Week*, November 13, 1989, HM20+.

48. Kory Grow, Judas Priest's Subliminal Message Trial: Rob Halford Looks Back," *Rolling Stone*, August 24, 2015, available online at https://www.rollingstone.com/music/music-features/judas-priests-subliminal-message-trial-rob-halford-looks-back-57552/.

49. Donna Gaines, *Teenage Wasteland: Suburbia's Dead End Kids* (New York: Pantheon, 1991), 249.

50. Walser, *Running with the Devil*, 150.

Chapter 7

1. Alan Di Perna, "Hard as a Rock," *Guitar World*, January 1993, 26–33.

2. Ibid.

3. Jesse Fink, *The Youngs: The Brothers Who Built AC/DC* (Edinburgh: Black & White, 2015), 63.

4. Bob Gulla, "Angus Young and the Fine Art of Ballbreaking," *Guitar*, December 1995, 30–32.

5. Martin Popoff, *AC/DC: Album by Album* (New York: Crestline, 2019), 10.

6. Clinton Walker, *Highway to Hell: The Life and Times of AC/DC Legend Bon Scott* (Portland, OR: Verse Chorus Press, 2001), 164.

7. Popoff, *AC/DC*, 67.

8. David Fricke, "AC/DC and the Gospel of Rock & Roll," *Rolling Stone*, November 13, 2008, 64–73.

9. Popoff, *AC/DC*, 59.

10. Di Perna, "Hard as a Rock," 26–33.

11. Gulla, "Angus Young," 30–32.

12. Fricke, "AC/DC," 64–73.

13. Gulla, "Angus Young," 30–32.

14. Fricke, "AC/DC," 64–73.

15. Popoff, *AC/DC*, 68.

16. Walker, *Highway to Hell*, 172.

17. Ibid., 47.

18. Ibid., 220.

19. Ibid., 246.

20. Fink, *The Youngs*, 23.

21. Popoff, *AC/DC*, 70.

22. Di Perna, "Hard as a Rock," 26–33.

23. Jefferson Cowie, *Stayin' Alive: The 1970s and the Last Days of the Working Class* (New York: New Press, 2012), 324.

24. Donna Gaines, *Teenage Wasteland: Suburbia's Dead End Kids* (New York: Pantheon, 1991), 181.

25. Danny Goldberg, *Bumping into Geniuses: Inside the Rock and Roll Business* (New York: Gotham Books, 2008), 123.

26. Ray Herbeck, "Unleashing the Grease on an Unsuspecting Public," *Billboard*, July 15, 1978, S-4.

27. George Lucas, Gloria Katz, and Willard Huyck, *American Graffiti: A Screenplay* (New York: Ballantine, 1972), 4.

28. Reebee Garofalo, *Rockin' Out: Popular Music in the USA* (Boston: Allyn & Bacon, 1996), 347.

29. Alice Echols, *Hot Stuff: Disco and the Remaking of American Culture* (New York: W. W. Norton, 2011), 214.

30. Steve Dahl, Dave Hoekstra, Paul Natkin, and Bob Odenkirk, *Disco Demolition: The Night Disco Died* (Chicago: Curbside Splendor Publishing, 2016).

31. Jesse Fink, *Bon: The Last Highway; The Untold Story of Bon Scott and AC/DC's Back in Black* (Edinburgh: Black & White Publishing, 2017), 27.

32. Walker, *Highway to Hell*, 229.

33. Steve Pond, "Faceless Bands," *Rolling Stone*, February 4, 1982, 37.

34. Michael R. Lee, "Facing an Identity Crisis," *Billboard*, March 27, 1982, 22.

35. Goldberg, *Bumping into Geniuses*, 120.

36. Robert Love, ed., *The Best of Rolling Stone: 25 Years of Journalism on the Edge* (New York: Doubleday, 1993), 395.

37. Nelson George, "Artists Demand Their Piece of the Rock," *Billboard*, December 21, 1985, 41–44.

38. John Pareles, "Who Decides the Color of the Music?" *New York Times*, May 17, 1987.

39. Pond, "Faceless Bands," 37.

40. Jonathan Cain, *Don't Stop Believin': The Man, the Band, and the Song that Inspired Generations* (New York: HarperCollins, 2018), 159.

41. Paul Stanley, *Face the Music: A Life Exposed* (New York: HarperCollins, 2014), 153.

42. Ibid., 57.

43. Jeff Kitts, "Smashes, Thrashes & Hits," *Guitar World*, August 1992.

44. Gene Simmons, *KISS and Make-Up* (New York: Crown Publishers, 2001), 108.

45. Goldberg, *Bumping into Geniuses*, 114–115.

46. Robert Walser, *Running with the Devil: Power, Gender and Madness in Heavy Metal Music* (Hanover, NH: Wesleyan University Press, 1993), 7.

47. Martin Popoff, *Rush: The Unofficial Illustrated History* (Minneapolis: Voyageur Press, 2016), 38.

48. Murray Engleheart and Arnaud Durieux, *AC/DC: Maximum Rock & Roll* (London: Aurum, 2009), 258.

49. Brian Johnson, *Rockers and Rollers: A Full-Throttle Memoir* (New York: HarperCollins, 2012), 9.

50. Di Perna, "Hard as a Rock," 26–33.

51. J. D. Considine, "Shout at the Devil" (album review), *Rolling Stone*, February 16, 1984.

52. Gulla, "Angus Young," 30–32.

53. Deena Weinstein, *Heavy Metal: A Cultural Sociology* (New York: Lexington Books, 1991), 114–115.

Chapter 8

1. Bruce Springsteen, *Born to Run* (New York: Simon & Schuster, 2016), 78–79.

2. June Skinner Sawyers, *Racing in the Street: The Bruce Springsteen Reader* (New York: Penguin Books, 2004), 65.

3. Fred Goodman, *The Mansion on the Hill: Dylan, Young, Geffen, Springsteen, and the Head-On Collision of Rock and Commerce* (New York: Vintage Books, 1998), 284.

4. Peter Ames Carlin, *Bruce* (New York: Touchstone, 1998), 286.

5. Dave Marsh, *Bruce Springsteen: Two Hearts, The Story* (New York: Routledge, 2004), 286.

6. Sawyers, *Racing in the Street*, 108.

7. Mark Kemp, *Dixie Lullaby: A Story of Music, Race, and New Beginnings in a New South* (New York: Free Press, 2006), 175.

8. Carlin, *Bruce*, 319.

9. Jon Meacham and Tim McGraw, *Songs of America: Patriotism, Protest, and the Music That Made a Nation* (New York: Random House, 2019), 204.

10. Robert Matheu and Brian J. Bowe, *Creem: America's Only Rock 'n' Roll Magazine* (New York: Collins, 2007), 213.

11. Ibid., 217.

12. Joe Smith and Mitchell Fink, *Off the Record: An Oral History of Popular Music* (New York: Warner Books, 1989), 411–412.

13. Jimmy Guterman, "Scarecrow," *Rolling Stone*, September 26, 1985, available online at https://www.rollingstone.com/music/music-album-reviews/scarecrow-86935/.

14. Jon Pareles, "Mellencamp Aims at the Heartland," *New York Times*, September 1, 1985.

15. "Willie Nelson Announces Farm-Aid Concert in Illinois," *Cedar Rapids Gazette*, August 17, 1985, 20.

16. Steven Greenhouse, "14-Hour Concert in Illinois Sept. 22 Will Seek $50 Million to Help Farmers," *New York Times*, September 15, 1985.

17. Kenny Aronoff, *Sex, Drums, Rock 'n' Roll!: The Hardest Hitting Man in Show Business* (Milwaukee: Backbeat, 2016), 129.

18. Ibid., 132.

19. Willie Nelson and David Ritz, *It's a Long Story: My Life* (New York: Little, Brown, 2015), 10.

20. Karen Schoemer, "Critic's Notebook: Farm Aid: Music Omits Message," *New York Times*, March 16, 1992.

21. Aronoff, *Sex, Drums, Rock 'n' Roll*, 69.

22. Jon Pareles, "Heartland Rock: Bruce's Children," *New York Times*, August 30, 1987.

23. Sean O'Hagan, "Cowboy Junkie Who Found High Sobriety," *Guardian*, October 28, 2001.

24. Charles M. Young, "George Thorogood" (interview), *Rolling Stone*, March 22, 1979.

25. Erin Lebar, "Bluesman of the People," *Winnipeg Free Press*, April 28, 2016, A&E 7.

26. Peter Goddard, "Thorogood on the Roar and Grind," *Toronto Star*, June 2, 2012, E6.

27. Michael F. Scully, *The Never-Ending Revival: Rounder Records and the Folk Alliance* (Urbana: University of Illinois Press, 2008), 107–108.

28. Smith and Fink, *Off the Record*, 336.

29. "Bob Seger Changes His Tune about Detroit" (interview), *NPR Morning Edition*, January 8, 2007.

30. Ray Waddell, "Return of the Road Warrior," *Billboard*, November 21, 2015, 54.

31. Steve Miller, *Detroit Rock City: The Uncensored History of Rock 'n' Roll in America's Loudest City* (New York: Da Capo, 2013), 77.

32. Smith and Fink, *Off the Record*, 336.

33. *NPR Morning Edition*, January 8, 2007.

34. Miller, *Detroit Rock City*, 77.

35. Springsteen, *Born to Run*, 403.

36. Dale Maharidge, Michael S. Williamson, and Bruce Springsteen, *Someplace like America: Tales from the New Great Depression* (Berkeley: University of California Press, 2013), ix.

37. George Packer, *The Unwinding: An Inner History of the New America* (New York: Farrar, Straus & Giroux, 2014), 52.

38. "Pop Music Shift," *National Review*, August 10, 1984, 17.

39. John Tierney, "Has the Boss Joined Ranks with the Limousine Liberals?" *New York Times*, June 14, 2000, B1.

40. Julian E. Barnes, "Springsteen Song about Diallo Prompts Anger from Police," *New York Times*, June 13, 2000, B3.

41. Springsteen, *Born to Run*, 436.

42. Maharidge, Williamson, and Springsteen, *Someplace like America*, 84.

Chapter 9

1. Dexter Filkins, *The Forever War* (New York: Alfred A. Knopf, 2008), 3.

2. Philip S. Meilinger, "Pump Up the Volume," *MHQ: The Quarterly Journal of Military History*, Winter 2012, 14.

3. Michael Herr, *Dispatches* (New York: Everyman's Library/Alfred A. Knopf, 2009 [1977]), 169.

4. Martin Popoff, *Contents under Pressure: 30 years of Rush at Home and Away* (Toronto: ECW, 2004), 72.

5. Liz Ramanand, "Avenged Sevenfold's M. Shadows on Performing for Troops," Loudwire, October 7, 2011, https://loudwire.com/avenged-sevenfold-m-shadows-performing-for-troops/.

6. Evan Serpick, "Tour of Duty: Bands Go to Iraq," *Rolling Stone*, May 31, 2007, 13–14.

7. Tom Shanker, "All's Loud and Rocking on Iraqi War Front," *Toronto Star*, April 14, 2004, F2.

8. "Zappa Speaks Up for Rock Lyrics," *Ottawa Citizen*, March 21, 1986, 79.

9. David Corn and Sam Munger, "Rockin' Rush: Radio Pirate," *The Nation*, August 25 / September 1, 1997, 26.

10. Ibid.

11. Benjamin Barber, *Jihad vs. McWorld* (New York: Crown, 1995), 111.

12. Brad Tolinski, "Quote-O-Rama," *Guitar World*, July 1990, 21.

13. Brad Tolinski, with Alan Paul, "Iron Men," *Guitar World*, August 1992, 45.

14. Timothy White, "Truth, Lies, and the Getting of Wisdom," *Billboard*, June 25, 1994, 3.

15. Craig McInnis, "Race & Hate and Rock 'n' Roll" *Toronto Star*, November 11, 1989, J1.

16. Jon Pareles, "There's a New Sound in Pop Music: Bigotry," *New York Times*, September 10, 1989.

17. McInnis, "Race & Hate," J1.

18. Pareles, "There's a New Sound."

19. Mick Wall, *W.A.R.: The Unauthorized Biography of Axl Rose* (New York: St. Martin's, 2008), 158.

20. Del James, "Axl Rose," *Rolling Stone*, August 10, 1989, 42.

21. Matt Pegan, "One in a Million: The Forgotten History of Hard Rock's Most Shameful Moment" *UWire*, September 5, 2016, 1.

22. Guns n' Roses, *G N' R Lies*, Geffen Records GHS 24198, 1988).
23. Andrew Blake, ed., *Living Through Pop* (London: Routledge, 2002), 167.
24. Dorian Lynskey, "Phil Collins Returns," *Guardian*, February 11, 2016.
25. Tolinski, "Quote-O-Rama," 20.
26. George Case, *Out of Our Heads: Rock 'n' Roll before the Drugs Wore Off* (New York: Backbeat Books, 2010), 85.
27. Ted Nugent, *God, Guns and Rock 'n' Roll* (Washington, DC: Regnery Publishing, 2001), 14.
28. Steve Hendrix, "Ted Nugent, Guitarist and Gun-Lover, Rocks the Political World," *Washington Post*, July 5, 2013.
29. Jay Root, "Bearing Arms and Cranking Up the Controversy," *New York Times*, May 4, 2012.
30. Anthony Bozza, "Eminem Blows Up," *Rolling Stone*, April 29, 1999, 42.
31. Lisa Robinson, "Eminem's World" *Vanity Fair*, December 2004, 370.
32. Mark Binelli, "Kid Rock on a Roll," *Rolling Stone*, September 2, 1999, 67.
33. Peter Ames Carlin, *Bruce* (New York: Touchstone, 2012), 413.
34. sam_webmaster, "Political / religious topics," Led Zeppelin Official Forum, November 15, 2015, https://forums.ledzeppelin.com/topic/23247-political-religious-topics/.
35. Sam Rapallo, email to author, August 7, 2019.
36. David Cantwell, *Merle Haggard: The Running Kind* (Austin: University of Texas Press, 2013), 4.
37. Charles K. Wolfe and James Edward Akenson, *Country Music Goes to War* (Lexington Kentucky: University Press of Kentucky, 2005), 208.
38. Kurt Cobain, *Journals* (New York: Penguin Putnam, 2002), 168.
39. Charles M. Young, "The Red Rocker," *Guitar World*, March 1997, 40–96.
40. Thomas M. Kitts, *Finding Fogerty: Interdisciplinary Readings of John Fogerty and Creedence Clearwater Revival* (Lanham, MD: Lexington Books, 2013), 185.
41. Ozzy Osbourne and Chris Ayres, *I Am Ozzy* (New York: Grand Central, 2011), 346.
42. Jonathan Ritter and J. Martin Daughtry, eds., *Music in the Post-9/11 World* (London: Routledge, 2013), 25.
43. John Berlau, "Antiwar Singers Out of Tune with Public," *Insight on the News*, May 13, 2003, 30.
44. Frank DiGiacomo, "One From the Heartland," *Vanity Fair*, February 2007, 108.
45. Ibid.
46. *The Journal Editorial Report*, April 19, 2008, transcript available online at https://www.foxnews.com/story/transcript-the-journal-editorial-report-april-19-2008.amp.
47. Ryan L. Cole, "Born to Rant," *Weekly Standard*, December 1, 2014.
48. Dorian Lynskey, *33 Revolutions per Minute: A History of Protest Music* (New York: Harper Collins, 2011), 522–523.
49. Ibid., 524.
50. Marky Ramone and Richard Herschlag, *Punk Rock Blitzkrieg: My Life as a Ramone* (New York: Simon & Schuster, 2016), 374.
51. Berlau, "Antiwar Singers," 30.
52. Root, "Bearing Arms," A21.
53. Amy Davidson Sorkin, "Ted Nugent's 'Subhuman Mongrel' Slur, in Translation," *New Yorker*, February 22, 2014, available online at https://www.newyorker.com/news/amy-davidson/ted-nugents-subhuman-mongrel-slur-in-translation.

54. Keith Richards with James Fox, *Life* (New York: Little, Brown, 2010), 542.

55. Emma Roller, "Can Republicans Rock Cleveland?" *New York Times*, July 19, 2016.

56. Neil Peart, *Far and Near: On Days Like These* (Toronto: ECW Press, 2014), 152.

Conclusion

1. B. B. King and David Ritz, *Blues All Around Me* (New York: Harper Collins, 1996), 186.

2. Kevin D. Williamson, "The Father-Fuhrer: Chaos in the Family, Chaos in the State," *National Review*, March 28, 2016, 30.

Further Reading

Though the particular subject of rock 'n' roll populism has rarely been addressed in a single study, there are numerous valuable works addressing different elements which comprise the phenomenon, which I consulted when writing *Takin' Care of Business*.

The decline of the North American industrial economy and its unionized workforce is well covered by Jefferson Cowie's *Stayin' Alive: The Seventies and the Last Days of the Working Class* (New York: New Press, 2010), while the political and economic upheavals that so affected the electoral moods of the United States and Britain during the period I track have humane treatments in a pair of titles by Dominic Sandbrook, *Mad As Hell: The Crisis of the 1970s and the Rise of the Populist Right* (New York: Alfred A. Knopf, 2011) and *State of Emergency: The Way We Were, Britain, 1970–1974* (London: Allen Lane, 2010). Michael Lind's *Land of Promise: An Economic History of the United States* (New York: Harper Collins, 2012) is an accessible guide to the people and circumstances defining America's agricultural, industrial, and postindustrial national character over three centuries. Today's legacy of that long transformation is addressed from various illuminating angles in Charles Murray's *Coming Apart: The State of White America, 1960–2010* (New York: Crown, 2012), Nancy Isenberg's *White Trash: The 400-Year Untold History of Class in America* (New York: Viking, 2016), George Packer's *The Unwinding: An Inner History of the New America* (New York: Farrar, Straus & Giroux, 2013), and most intimately in Dale Maharidge and Michael Williamson's *Someplace Like America: Tales from the New Great Depression* (Berkeley: University of California, 2011).

I've been reading about rock and other musical genres for many years, and there's a wide range of material for fans like me to enjoy, from sleazy tell-alls and quickie photo compendia to deeply researched biographies, honest memoirs, knowledgeable musical analyses, and even the rare title that takes care to include a perspective from outside of popular music itself. For *Takin' Care of Business* I found, besides solid source material, good stories and surprisingly good writing in the autobiographies of Bruce Springsteen (*Born To Run*, Simon & Schuster, 2016), Bruce Dickinson (*What Does This Button Do?*, Dey Street, 2017), and John Fogerty (*Fortunate Son*, Little, Brown, 2015)—those guys could actually quit their day jobs. Another good Boss bio is Peter Ames Carlin's *Bruce* (New York: Touchstone, 2012). Mark Kemp's *Dixie Lullaby: A Story of Music, Race, and New Beginnings in a New South* (New York: Free Press, 2004) is an original and personal take on the southern rock of the Allman Brothers and Lynyrd Skynyrd, while Steve Miller's *Detroit Rock City: The Uncensored History of Rock 'n' Roll in America's Loudest City* (New York: Da Capo, 2013) contains gems of recollection from Michiganders Ted Nugent, Bob Seger, and members of Grand Funk Railroad. The story of the artists who transformed country music in the 1970s is captured in *Outlaw: Waylon, Willie, Kris and the Renegades of Nashville*, by Michael Streissguth (New York: It Books, 2013), and the Cosmic Cowboy also has a worthy bio in Joe Nick Patoski's *Willie Nelson: An Epic Life* (New York: Little, Brown, 2008). A celebrated pair of rock 'n' roll casualties are given their rightful due in Graeme Thomson's *Cowboy Song: The Authorized Biography of Philip Lynott* (London: Constable, 2016) and Clinton Walker's *Highway to Hell: The Life and Times of AC/DC Legend Bon Scott* (Portland, OR: Verse Chorus, 2001).

Wider studies of the entire music business, such as it was, and subcategories within it can be gained from Michael Walker's *What You Want Is in the Limo: On the Road with Led Zeppelin, Alice Cooper, and the Who in 1973, the Year the Sixties Died and the Modern Rock Star Was Born* (New York: Spiegel & Grau, 2013) and Dean Budnick's *Ticket Masters: The Rise of the*

Concert Industry and How the Public Got Scalped (Toronto: ECW, 2011). The landmark print and electronic journalism of *Rolling Stone* is pretty much indispensable for anyone writing on rock 'n' roll, but I've always had a soft spot for the more specialized interviews and reportage of *Guitar World* magazine; likewise, Robert Walser's *Running with the Devil: Power, Gender, and Madness in Heavy Metal Music* (Hanover, NH: Wesleyan University Press, 1993) has long been a personal favorite for its scrupulous critical research into an often critically dismissed branch of rock. And, while it's not specially concerned with the music and eras of *Takin' Care of Business*, the late Ian MacDonald's *Revolution in the Head: The Beatles' Records and the Sixties* (London: Pimlico, 1995) remains a pinnacle to which any writer on rock 'n' roll, politics, and culture can only aspire. Further titles of interest will be found throughout the Notes below. Read, and rock, on.

Index